Non-Religious Pastoral C

This ground-breaking book is a guide to non-religious pastoral care practice in healthcare, prisons, education, and the armed forces in the UK. It brings a new perspective to our understanding of care services traditionally offered by chaplaincy departments. The book charts the progress from a Christian to a multi-faith and on to a fully inclusive care service. Compelling evidence is presented showing strong and broad support for non-religious pastoral care provision.

A practical guide, it outlines the beliefs and values on which this care is founded and its person-centred approach. The role, skills, competencies, and training requirements for non-religious pastoral carers are described. Institutions need to consider their policy responses to the rapid development of non-religious pastoral care provision. A number of policy aspects are explored, including understanding service users' needs, recruitment, and communications.

This book is essential reading for non-religious pastoral carers and those thinking of entering this field. Chaplains and institutional managers responsible for chaplaincy or spiritual care departments will find this book gives them valuable insights into the positive contribution non-religious pastoral carers can make in building stronger, more inclusive pastoral, spiritual, and religious care services.

David Savage took a leading role in establishing the non-religious pastoral care programme at Humanists UK. In 2012 he started to provide pastoral care at Guy's and St Thomas' NHS Foundation Trust and was the first non-religious person to successfully complete their spiritual healthcare department's two-year professional training course. He continues to provide care at the Trust and is helping to found a non-religious pastoral care role at the University of Surrey. Dr Savage is chair of the board of the Non-Religious Pastoral Support Network.

'This is a much-needed intervention on the growing phenomenon of non-religious pastoral care within chaplaincy contexts. It will undoubtedly raise challenges for chaplaincies and institutions across a wide range of settings in British public life.'

Ben Ryan, Researcher at Theos Think Tank, author of A Very Modern Ministry: Chaplaincy in the UK

'This timely book sketches an innovative and inspiring view of pastoral care that is relevant for professionals and managers involved in spiritual/pastoral care provisions and chaplaincy, both within and beyond the UK. Using both scientific evidence and case examples, David Savage makes a well-founded and passionate plea for a more inclusive pastoral care service in which pastoral care needs of all people are taken seriously and can be addressed.'

Carmen Schuhmann, Assistant Professor, Dep. Globalization and Dialogue Studies, University of Humanistic Studies

Non-Religious Pastoral Care

A Practical Guide

David Savage

Pip, Best wishes.

David.

Routledge
Taylor & Francis Group

LONDON AND NEW YORK

First published 2019
by Routledge
2 Park Square, Milton Park, Abingdon, Oxon OX14 4RN

and by Routledge
711 Third Avenue, New York, NY 10017

Routledge is an imprint of the Taylor & Francis Group, an informa business

© 2019 David Savage

British Library Cataloguing in Publication Data
A catalogue record for this book is available from the British Library

Library of Congress Cataloging in Publication Data
Names: Savage, David, 1944- author.
Title: Non-religious pastoral care : a practical guide / David Savage.
Description: Abingdon, Oxon ; New York, NY : Routledge, 2018. | Includes bibliographical references and index.
Identifiers: LCCN 2018023213| ISBN 9781138578395 (hardback) | ISBN 9781138578401 (pbk.) | ISBN 9781351264488 (ebook)
Subjects: LCSH: Pastoral care--Great Britain.
Classification: LCC BV4011.3 .S28 2018 | DDC 206/.1--dc23
LC record available at https://lccn.loc.gov/2018023213

ISBN: 978-1-138-57839-5 (hbk)
ISBN: 978-1-138-57840-1 (pbk)
ISBN: 978-1-351-26448-8 (ebk)

Typeset in Times New Roman
by Taylor & Francis Books

To Jo

Contents

Illustrations

Figures

Tables

Foreword

Last year, when both my grandparents were in hospital towards the end of their lives, they were approached by religious chaplains. The encounters were harmless in themselves. Having politely been told that they were not needed, thank you, the chaplains melted gently away and out of the ward. At least, therefore, my grandparents were not bothered with inappropriate offers of care.

My grandparents were hardly ever alone – they had family with them almost all of the time. This was not true of everyone on the ward, but what they did have in common with my grandparents was that they too politely declined the offer of religious support.

Most people in the UK today do not have a religious identity; most people do not have religious beliefs; most people do not engage in any sort of religious practice. But of course, we have beliefs, we have an approach to life, we have the same need as every human being to make sense of what is happening to us and to connect with like-minded people. In difficult times we need support. Someone less than a counsellor, more than a friend, who can listen and be present with us.

Inspired by such thoughts and by her own experience, my mother trained as a humanist pastoral carer in the programme designed by Dr Savage, the author of this excellent book. Her experiences in just a short time of practice have brought home the distinctive needs that non-religious people have when dealing with the moments of crisis, and she has in turn found great personal fulfilment from the care she has provided.

This excellent book captures both the context in which this care is necessary, and the policy environment in which it is delivered, far better than anecdotes from personal experience can do.

As Dr Savage's excellent book illustrates, people who do not wish for religious pastoral care may nonetheless need distinctive pastoral care. Until recently that need has not been met. Through the efforts of the author of this book and others, this is a lack now being made good, and this book is an excellent elucidation of both why this is necessary and how it can be accomplished. It tells the story of these developments with panache, and is invaluable for anyone interested in learning more about how so many public service sectors, from prisons to universities to healthcare, should and can respond to unprecedented social change.

But this volume is subtitled *A Practical Guide* and that is really what it is – and what is needed. No doubt in time, as humanist pastoral support in the UK continues to grow and develop, it will acquire the same sort of theoretical and academic substance that it has in countries such as the Netherlands, where one can graduate in it. This is not to say that Dr Savage does not give attention to the academic and theoretical debates – he does, and with flair and depth. At the moment, however, the urgency is to get it going. With clarity and insight, drawing from a deep well of personal professional experience, the author turbo-charges that possibility with this book.

It was one of my proudest initiatives to introduce the pastoral care pro-gramme at Humanists UK. Dr Savage was the pioneer and founder of that work, and it is an honour to write this foreword to a landmark volume in what deserves to be – and, I'm sure, will be – a growing and thriving field of study and practice. Everyone, from a general reader with the mildest interest to the most seasoned care practitioner from any sector, will benefit from reading it.

Andrew Copson
Chief Executive, Humanists UK
Nuneaton, April 2018

Acknowledgements

The growth of non-religious pastoral care was made possible through the desire of hundreds of humanists to give their time and energy to provide such care, and through the generosity of thousands of humanists who donated funds. Humanists UK, its Trustees, and its Chief Executive gave long-term strategic support to this development. They also commissioned an important survey into public attitudes and understanding on non-religious pastoral care and on chaplains. The board of the Non-Religious Pastoral Support Network brought wisdom, experience, and expertise to help build a network of accredited non-religious pastoral support providers and to foster a mutually supportive community of practice.

The provision of high-quality non-religious pastoral care is being built on solid foundations. One of those foundations is the Humanist Ceremonies network. They have established a justifiably high reputation based on excellent training and continuing professional development, effective quality assurance, and good governance. Their experiences and practices have been used to help ensure that equally high standards will be maintained in non-religious pastoral care. The Humanistisch Verbond and the University of Humanistic Studies in the Netherlands have been very supportive. With decades of experience of providing professional non-religious pastoral care, they have been able to demonstrate the benefits of providing such care in the armed forces, prisons, and hospitals. This provides a foundation of evidence and of confidence. If non-religious pastoral care provision could be established throughout our institutions, both the individuals in those institutions and the institutions themselves would benefit.

There are many individuals who have made this development possible, too many to name. Three pioneers are due special thanks. Bill Stephenson designed an excellent induction/training course. The success of this training results largely from his insightful understanding of the role of pastoral carers, and the skills and competencies that they need. Much of part II of this book is based on his work. Carrie Thomas has experience in both hospices and prisons. Her personality and counsel have helped ensure that all our work has been imbued with compassion, empathy, and a deep concern for the individual. Amy Walden pioneered our work in prisons. Setting out on this journey was not easy, but her kind, unrelenting tenacity has laid a trail for others to follow. My personal journey of learning and non-religious care practice was encouraged and strengthened by those in the Spiritual Health-care team at Guy's and St Thomas' NHS Foundation Trust, in particular the Hospitaller Revd Mia Hilborn, my training supervisor Revd Rosemary Shaw, and my mentor Revd William Sharpe. They all shared their extensive experience and, importantly, gave excellent pastoral care to me when needed. My thanks to those who provided case studies, they must remain anonymous in order to protect confidentiality. I am indebted to Andrew Copson, Chief Executive of Humanists UK, for his generous Foreword, and to Rebecca Hewitt and Simon O'Donoghue for their perceptive reading of my manuscript. It was a pleasure to work with the editorial and production staff at Routledge.

Last, and by no means least, I want to acknowledge those institutional managers, leaders of 'chaplaincy' bodies, managing 'chaplains', and others who had the vision, open-mindedness, and resolution to foster the development of non-religious pastoral care. In their various ways they have helped to ensure that issues of equality and diversity are addressed, championed non-religious pastoral carers joining their teams as volunteers or in paid posts, publicly recognised the value of such care, and given indispensable, sage advice.

My thanks to all of you.

Chapter 1

Introduction

This book is about care, more specifically about pastoral, spiritual, and religious care. The emphasis is on the care of people in prisons, hospitals, hospices, the military, and educational establishments. In all these places, there are times when people may feel anxious, lost, in pain, or isolated, and may experience a myriad of other feelings and thoughts that accompany all of us on our journey through life. Some may be trying to find meaning, purpose, and identity in difficult circumstances or looking for some source of hope. At such times, it can be helpful to talk to someone who is compassionate, empathic, confidential, and like-minded, perhaps to share or explore those thoughts and feelings, perhaps to pray, perhaps to reflect. Some people gain strength and comfort from appropriate rituals, memorials, and remembrance services.

Whilst help can come from a number of sources, many 'chaplains'[1] have seen themselves as specialists in providing such care, often describing it as spiritual care or simply 'chaplaincy'. Whatever the description, most 'chaplains' offer such care to everyone in their institution, irrespective of that person's religion or belief. They do so with commitment and sincerity. However, society is changing, the number of people with non-religious beliefs and values is growing, and that growth is likely to continue. This book presents evidence that many non-religious people want to receive this sort of care, here described as pastoral care, but that they would prefer that care to be provided by a trained pastoral carer rather than a religious 'chaplain'.

It is a central premise of this book that people with non-religious beliefs should have the same opportunities to access like-minded pastoral care as people with religious beliefs, and that people with non-religious beliefs should have the same opportunities to provide that care. This is a simple statement of choice, opportunity, fairness, and equality. In most areas of care these principles are followed and well established. Sadly, this has not been the case with spiritual care and 'chaplaincy'. Survey data show that people who identify themselves as non-religious do not access such care to the same extent as those who identify themselves as Christian. Recruitment practices in 'chaplaincy' departments have prevented non-religious people from applying for salaried posts to provide that care. But some progress has been made.

Historically, this care service was provided by Anglican Christians, this was then extended to other Christian denominations, and in recent years to other religions with the development of a multi-faith care service. It is now time to take the next step and move from a multi-faith care service to one that embraces non-religious pastoral care. The ability to take this next step is being enhanced by hundreds of very capable and committed people undertaking volunteer and postgraduate training in non-religious pastoral care. Welcoming them will help create a better, stronger, and genuinely inclusive care service.

This book is written from one non-religious perspective, not 'the' non-religious perspective. Just as there are many different religious perspectives, so there are many non-religious ones. Inevitably, comparisons are made between these two different perspectives, and of course they overlap. Nevertheless, they are different ways of seeing. It is not that one perspective is right and another is wrong; it is that some things can be seen clearly from one perspective but are difficult to perceive from another. A non-religious person may learn about the ten Sikh gurus but cannot know what it feels like to live as a Sikh. They may take part in mindfulness classes but cannot know if their experience is the same as that of a Buddhist monk practising Dhyana. Similarly, a religious person who has always believed in reincarnation can understand that a non-religious person does not believe in life after death, but they cannot know what it feels like to live life on that basis. A member of a Christian church may understand that a humanist may feel upset that they cannot be represented at Remembrance Day commemorations at the Cenotaph, but they will not experience their sense of rejection and discrimination. Despite these limitations, this non-religious perspective does try to understand and appreciate some religious perspectives. It may help non-religious pastoral carers to better understand the perspectives of many 'chaplains', and help 'chaplains' to have a better understanding of the perceptions of people with non-religious beliefs.

The scope of this book is limited for a number or reasons. The provision of this sort of non-religious pastoral care is a recent development, so practitioners have limited experience. Geographically, it is largely restricted to the United Kingdom, although it does draw on the wealth of knowledge and experience of non-religious pastoral care practice in places such as the Netherlands and Belgium. There are few academic references, and where references are given they should be reasonably accessible to most readers. Whilst prisons, healthcare, the military, and education are highlighted, most of the ideas discussed are equally relevant to other institutions and to community engagement. As non-religious pastoral care practice continues to develop, new research and new publications will extend these boundaries and fill some gaps.

Those with an interest in providing non-religious pastoral care as volunteers or professionals, those who want to understand what non-religious pastoral carers can offer, and those with responsibility for policy development and implementation should gain some useful insights from this book.

Throughout the book there are real examples. People's name, and in some cases their sex and circumstances, have been changed to protect their identity, but as far as possible the essence of the encounter has been retained.

The book is in three parts. Part I begins by examining the critically important role religious perspectives have played in the development and practice of 'chaplaincy' and spiritual care (chapter 2). A more specific focus follows in chapter 3 on the public's views of non-religious pastoral care and 'chaplaincy'. It shows that people of all religions and beliefs support better provision of non-religious pastoral care, and many non-religious people would prefer to receive care from a non-religious pastoral carer rather than a 'chaplain'. Chapter 4 explores the complexities of surveying and under-standing people's religious and non-religious beliefs. It stresses that good pastoral care can be given only if non-religious people are seen positively, as people *with* non-religious beliefs and values, rather than negatively, as people *without* religious beliefs. This positive perception informs the rest of the book.

Part II explores the non-religious pastoral care practice. It begins by out-lining in chapter 5 some of the beliefs and values on which non-religious care practice is grounded. The humanist approach to life is described. The value of a person-centred approach is highlighted and maintained as a foundation of good pastoral care. Skills, capabilities, and training are explored in some detail in chapter 6. Concepts familiar to 'chaplains', for example 'staying with' and 'being alongside', are seen as central. Some religious people have asked how a non-religious pastoral carer can talk to a dying person if they don't believe in an everlasting soul. How can they give a dying person hope if they don't believe in heaven? Aspects of death and loss are discussed from a non-religious perspective in chapter 7. The importance of ritual to non-religious as well as religious people is underlined. Pastoral, spiritual, and religious care practices inevitably raise some ethical issues (chapter 8). What should a non-religious pastoral carer do if they are asked to pray for someone? Is it ethical to require a non-religious person to call themselves a 'chaplain'? These and other ethical questions are raised.

Part III looks at the role of institutions, particularly the crucial role played by their senior management. All the institutions discussed in this book have made clear that their pastoral, spiritual, and religious care provision should be available to everyone, irrespective of the person's religion or belief. The days of this being a purely religious care service, provided only by religious people and only for religious people, should be long gone. It is clear that a fully inclusive pastoral, spiritual, and religious care service can develop only if the senior management in institutions take responsibility for that develop-ment (chapter 9). It cannot be delegated to 'chaplains', 'chaplaincy' organi-sations, or religious bodies. Gaining a better understanding of service users' needs and priorities should be a cornerstone of policy development (chapter 10). Effectively communicating what care services are provided by an institu-tion is essential if everyone is to properly understand how they may benefit from them. Some forms of expression, such as describing a care service simply as 'chaplaincy', can act as barriers to effective communication. Some alternatives approaches are suggested in chapter 11. Restrictions on recruitment have produced a service provider demographic which fails to reflect that of institutions' communities in terms of religion or belief (chapter 12). The legal framework for recruitment is explained, and some good practices proposed. Finally, the processes for development and implementation of improved pastoral, spiritual, and religious care policies in each of the institutions examined are briefly discussed in chapter 13.

More and more non-religious pastoral carers are setting out on their journey to provide care. Increasingly, they are being welcomed into institutions as their contributions are being recognised by both service users and management. If this book helps to make their journey a little easier, it will have achieved one of its purposes. Institutions are also setting out on a journey – one that puts service users' needs and priorities at the heart of policy development; that sees non-religious people in a positive way as people *with* sincerely held, meaningful beliefs and values; and that wants to help build strong, inclusive teams. If this book helps to make *their* journey a little easier, it will have achieved another of its purposes. If an outcome is that everyone, irrespective of their religion or belief, can have better access to good quality, like-minded pastoral, spiritual, and religious care, it will have made the journey in writing this book worthwhile.

Note

1 In this book, the term chaplain without quotation marks refers to a Christian person; 'chaplain' in quotation marks refers to a religious person who may be Christian or non-Christian.

Part 1

The social and institutional environment

Chapter 2

The development of pastoral, spiritual, and religious care practice

The importance of religious perspectives

It may seem a little strange for a book about non-religious pastoral care to discuss the importance of religious perspectives. In most areas of care – including psychotherapy, nursing, rehabilitation, adult social care, and counselling – aspects of religious beliefs may be present, but would not be dominant. When care organisations such as Cruse, Samaritans, and Age UK recruit, they do not emphasise the importance of the religious affiliations of potential applicants. Instead, the emphasis would be on the applicants' skills, capabilities, and experience in delivering the relevant type of care.

Although many 'chaplains' describe their main activity as pastoral care, it is the religious aspect that often seems to be dominant in their practices, culture, and service provision. For many 'chaplains' an emphasis on religious aspects is natural, long-established, and essential to their provision of high quality, authentic care. There are many reasons for this emphasis. As integral and constructive members of a care team, it is important for non-religious pastoral carers to understand these reasons and, where appropriate, to appreciate them. It may also be helpful for 'chaplains' to understand what 'chaplaincy' can look like from a non-religious perspective.

The emphasis on religion is partly historical and traditional. Chaplains, as Christian clerics, have a long history going back to the 8th century. Harting-Correa (1996) refers to the Frankish kings who took the half-cloak of St Martin into battle with them, believing that it would help them to victory. This cloak, together with other venerated saints' relics, was carried by clerics. These clerics became known as *cappellani* (chaplains) from *cappa*, meaning cloak. The belief that saintly relics have some power to change events is no longer very prevalent. Today, Christian chaplains accompanying armed forces into battle do not do so in the belief that 'God is on their side' in the conflict; such beliefs are themselves largely relics of history. However, some legacies of the past remain. The earliest appointed chaplains in prisons, hospitals, and universities were all Christian, and members of the Established Church. This remained the case for hundreds of years, with Church bodies controlling the recruitment, training, and practices of chaplains. The institutions in which they provided care played a limited role. Over the centuries, chaplains and Christian churches have gained a massive amount of worthwhile experience in delivering religious care. They have obtained an insight into people's care needs and have built up a good understanding about the institutions themselves. Non-religious pastoral carers have much to learn from them.

The tradition of an almost wholly Christian chaplaincy service was maintained until very recently. It was not until the 1990s that extending provision was seriously considered. Olumide (1993) wrote about equitable provision of spiritual, religious, and cultural care in the NHS, and a few years later Beckford and Gilliat (1998) carried out a study of relationships between the Church of England and other faiths in the Prison Service Chaplaincy. Their book, *Religion in Prison: 'Equal Rites' in a Multi-Faith Society*, highlighted the struggle for those from non-Christian backgrounds to achieve equal opportunities. It considered the somewhat controversial role Anglican chaplains played as gatekeepers in facilitating non-Christian pastoral, spiritual, and religious care provision. Non-Christian provision had to operate within the Christian traditional and cultural model. For example, the Christian word 'chaplain' was used as a descriptor for the appointed Buddhists, Hindus, Muslims, and Sikhs. Yet, as shown in chapter 3, almost all members of these traditions regard the term chaplain as a Christian description. Although the second largest group after Christians at this time was non-religious people, these studies effectively ignored the pastoral care needs of people with non-religious beliefs and values. The traditional emphasis on religion remained. Since the 1990s, there has been a positive development from a Christian to a multi-faith care approach, and this is to be welcomed. However, the following examination of practice in different institutions shows that this development has been quite limited. The current situation is still strongly influenced by the historical and traditional Christian approach. Whilst it is important to understand this tradition, it would be quite wrong to let tradition become a barrier to progress.

Another reason for the emphasis on religion is that the overwhelming majority of people working and volunteering in pastoral/spiritual care and 'chaplaincy' departments are religious. Until recently, virtually all recruitment into salaried posts has been restricted to religious people. Many will be ordained clergy, and many will be active in their local religious community. In almost all cases, their religion and religious practice will be very important to them. Whilst most of them will want to care for all people, irrespective of their religion or belief, it would not be surprising to find that they see and feel from a religious perspective. This religious perspective is also likely to apply to the department as a whole. Many voluntary chaplaincy organisations are composed of religious people, with senior roles predominantly Christian. In such circumstances, it has often been difficult for a non-religious perspective to be effectively represented or considered. Having both religious and non-religious perspectives represented in discussions and in policy development is essential if a fully inclusive care service is to be developed. The senior management in institutions need to be proactive to ensure this happens.

Religious care is vital for some people, and this care can take many forms. Accessing the sacraments, such as Anointing the Sick, and Baptism, is an important aspect, so there needs to be a capability to call on a range of qualified people to conduct those sacraments. Opportunities to pray and worship can help bring comfort and hope. Saying a private prayer with a 'chaplain' at the bedside, attending Friday prayers in prison with an imam, or taking part in Holy Communion at a military base in a war zone all provide such opportunities. Recitation of the Kaddish or chanting of Hindu mantras can bring reassurance and strength to people at acute times of need. Being with someone of one's own religion can allow the exploration of those beliefs, encouraging reflection, for example, on their God's love and purpose.

So far, we have talked of a care service. But from the perspective of many religious chaplains their work may not be seen as (or just as) a care service, but as one of mission. For the Church of England (2017a), its mission is described as carrying forward the work of Jesus Christ into all aspects of people's lives in society. In guidelines for new chaplains in universities, it tells them that they are at the cutting edge of ministry, that as chaplains they are part of the Church and have a responsibility to it (Church of England 2017b, p.6). The Catholic Church is quite explicit: a Catholic chaplain is an agent of the bishop (Catholic Bishops' Conference 2007, p.6). Methodists have a very similar perspective: 'chaplains minister in the secular world with a status that is conferred by the Church and with a huge representative role – of God, of the Church and of the whole Christian cause' (Jones 2010, p7). In a real sense, chaplains are 'sent' by the Church to carry out its work in another building. This sense of mission can be very motivating and empowering, as can be seen in the commitment and dedication of many chaplains.

Of course, many people, including non-religious pastoral carers, can and do show the same dedication and commitment without any sense of religious mission. Apart from the motivational aspects, mission has several other important practical implications. Perhaps the most important is that, for many, their role is not just to provide care, but to be a representative of their Church, God, and religion. This is quite different from the roles of most people who are employed in institutions. The professor, the major, the doctor, or the prison governor may well feel that they are, in some way, a representative of their institution. But even if they have a strong religious belief and are motivated by it, they probably do not feel that it is part of their role to be a representative of their church, religious community, or religion in that institution. Another important implication of mission is that of dual responsibility. Some chaplains see themselves as having a responsibility to the institution and a responsibility to the Church and its authorities, such as a bishop or Canon Law. For the most part, these responsibilities and their work for the institution are mutual activities, but not always. This can lead to tensions or a feeling of a lack of support by some chaplains. Todd (2013a) explores tensions felt by some military chaplains due to differences between their moral outlook and that of their 'sending church'. Slater (2015), a community chaplain, looks at some tensions between serving the community and supporting those in the parish who attend church. This duality of responsibility can have a substantial effect on the culture and practices of chaplains. Most non-religious pastoral carers have worked in secular institutions without the same concept of mission and without the same duality of roles and responsibilities. It is important for non-religious pastoral carers to be aware of the dual roles and responsibilities of chaplains, and to appreciate the tensions that sometimes result.

Whilst religious care is a vital part of the care service, it is just one part of a much more holistic pastoral, spiritual, and religious care service. For those who identify themselves as non-religious, religious care may be irrelevant. The relative importance of the religious care element should be determined by the needs and wishes of users and potential users of the service, rather than by the providers of the service.

The influence of religion on pastoral care in institutions

The extent to which history, tradition, and mission play a part in determining the culture, policy, and practices of pastoral/spiritual care and 'chaplaincy' departments varies from institution to institution. For non-religious pastoral carers joining a department's care team, it is helpful to gain an understanding of how these aspects influence different institutions, and *A Handbook of Chaplaincy Studies: Understanding Spiritual Care in Public Places* (Swift 2016) offers an excellent insight. Whilst cognisant of people with non-religious beliefs and values, it is written from an essentially religious perspective. 'Chaplaincy' departments can look and feel somewhat different from a non-religious perspective. The following sections highlight some aspects that are noticeable from a non-religious perspective but may be less apparent from a religious perspective. It is stressed that both perspectives are needed to get a full picture.

Prisons

Prisons in England and Wales are still governed by the Prison Act (UK Government 1952),[1] which offers some insight into the thinking prevalent in 1952. It is a legal requirement that every prison shall have a chaplain (p.3). The chaplain was seen as a key post in the prison. The term chaplain applies only to a clergyman of the Church of England (p.4), no other denomination or religion. Ministers from other denominations are allowed to visit prisoners of that denomination, but are not called chaplains. The concept of 'chaplaincy', as a department or team of 'chaplains', was not well established in 1952. In part this was because it was envisaged that there would be only one employed chaplain, perhaps with an assistant, per prison. The Act treats the Church of England differently from other Christian denominations and from other religions or beliefs. This is discriminatory, but was clearly considered to be acceptable by the Church of England and the State in 1952. Beckford (1999) records that in 1996 leaders of non-Christian religions tried to persuade the Secretary of State at the Home Office to change the legislation, saying: 'the central role of one particular religious denomination in the prison system is unacceptable ... when legislation is brought forward, it must ensure that all religions are treated equally' (p.64).

Interestingly, Beckford (1999) goes on to say that 'Their aim was nothing less than the abolition of the "special privileges" enjoyed by Church of England chaplains in prison chaplaincy' (p.64). Here we see two different perspectives: the quotation from leaders of non-Christian religions makes a proposal about equality; the quotation from Beckford sees the proposal in terms of the abolition of Church of England 'special privileges'. Of course, both perspectives have validity. Beckford is right to say that the proposed law change would remove the legal duty to appoint a chaplain who must be of the Church of England, abolishing its privileged position. But there is no evidence to suggest that abolishing Church of England privileges was the main aim of the leaders in making their proposal. Rather, it seems that their proposal was motivated by concerns for the care and equal treatment of non-Christians.[2] Perspectives matter. The Government did not change the legislation, and the 1952 Act remains extant. However, Beckford and Gilliat (1998) had criticised the prison chaplaincy service and the over-dominant role of the Church of England, saying:

> we believe that religious care should be available to all prisoners, equally, regardless of their particular faith ... If the provision is not perceived to be even-handed, accusations may be made about discrimination ... the fact that responsibility for administering the provision of religion to prisoners rests mainly with the clergy of the Church of England gives rise to difficult questions about the equal opportunities for non-Christians. (p.7)

It is encouraging to see that the prison chaplaincy service responded to these criticisms in a constructive and progressive way, at least in relation to the 9% of the prison population that were non-Christian at that time. (The 27% who were non-religious were largely ignored by Beckford, Gilliat and the chaplaincy service.) A new Chaplain General, William Noblett, was appointed. Noblett (2001) recognised the validity of the criticisms, commenting:

> I advocate a move to a more inclusive, multi-faith chaplaincy. I suggest Church of England predominance in publicly funded chaplaincies belongs to the past; that chaplaincy needs to be inclusive, not

exclusive; … to acknowledge the equality of people created in the image of God. (p.39)

At the time this was described as a paradigm shift. The move from a Christian chaplaincy service to multi-faith provision has been very positive. Now is the time to make another paradigm shift: from a multi-faith to a fully inclusive pastoral, spiritual, and religious care service. There are some signs that this is happening.

In part, this progress is due to the organisation of 'chaplaincy' being fully integrated within Her Majesty's Prison and Probation Service (HMPPS).[3] HMPPS employs a Chaplain General at its headquarters. This helps ensure that there is good dialogue between the 'chaplaincy' function and HMPPS senior management, that HMPPS priorities and values are reflected in the work of the 'chaplaincy' department, and that the importance of pastoral, spiritual, and religious care is recognised. The Chaplain General has a group of advisers covering different religions, so benefiting from a range of perspectives, albeit with no non-religious member of the group, as yet. This structure ensures that all prisons, public and private, adhere to Prison Service Instructions (PSI). PSI 05/2016 'Faith and Pastoral Care for Prisoners' sets out the responsibilities of prison chaplaincy staff (National Offender Management Service, 2016). It is important to stress that the prison service and its 'chaplains' recognise that they are there to provide a service to *all* prisoners, irrespective of their religion or belief. This is reflected not only in the PSI but, more importantly, in the attitudes and actions of the 'chaplains' themselves. This concept is built in to the ethos and culture of the organisation. In a very constructive development, the PSI now specifically recognises humanism (p.56), and that humanists should be able to request humanist pastoral care. HMPPS has encouraged and supported accredited humanist pastoral carers providing specific and generic care in prisons. The Chaplain General (Kavanagh, 2016) notes that:

It can be especially valuable where humanists are part of the chaplaincy team. Including them can help some prisoners whose sense of themselves may not involve a 'higher power' but rather a renewed sense of faith in human potential to do good and of the dignity of human being apart from any notion of transcendence. (p.265)

This is a very encouraging and insightful statement. This insight now needs to be fully reflected in the Prison Service Instructions. These refer to the rights of prisoners to practise their 'faith', and for appointments to reflect the 'faith' make-up of the prison population. These references to 'faith' need to be replaced with references to 'religion or belief', a term that includes non-religious people. Specifically recognising the needs of prisoners with non-religious beliefs and values would be a significant step forward. Non-religious prisoners are the second biggest group after Christian prisoners (House of Commons Library, 2017). Table 2.1 compares the religion or belief demographics of the prison population with that of the 'chaplains' who are there to care for them.

Despite cuts elsewhere in the prison service, it appears that the number of full- and part-time 'chaplains' has increased significantly since 2011.[5] It should be stressed that 'chaplain' figures are for the number of full- and part-time staff, not the number of hours worked. They also exclude sessional 'chaplains' and volunteers. Nevertheless, it is possible to draw some general conclusions. There are big disparities between the profile of the prisoners and that of the 'chaplains'. This should be a cause for serious concern by HMPPS. How can its policies and practices be satisfactory if such large discrepancies exist? Christian chaplain representation is much higher than that of the prisoner population. It is not clear to what extent this over-representation of Christians is a traditional legacy. For example, when a Christian chaplain leaves, just recruiting for another Christian will maintain the inequality. In this context, it is interesting to note that all Chaplain General appointments have been of Anglicans, and that these appointments have been made in full consultation with the Church of England. Will this process be maintained when the next Chaplain General is appointed? Will HMPPS and the Church of England consider that they are jointly responsible for the appointment, or will the role be open to any person with the appropriate skills and capabilities, irrespective of their religion or belief?

Muslim 'chaplains' are also over-represented. It would be good to think that this was only the result of HMPPS wanting to provide very good pastoral, spiritual, and religious care of Muslim prisoners. However, it is likely that external actions in relation to the Government's Prevent agenda and its wish to reduce radicalisation in prisons has played a part. What the figures on the percentage of Muslim 'chaplains' do show is that, if there is the political will, it is possible to adopt recruitment and training practices to effectively correct disparities. Encouragingly, many Muslims have been successfully appointed to managing 'chaplain' roles. This suggests that such roles can be filled by people of any religion or belief, including those with non-religious beliefs. Sadly, in the absence of a Prevent agenda, these positives have not

Table 2.1 Prison and 'chaplain' populations (2017)

Religion or belief	Prisoners (%)	'Chaplains' (%)
Christian	48	74
Non-religious	31	0
Muslim	15	24
Other non-Christian	6	2

Source: data from House of Commons Library, 2017; Freedom of Information Act Request 112352[4]

been replicated for other non-Christian 'chaplains'. They have been unable to establish any sort of significant presence in full- or part-time posts. In this respect, the paradigm shift to a more inclusive multi-faith 'chaplaincy', advocated by Noblett a decade earlier, has not been achieved in full.

The biggest discrepancy between the prisoner and 'chaplain' populations is in the non-religious category. Despite this being the second biggest group for several decades, the prison service 'chaplaincy' had not taken any initiative to train and recruit full-time or part-time non-religious carers, and it has taken external players to press for a move toward multi-faith 'chaplaincy'. It seems that external players, such as the Non-Religious Pastoral Support Network, will need to play an important role in support of those prisoners with non-religious beliefs and values. Of course, this requires a shift in perspective; for example, recruitment cannot be limited to religious providers. The need for this shift in perspective is supported by the fact that it is pastoral care that is seen as the primary role of 'chaplains'.

This is confirmed by Todd and Tipton (2011):

> All constituencies (chaplains, prisoners and prison officers) identified the primary role of the chaplain as being pastoral. This meant especially providing one-to-one support to prisoners, in a non-judgemental way, irrespective of their beliefs. (p.4)

In the words of Dearnley (2016), an HMPPS chaplain, 'At the heart of prison chaplaincy is the understanding that chaplains are there pastorally for prisoners and staff of all faiths and none' (p.247).

Perhaps HM Prison Chaplaincy Statement of Purpose captures its current ethos:

> By celebrating the goodness of life and exploring the human condition we aim to cultivate in each individual a responsibility for contributing to the common good. We will contribute to the care of prisoners to enable them to lead law-abiding and useful lives in custody and after release. (National Offender Management Service, n.d., p.2)

This ethos is entirely consistent with building a fully inclusive pastoral, spiritual, and religious prison care service. With goodwill on the part of HMPPS, and of those external organisations seeking to support non-religious prisoners, there is every hope that good progress will be made in building such an inclusive service.

Healthcare

The discussion here is largely limited to the NHS in England and the NHS in Scotland. This is because there is a reasonable amount of evidence and significant comparisons can be made. However, much is relevant to other geographical and healthcare areas. Unlike prisons, there is no legal duty for hospitals to employ a chaplain. There is no duty to have a 'chaplaincy' department. There is a contractual requirement for providers 'to take account of the spiritual, religious, pastoral and cultural needs of Service Users' (NHS, 2016, p.15). This contractual requirement is expected to remain. The extent to which providers 'take account' of these needs, or how they meet these needs, is not specified or prescribed. Many people, not just those in pastoral/spiritual care or 'chaplaincy' departments, will contribute to meeting these needs, so providers need to take a holistic and service user-driven approach. More specifically, in England trusts 'must have regard to the NHS Chaplaincy Guidelines' (NHS, 2016, p.15). However, these guidelines are advisory and trusts do not have to follow them. Indeed, most trusts do not meet the guidelines in some key areas, for example, in relation to recommended staffing levels.

Whilst contracts and guidelines play a part in shaping pastoral, spiritual, and religious care provision, historical and cultural aspects continue to have influence. Just as Beckford and Gilliat's (1998) book *Religion in Prison: 'Equal Rites' in a Multi-Faith Society* was persuasive in changing attitudes in prisons, so Orchard's (2000) report *Hospital Chaplaincy: Modern, Dependable?* asked serious questions about the state of hospital chaplaincy. She asked, 'What formal and informal arrangements have been put in place to address the challenge of equity of access for all patients and to what extent are they effective?' (p.13). The report noted that Anglican chaplaincy was still a dominant presence in 1999. In 1992, the Department of Health issued guidelines stating that, in providing for the spiritual needs of patients and staff, the welfare of both Christians and non-Christians should be recognised as far as reasonably possible. An accompanying press release made it explicit that there was a need to provide for patients of all religions. Of course, there was no mention of patients who were not religious but, at least, this was the first time that such explicit mention of non-Christians was given (Beckford and Gilliat, 1996).

In 1999, in practice, 99.7% of full- and part-time chaplains were Christian, and 83% of these were Anglican.[6]Orchard (2000) concluded 'The lack of urgency in creating inclusive structures ... able to respond to the needs of all patients and relatives is lamentable' (p.152). There was a positive response to these criticisms. A Multi-Faith Group for Healthcare Chaplaincy was formed. This group made an important contribution to the 2003 guidance, *NHS Chaplaincy: Meeting the Religious and Spiritual Needs of Patients and Staff* (Department of Health, 2003). The Chief Nursing Officer wrote that 'One of the key aims of this guidance is to enable chaplaincy services to meet the needs of today's multi-cultural and spiritually diverse society' (p.3). The guide was more inclusive, recommending that 'Adequate arrangements are made for the spiritual, religious, sacramental, ritual, and cultural requirements appropriate to the needs, background and tradition of all patients and staff, including those of no specified faith' (p.8). It is clear that by 2003 the NHS was no longer talking only about a religious care service, only for religious people; but recruitment was still restricted to religious people.

Following reorganisations, more responsibility was devolved to four autonomous regions: England, Scotland, Wales, and Northern Ireland. Their guidelines and arrangements can differ significantly from region to region. NHS Scotland and NHS England are compared below.

In Scotland, history, tradition, and culture played a big role in pastoral, spiritual, and religious care provision. The Church exerted considerable influence on the NHS spiritual care policies and practices. Even though NHS Scotland, as a public body, paid for chaplains, it was customary for the Church of Scotland to employ them. The Church of Scotland selected and recruited all full-time chaplains in the NHS in Scotland, irrespective of denomination.[7] The Church then had its costs reimbursed by the local NHS organisation. There are some obvious risks in this approach. Can such a body act in a neutral way with respect to all denominations? This unsatisfactory situation changed only when NHS Scotland took more direct management responsibility for its own spiritual care service. In 2003, it set up a central Spiritual Care Development Committee whose role was 'the development of spiritual care in both understanding and practice in the NHS Scotland' (Scottish Government, 2009, p.19). Importantly, non-Christian religious groups and humanists were members of the committee in their own right. In 2006 NHS Scotland went further and took direct responsibility for the employment of chaplains (Scottish Executive, 2006). Like HMPPS, it set up its own spiritual care training and development, started to revise its own guidelines, and set up a guidelines working group. Interestingly, of 13 members, six were not from religion or belief groups so the working group was not dominated by religious perspectives. A humanist perspective was provided by the Humanist Society of Scotland. The 2009 Spiritual Care and Chaplaincy Guidelines made some very progressive changes. They focused more on spiritual care than on chaplaincy, and included a more inclusive recruitment policy, stating that 'Chaplains will normally be appointed on the basis of their qualifications, pastoral skill and experience rather than any particular denominational or faith community basis' (Scottish Government, 2009: Annex B, p.14). It was noted that 'Elsewhere the denominational aspects are stronger and there is less commitment to those with no declared faith' (Appendix B, p.19). By listening to a range of perspectives, NHS Scotland developed more inclusive guidelines. The learning from this is discussed in chapter 13.

NHS England, a commissioning organisation, has a responsibility for advising on the spiritual, religious, pastoral, and cultural needs of service users in England. But, unlike the prison service, it does not employ the equivalent of a Chaplain General, nor has it had the equivalent of NHS Scotland's Spiritual Care Development Committee. Instead, it has relied

heavily on 'chaplaincy' organisations and religion or belief grou|
advice, and to conduct work on its behalf. For example, a review ᴏ₁ ᴛ…
NHS England Chaplaincy Guidelines was led by a chaplain in consultation
with the Chaplaincy Leadership Forum.[8] The executive members of the
Forum were all Christian so, unlike NHS Scotland, this review was undertaken from a largely religious and Christian perspective. However, the
review had to meet the requirements of the Equality Act 2010. Having taken
legal advice, the British Humanist Association responded to the draft
guidelines, considering them to be seriously deficient in that NHS England
had failed have due regard to advancing the equality of opportunity of non-
religious people. The NHS was asked to reconsider. It did. For the first time,
its 2015 Chaplaincy Guidelines explicitly referred to non-religious pastoral,
and spiritual care providers (Swift, 2015). This was a major step forward,
albeit coming 15 years after Orchard had complained about a lamentable
lack of urgency.

The need for greater inclusion was still not fully recognised. The equality
analysis that accompanied the guidelines failed to mention, let alone address,
the massive inequalities in staffing and recruitment (Durairaj, 2015). Ongoing
recruitment practices were preventing a reduction in inequality. The executive
of the Chaplaincy Leadership Forum had rejected a proposal to consider
matters of equality and inclusion in its work programme. The British Humanist Association was challenging recruitment advertising where it considered
that non-religious people were unjustifiably being excluded from applying.
NHS England needed to assume real responsibility for its own pastoral,
spiritual, and religious care service.[9] It has started to do so, with very
encouraging results. The Non-Religious Pastoral Support Network are now
full members of a renamed Network for Pastoral, Spiritual and Religious
Care in Health. There have been NHS England-sponsored work programmes
and workshops on equality and recruitment. More advertised posts are open
to non-religious people. Accredited non-religious pastoral carers are being
recruited and being recognised as making a positive contribution to pastoral,
spiritual, and religious care teams in acute hospitals, mental hospitals, and
hospices. There are some outstanding issues, for example about the use of the
word chaplaincy (see chapter 11). However, there is a formal commitment by
NHS England to address these in a future review.

The religion or belief of people in a hospital's catchment will differ from
region to region; the age profile also differs in different types of healthcare
unit. The measurement of people's religion or belief also depends on the
question asked. Taking these aspects together, it seems that *very roughly* 20%
to 40% of patients are non-religious.[10] Table 2.2 shows the religion or belief of
patients based on Care Quality Commission (2016, 2017) data for NHS
England. They use the census question, so the percentage of non-religious
people recorded is lower than when using better questions. These figures are
compared with those of paid substantive NHS chaplains.[11]

Table 2.2 NHS England inpatients and paid substantive NHS 'chaplain' populations (2015)

Religion or belief	Population (%)	'Chaplains' (%)
Christian	64–78	94
Non-religious	15–24	0
Muslim	2–3	4.6
Other non-Christian	2	1.4
Other/would not say	3–7	

Sources: data from Care Quality Commission (2016, 2017); College of Health Cars Chaplains (2016).

It is quite clear that NHS 'chaplaincy' remains overwhelmingly Christian, and does not reflect the make-up of our patient population. It is difficult to understand how this dominance can be justified. As with prisons, Muslim 'chaplain' employment is also over-represented, and other non-Christian religions are under-represented.[12] But the largest under-representation is in relation to people answering 'no religion'. As discussed earlier, this Christian dominance is likely to be the result of many influences: history, tradition, culture, restrictive recruitment, and inadequate policies. Whatever the reasons, such big discrepancies should be a cause for serious concern for the NHS.

The number (full-time equivalent) of paid substantive chaplains increased significantly when the NHS took responsibility for their employment. Further significant expansion occurred in the 1960s and following the 1991 'Patient's Charter'. Since then, growth has been slower (see Table 2.3).[13][14]

It is worth noting that numbers have remained broadly level for the past 20 years despite a reduction in the number of beds, much shorter stays in hospital, and a decline in Christian affiliation. Whilst overall numbers have been reasonably consistent, there have been significant changes in the demographics. The proportion of Anglican chaplains has fallen from over 80% in 1999 to about 50% today, whilst the percentages of Free Church and Catholic chaplains have increased. The biggest changes have been within the Christian chaplaincy community, rather than a move to a multi-faith or fully inclusive care service.

Table 2.3 Number of NHS 'chaplains' (full-time equivalents)

1948	28
1990	266
1996	350
1998	354
2009	390
2015	385

Sources: Swift, Cobb and Todd (2016); Orchard (2000); College of Health Care Chaplains (2016).

Good evidence of how much time 'chaplains' spend on different aspects of their work is very hard to find. A now out-of-date 2002 document prepared by chaplains for the Scottish Executive Health Department gives detailed estimates for the time required each week for various chaplaincy duties, including worship service, bedside services, sacraments, etc. (Scottish Government, 2009). The figures suggest that these constitute about a tenth of a chaplain's work load. These are average figures, so for some chaplains the time spent conducting rituals, sacraments, and worship may be higher, and for some lower. It should be stressed that although these activities are minor in terms of time, they may be particularly important to those receiving this religious care, and to the chaplains providing it. Nevertheless, it does seem that paid substantive 'chaplains' spend most of their time in providing pastoral and spiritual care.

Military

As may be expected from military organisations, pastoral, spiritual, and religious care provision is covered by regulations, in this case Queen's Regulations (QRs). The 1975 QRs for the Army, the 1999 RAF regulations, and the recent 2016 Navy regulations are compared (Ministry of Defence, 1996; Queen's Regulations, 1999; Royal Navy, 2016). By examining these in turn we can see the historical development of military attitudes to pastoral, spiritual, and religious care over time. In the 1975 Army QRs, commissioned chaplains are specifically Christian but not limited to Anglicans. The chaplains' role, as well as providing 'religious ministrations', is to 'promote ... the spiritual and moral welfare of the entire military community' (p.4B-1). The community is tacitly seen to be Christian or Jewish. J5.267 states 'Provision is to be made for the care of personnel of the Jewish faith as occasion arises' (p.5/7–1). No mention is made of other religions and certainly not of non-religious people. The chaplains' role is quite wide and includes 'Giving religious instruction to the personnel of the armed forces and to their families and children living with them' (p.5/7–2). Note that chaplains give religious instruction, not religious education.

Perhaps the most striking part of the QRs is the role of commanding officers. They are 'to encourage religious observance by those under their command and are to set a good example in this respect ... Commanding officers will at all times encourage attendance [at divine service]' (p.5/7–1). Attendance at divine service was not compulsory but there were exceptions. For example, those under 17 years could be ordered to attend divine service of their own denomination. Of course, the regulations do not say what should happen if a 17-year-old does not have a denomination, which is the case for most 17-year olds today. For the Army, 'religion in the armed forces is of the highest importance' (p.5/7-1). This may well be linked to ideas of morality. It was, and remains, crucial that soldiers act with high moral values during times of armed conflict. The Royal Army Chaplains' Department is responsible for promoting the moral welfare of the entire military community. How this works when many of the moral values advocated by the main Christian churches are often at odds with most of the population is unclear. What is astonishing is that the regulations require those in command to encourage religious observance. Where is the moral concept of freedom of conscience?

Over 20 years later, the RAF issued its revised QRs (Queen's Regulations, 1999), showing some limited progress. The basic attitudes of the armed forces and the RAF appear not to have changed. 'The reverent observance of religion in the armed forces' remains 'of the highest importance', and RAF commanding officers are 'to encourage religious observance by those under their command and are themselves to set a good example in this respect' (p.13-10). So even as late as 1999 all commanding officers in the RAF are required to show, by example, that they encourage religious observance. But there has been some progress. Those under 17 years old cannot be ordered to attend divine service. More significant is a change in the role description, 'Christian Chaplains are ... to provide for the spiritual wellbeing, pastoral care and moral teaching and guidance of Service personnel and their families, regardless of faith or profession of no faith' (p.13-10). This is no longer just a religious care service, just for religious people. The importance of wellbeing and pastoral care is noted. At last, there is recognition that there are people in the RAF who profess 'no faith'. However, only Christians can become commissioned chaplains. By this time, the Ministry of Defence had appointed five Civilian Chaplains and a Jewish Officiating chaplain to the whole of HM Forces 'to ensure appropriate consideration is given to Recognised World Faiths other than Christian' (p.13-10). These are Buddhists, Hindus, Jews, Muslims, and Sikhs. At this time, there was much discussion on the wearing of religious dress, days off for religious festivals, and dietary requirements. There has been real progress: for example, Sikhs are normally permitted to wear the five Ks; male Sikhs can also wear a turban; Jews can wear a yarmulke; Muslim men can normally wear a short beard, and halal and kosher meals are now available. However, unlike the non-Christian world faiths, no-one was appointed to ensure appropriate consideration be given to people with non-religious beliefs. People with non-religious beliefs were seen to exist, but not seen as a group worthy of specific or equal consideration.

The most recent regulations on religion and belief, produced by the Royal Navy (2016), may reflect the latest thinking in the armed forces. Importantly, these regulations try to take into account the Equalities Act of 2010. They are a significant step forward from the RAF's 1999 regulations. These regulations treat religious belief as a private matter. There are no references to religion remaining of the highest importance in the armed forces, or to requiring commanding officers to encourage religious observance by those under their command. The description of the chaplains' role has changed somewhat to include:

(1) Delivery of 'all souls ministry' to those of all faiths and those of none.
(2) Practical pastoral care for Service personnel and their families:
  (a) Delivering as guardians of the Service's moral compass.
  (b) Behaving as the indispensable and confidential 'friend and advisor to all.
  (c) Ensuring that their conduct and way of life reflects their sacred calling and maintaining the highest standard of professionalism, leadership and personal example'. (p.31-8)

The idea that chaplains can properly serve 'all faiths and those of none' is still assumed but there is more emphasis on practical pastoral care. Chaplains no longer have responsibility for moral teaching and guidance, rather they are guardians of the Navy's moral compass. For the first time the regulations make explicit an increasingly important and indispensable role, that of a confidential friend and advisor. However, while in principle, the provider of this role does not need to be Christian, or indeed religious, the regulations do not reflect this. Indeed, the regulations go on to say 'Commissioned Armed Forces Chaplains ... are currently drawn from the main Christian denominations to which the majority of Service personnel belong' (p.31-6). The regulations do not say if this *should* be the case. The implication is that if the majority of service personnel are Christian then all commissioned chaplains should be Christian. There is certainly no mention of any wish or intent to ensure that the provision broadly matches the religion or belief of the Navy community. The non-Christian world faith appointees are now called 'chaplains' but they are treated differently from Christian chaplains: they are there to provide internal advice and raise awareness of their faith. They are civilians, not commissioned officers. Recruitment into commissioned roles still seems to be restricted to Christians. It is difficult to see how this situation can be consistent with the Equalities Act. The Navy regulations state:

The Equality Act protects everyone from discrimination on grounds of their religion or belief including Christians, Muslims, Jews, Hindus, Sikhs, Buddhist and members of other religions, *as well as humanists and atheists.* (p.31-3) [my italics]

The protection of the Equalities Act goes well beyond 'humanists and atheists', it covers all those with a lack of religion and all those with a lack of belief. This is a much bigger group than that of atheists and humanists. The most recent census recorded 24.7% as 'no religion' but only 0.2% as atheist or agnostic (Office for National Statistics 2011). The fact that the Navy regulations do not make it clear that people who are non-religious cannot be discriminated against should be a source of concern to the Navy and the armed forces in general. The development of Queen's Regulations does show some limited progress, but these regulations do suggest that those in command of our armed forces have found it difficult to make an appropriate response to both the equality issues and the provision of like-minded pastoral, spiritual, and religious care.

A report for the Church of England in 2010 showed that the armed forces employed about 470 chaplains, with nearly 70% in the Army and 15% in each of the Navy and Air Force (Church of England, 2010). Unlike the NHS and the prison service, the armed forces did not develop a genuinely multi-faith pastoral, spiritual, and religious care service where non-Christian care providers were treated in the same way as Christian chaplains. In relation to armed forces personnel with non-religious beliefs, a report by King (2013) of the Royal Army Chaplains' Department found that on Operation HERRICK15 one in five of front-line troops were non-religious.[15] This tends to refute the apocryphal assertion that 'there are no atheists in fox-holes'. Indeed, the number of non-religious people in the armed forces has grown rapidly in recent years from 14.7% in 2012 to 25.5% in 2017 (Ministry of Defence, 2017).[16] Given the age profile of the armed forces, it is expected that non-religious personnel will be a very significant part of the armed forces. Ensuring that there are like-minded pastoral carers to meet their needs requires serious attention.

One particular aspect of the role of a commissioned chaplain is to be the guardian of the service's moral compass or to provide moral teaching and guidance of service personnel. As all commissioned chaplains are Christian, it is likely to be Christian moral guidance. This may be a problem to many in the armed forces who do not accept the moral guidance of Christian churches on such things as sex before marriage, gay marriage, assisted suicide, and so on. It may also be a problem for the chain of command, who are increasingly governed by legal principles such as the Law of Armed Combat. When someone is about to give an instruction to deploy a Reaper missile from a drone, they cannot debate the relative moral merits of the Law of Armed Combat versus the chaplain's Augustinian concepts of a just war.

The real tensions and sincere concerns are discussed in *Military Chaplaincy in Contention* (Todd, 2013a). For example, chaplains want to be a committed and constructive part of their military unit, but may have values that are occasionally inconsistent with some of the team's actions. This can result in tension between the chaplain's wish to support the team and the need to act according to his highest moral values. Sedgwick (2013) discusses this in relation to the Baha Mousa inquiry and the chaplain's role, saying: 'Once again the chaplain is caught between the demands of the institution they serve and the demands of the gospel, and that tension is irreducible' (p.80). Tensions can arise between the Church and the military command. In 1999, the Army carried out a review of spiritual needs, which examined the extent to which chaplains' activities should be determined by the Church, and by the military command. McGill (1999), cited by Howson (2013), found it necessary to assert that 'The priority for a chaplain to be with soldiers, rather than involved with church affairs, needs restating' (p.108). It is perhaps inevitable that there should be some tension if two different organisations feel that they each have a role in determining the activities of chaplains. There can also be tensions between some chaplains and their 'sending churches'. Some sending churches or church leaders have strongly opposed military action by UK forces in Afghanistan and Syria. Howson (2013) mentions the Church of Scotland's long-standing view that having nuclear weapons is contrary to God's word, yet the same church authorised chaplains to serve in our nuclear navy. This can sometimes make military chaplains feel somewhat isolated from the church which should be there to support them. These situations arise, in part, from the dual role and responsibilities of some chaplains in practising their ministry. It is important for non-religious pastoral carers to be mindful of the tensions that their chaplaincy colleagues in their care team may be facing, and to help where possible.

One of the areas where this tension does not seem to exist is in the provision of pastoral care. We have seen how the development of regulations has increasingly recognised the importance of pastoral care. This is also an area where the sending churches fully recognise the value of the chaplains' work. For example, the Church of Scotland, whilst condemning nuclear weapons, went on to 'recognise the pastoral needs of those servicemen, servicewomen and civilians serving with the nuclear weapons programme' (Howson, 2013, p.97).

Whilst recognising the need for fully inclusive pastoral, spiritual, and religious care, the armed forces have retained an essentially Christian model of care provision. This seems to be both morally and legally unsustainable. Clearly, the commanders of the armed forces need to address this issue. Humanist and other organisations can encourage and help the armed forces management find a constructive way forward, perhaps learning from the experience of their Dutch colleagues. The Dutch armed forces have successfully provided a humanist care service for many decades (see chapter 13).

Education

Our earliest universities, Oxford and Cambridge, required students to subscribe to the Thirty-Nine Articles of the Church of England on graduation or matriculation, effectively excluding so-called dissenters from university education. In 1826, in the face of strong opposition from the Church of England, London University (now University College London) was founded as a secular alternative to Oxbridge. London University was more inclusive, enabling students who were not members of the Church of England to access university education. It was also the first university in the UK to admit women to its degrees. Fortunately, these ideas of inclusivity were adopted by other universities. The Universities Tests Act was passed in 1871, abolishing religious tests at Oxford, Cambridge, and Durham and allowing non-Anglicans to take up teaching appointments. Today all our universities admit students and appoint staff without discrimination based on their religion or belief. However, the Universities of Oxford and Cambridge Act 1923 allowed these universities and their colleges to draw up their own memoranda, and almost all of them stipulated that religious provision should be Christian and Anglican.

Each university cherishes its independence, and 'chaplains' are funded in a variety of ways. These factors have resulted in a much looser organisational structure than in hospitals, prisons, and the military. The older established university colleges will fund chaplains from their own endowments; charities fund a few chaplains; churches fund some; and universities fund others. Often funding will be shared by the churches and the university, for example with the university paying for buildings and administrative support. In some cases the university will have management responsibility for 'chaplains', and some will formally review their work. In 2008 about 98% of paid 'chaplains' were Christian (Clines, 2008, p.13). Interestingly, about a third of unpaid 'chaplaincy' volunteers were non-Christian, a high proportion. It is not clear to what extent the Christian dominance in paid roles is due to Christian church funding, the difficulty for non-Christian bodies to fund such roles, or universities' recruitment practices favouring Christians. Whatever the reasons, universities, their staff, and their students may wish to give serious consideration to increasing diversity in this area.

Unlike in prisons, hospitals, and military bases, people at university can integrate more easily into their local area. This means that pastoral, spiritual, and religious care is provided by many organisations. Universities are becoming more conscious of the need to provide pastoral and spiritual support to students. Some tutors have specific pastoral support responsibilities. Student welfare services provide counselling and related support. Religious support may be provided at local community places of worship, gurdwaras, temples, synagogues, mosques, churches, etc. Student religion or belief societies can be effective in giving peer-to-peer support and friendship. Some of these societies, such as the Student Christian Movement, are long established; others, such as the National Federation of Atheist, Humanist and Secular Student Societies (now Humanist Students), are more recent.[17] 'Chaplaincy departments' are not the only, and often not the main, source of pastoral, spiritual, or religious care.

Guest et al. (2013) state that 'Chaplaincies retain historical privilege and in some cases institutional advantage, but often achieve very low levels of student engagement' (p.196). Their survey showed that only 2.7% of Christian students were usually involved with university chaplaincy in term time, compared with 10% who were involved with the Christian Unions. Of course, student engagement is not the only role of the pastoral, spiritual, or religious care provided by 'chaplaincy' departments. This role can vary significantly from university to university, and even within a university. The Church of England (2017b) has produced an excellent document, *Guidelines for Beginning in Chaplaincy*, which describes the higher education scene and the different roles a carer may play. Almost all the guide is relevant to non-religious pastoral carers. Of course, statements in the guide such as 'Whether you are "lay" or ordained, you are part of the Church and have a responsibility to it' (p.6) are not relevant. Such statements do show the dual responsibilities of a Church of England chaplain to both the university authorities and the church authorities.

Historically, almost all schools were parish or chapel schools with either a priest or minister having an active role. Some of these schools would also have had a chaplain. Today the presence of a chaplain in a school is more likely to be limited to fee-paying independent schools, Voluntary Aided, and Voluntary Controlled church schools. Caperon (2011) found that about two-thirds of all chaplains were employed in independent schools, the remainder in maintained schools or academies.[18] The Church saw school chaplaincy as an essential element of its mission to young people. Very few children attend church. Chaplains can reach far more young people in church schools, independent schools, and schools with a religious character or ethos. Here their role is seen as one of ministry, possibly leading-edge ministry (p.2). The Church of England commissioned a report titled *The Public Face of God*, which referred to chaplains working in Anglican schools in England and Wales. The report stated that there has been significant growth in school chaplain numbers since the Dearing Report of 2001 (Church of England (2014, p.1).

The number of school chaplains is difficult to estimate, with various reports coming to different conclusions. Todd, Slater and Dunlop (2014) estimated that there were 181 Church of England school chaplains. In 2015 the Association of Catholic Chaplains in Education stated that it had 100+ chaplains within Catholic education in England and Wales (Polisano, 2015). Most Church of England secondary schools and academies employ a Christian chaplain, or team of chaplains. The majority are ordained ministers. Almost all are directly funded by public money through the school's own budget. Even though these chaplains are visibly religious people working in schools with a declared religious ethos, chaplains consider pastoral care to be the most important aspect of their work. 'School chaplains place the pastoral dimension of their vocation as its heart: it is a ministry involving a range of functions, but pastoral care for the person is what matters most' (Caperon, 2011, p.10).

Most school pupils do not go to independent fee-paying schools or schools with a religious character. They go to state-funded schools that do not discriminate in their admissions policies based on religion or belief. Very few of these schools have a paid chaplain, yet these pupils receive pastoral, spiritual, and religious support. Some of this is specifically provided within the teaching curriculum, for example within spiritual, moral, social, and cultural education. In recent years there have been significant developments in the provision of pastoral care in all schools, both independent and state-funded. The Independent (2013) cites a report from the Independent Schools Inspectorate:

> Decades ago, pastoral care barely existed, but independent schools and even many academic hothouses are now making huge efforts to create a nurturing and supportive setting ... Pastoral care is rarely less than good, and often excellent, which reflects the emphasis schools tend to place on this area.

In schools, pastoral care is likely to take a holistic approach with the school addressing the personal, social, emotional, and intellectual needs of pupils, so that they can fully participate and benefit from everything the school offers, not only its academic education. The development of best practice in such pastoral care is being supported by organisations such as the National Association for Pastoral Care in Education. Some idea of the nature and scope of their work can be seen from articles in the journal *Pastoral Care in Education: An International Journal of Personal, Social and Emotional Development.* [19] A selection of titles from the 2017 volume includes:

> Learning through observations: the potential of collective worship in primary schools.
>
> The success of a planned bereavement response – a survey on teacher use of bereavement response plans when supporting grieving children in Danish schools.
>
> An interactional analysis of one-to-one pastoral care delivery within a primary school.
>
> A person-centred life in action. A perspective on my life and work.
>
> Teachers' views on spirituality for adolescents in high schools across countries.
>
> Three quality professional documents to guide teachers for puberty, relationships and sexuality education.

Even this snapshot shows the scope and depth of work on pastoral care in education. The concept of pastoral care in schools is becoming well established. Most importantly, generations of younger people will go through school not only with an understanding of pastoral care, but with experience of it. The term pastoral care will have personal meaning for them. This is in contrast with 'chaplaincy'. A very small minority of school pupils will have experience of a chaplain or have any understanding of what they do. As we have seen, very few students at university are involved with chaplains. Over time, more pupils will experience pastoral care at school, and for many university students the concept of pastoral care will become more established. Conversely, as fewer young people affiliate to a religion or attend church, their contact with chaplains will decline. This trend will have important strategic implications in terms of the provision of pastoral, spiritual, and religious care.

Conclusions

In current pastoral, spiritual, and religious care practice there is a strong emphasis on religious care, for religious people, delivered by religious providers. There are many reasons for this emphasis, from history and tradition to the overwhelming proportion of religious, mainly Christian, providers. For some people, being able to receive that religious care can be an essential part of their wellbeing. As well as providing religious care, most 'chaplains' will see it as part of their role to provide pastoral and spiritual care to all those who may need it, irrespective of that person's religion or belief. That includes people with non-religious beliefs and values. 'Chaplains' aim to provide that care with commitment, compassion, and sincerity. Some religious carers may have concluded that, because they are there to serve 'all faiths and none', there is no need for non-religious pastoral carers. Of course, this view is not justified. Just as a person with Islamic beliefs may want to receive like-minded care from a Muslim carer, or a person with Catholic beliefs may want to receive like-minded care from a Catholic priest, so a person with non-religious beliefs may want to receive care from a like-minded non-religious pastoral carer.

Gradually, provision has progressed from that of purely Christian religious ministry to a care model including pastoral, spiritual, and religious care elements. Importantly, all the institutions have stressed that such care should be available to everyone, including non-religious people. Sadly, this change in approach and ethos has still to be fully reflected in the policies and practices of the institutions. One obvious manifestation of the absence of change is the over-representation of Christians in pastoral/spiritual care and in 'chaplaincy' departments. Whilst there has been some progress in moving from a Christian to a multi-faith care service, development has been slow and mainly directed to Islamic provision. Until very recently, progress towards a fully inclusive service that embraces non-religious care provision has been almost non-existent.

This lack of diversity and presence of inequality should be a serious cause for concern for management in all institutions. It has meant that service users have not been able to choose a non-religious pastoral carer, and non-religious pastoral carers have not had the opportunity to be employed to provide that care. Fortunately, this situation is improving. Good progress is being made where the senior management of institutions are taking ownership and responsibility for their pastoral, spiritual, and religious care services, rather than delegating responsibility to existing service providers. Choices and opportunities are increasing as more and more non-religious pastoral carers seek roles in institutions. Most institutions are responding positively. These non-religious pastoral carers, and the care teams of which they are a part, are finding that they can make a significant contribution to their institution's care provision.

Despite public spending cuts, an increase in the proportion of non-religious people, and a decline in religious observance, the number of 'chaplains' providing pastoral, spiritual, and religious care has proven to be remarkably robust. In part this is because the pattern of care being delivered has changed. What shines through this review is the importance and centrality of pastoral care to both 'chaplains' and institutions.

Of course, understanding the views of 'chaplains' and institutions as expressed in this review is important. But from a person-centred non-religious pastoral care perspective, it is the views of those receiving, or wishing to receive, pastoral, spiritual, and religious care that are fundamental.

Notes

1 Scotland has similar legislation in the Prisons (Scotland) Act 1989.
2 Angulimala, a Buddhist 'chaplaincy' organisation, wrote that 'Our sole interest has been to make Buddhism available in the prisons of the United Kingdom and we have tried to make this offering and to go about it in the spirit of Dana or Giving...All we have ever asked for are reasonable facilities and the right to go about our business unhindered' (Forest Hermitage 1996, cited in Beckford and Gilliat (1998, p.222).
3 On 1st April 2017, the National Offender Management Service became Her Majesty's Prison and Probation Service (HMPPS). Some of the reference documents refer to the National Offender Management Service.
4 The number of 'chaplains' is based on a Freedom of Information Act Request 112352. Number of prison chaplains by religion, as at 31 March 2017:

Religion	Managing (full-time)	Chaplains (full-time)	Chaplains (part-time)	Total	Percentage
Christian	30	89	196	315	74
Muslim	23	37	34	101	24
Sikh		4	2[*]	6	1.4
Hindu		2[*]	2[*]	4	1
Unknown	37	2[*]	3	42	

[*]This is a maximum number. Table 2.1 does not include the unknowns.

5 Todd (2013b) agreed with the National Offender Management Service that by 2011 there were 357 employed full- or part-time 'chaplains'. This had increased to about 468 in 2017.
6 This information is from the Hospital Chaplaincies Council, a Church of England body reporting to the General Synod. Orchard (2000) points out that numbers are not easy to reconcile (p.21). However, they are probably adequate to show the dominant position of the Church of England. The Hospital Chaplaincies Council has been disbanded.
7 The Catholic and Scottish Episcopal Churches employed some part-time NHS chaplains on the same basis.

8 The Chaplaincy Leadership Forum was a forum for dialogue between the College of Healthcare Chaplains, the Association of Hospital and Palliative Care Chaplains, the UK Board of Healthcare Chaplains, the Health Care Chaplaincy Appointment Advisers, and the Healthcare Chaplaincy Faith and Belief Group.

9 NHS England does not have a direct responsibility for the provision of pastoral, spiritual, and religious care. However, it can have a significant influence on policies and practices.

10 The Care Quality Commission community mental health survey for NHS England found that 64% of respondents were Christian and 24% were of 'no religion' (Care Quality Commission, 2017). Its Adult Inpatient Survey (Care Quality Commission, 2016) showed that 78% of respondents were Christian and 15% were of 'no religion'. This was in response to the Census question 'What is your religion?'. If a non-leading question was asked, such as that used in the British Social Attitudes survey, the number responding 'no religion' would have been higher, probably about 40% on average.

11 'Chaplain' data are from the Annual Report of the College of Health Care Chaplains (2016, p.8).

12 It is not entirely possible to explain the over-representation of Muslims, but it may be for the same sort of reasons that influenced the prison numbers. This effect may have been partly indirect. The Muslim community were encouraged to provide 'chaplaincy' services. To help with this, the Markfield Institute of Higher Education established an MA course in Muslim Chaplaincy. (Markfield Institute, n.d.) This would have helped to encourage the employment of Muslim 'chaplains' in all institutions, not just prisons.

13 Note that there is no consistent basis for collecting these numbers, so they should be regarded only as a guide. Sources are: for year 1948, Swift, Cobb and Todd (2106); for 1990–1998, Orchard (2000); for 2009 and 2015, College of Health Care Chaplains (2016).

14 The National Archives (2016) show that the headcount numbers have fallen from 1,107 in 2010 to 916 in 2015. It is not clear to what extent this fall is due to full-time posts replacing several part-time posts as the service attempts to 'professionalise', or to what extent it is a reduction in full-time equivalents. The Health and Social Care Information Centre points out that the data have not been subject to its usual validation processes, so these figures should be used with care.

15 UK operations in Afghanistan were conducted under the name Operation HERRICK.

16 This figure is for Regulars. The figure for Future Reserves is 22.1%.

17 The Student Christian Movement was set up in 1889; the National Federation of Atheist, Humanist and Secular Student Societies had its press launch in February 2009. Details available from: http://www.movement.org.uk/about-us/history and http://ahsstudents.org.uk/about/history.

18 This was based on a limited survey, so the findings need to be treated with some caution.

19 For further details see http://www.napce.org.uk/ and https://www.tandfonline.com/toc/rped20/35/4 [Accessed 26th April 2017].

References

Beckford, J.A. (1999) The Management of Religious Diversity in England and Wales with Special Reference to Prison Chaplaincy. *International Journal on Multicultural Societies* 1(2), 55–66.

Beckford, J.A., Gilliat, S. (1996) 'The Church of England and other Faiths in a Multi-Faith Society. Volume II. Healthcare Chaplaincy'. University of Warwick, unpublished.

Beckford, J.A., Gilliat, S. (1998) *Religion in Prison: 'Equal Rites' in a Multi-Faith Society*. Cambridge, Cambridge University Press.

Caperon, J. (2011) *School Chaplaincy: What Does Research Tell Us?* Project Papers 45. Cuddeston, The Bloxham Project. Available from: http://www.scala.uk.net/dyn/pages/research-project-report-for-2011-conference-2.pdf [accessed 25th April 2017].

Care Quality Commission (2016) Adult Inpatient Survey 2016. Open Data, National Tables. Available from: http://www.cqc.org.uk/publications/surveys/adult-inpatient-survey-2016 [accessed 2nd December 2017].

Care Quality Commission (2017) Community Mental Health Survey 2017. Open Data, National Tables. Available from: http://www.cqc.org.uk/publications/surveys/community-mental-health-survey-2017 [accessed 2nd December 2017].

Catholic Bishops' Conference (2007) *Caring for the Catholic Patient: A Guide to Catholic Chaplaincy for NHS Managers & Trusts*. London, Incorporated Catholic Truth Society. Available from: http://www.cbcew.org.uk/content/download/34847/258815/file/CCP_Guide_to_NHS_Managers_and_Trusts.pdf [accessed 8th April 2017].

Church of England (2010) *Presentation on Military Chaplaincy*. GS 1776. Available from: https://www.yumpu.com/en/document/view/51145194/presentation-on-military-chaplaincy-church-of-england [accessed 1st July 2018].

Church of England (2014) *The Public Face of God, Chaplaincy in Anglican Secondary Schools and Academies in England and Wales*. London, Church of England Archbishops' Council Education Division. Available from: https://www.churchofengland.org/sites/default/files/2017-10/2014_the_public_face_of_god_web_final.pdf [accessed 25th April 2017].

Church of England (2017a) *Our Faith: Mission*. Available from: https://www.churchofengland.org/our-faith/mission.aspx [accessed 8th April 2017; no longer available online].

Church of England (2017b) *Education and National Society: Guidelines for Beginning in Chaplaincy*. Available from: https://www.churchofengland.org/educations/colleges-universities/he/chaplaincy-resources/getting-started.aspx [accessed 8th April 2017; no longer available online].].

Clines, J.M.S. (2008) *Faiths in Higher Education Chaplaincy*. London, Church of England Board of Education. Available from: https://www.fbrn.org.uk/sites/default/files/files/faiths%20in%20higher%20ed%20exec%20summary.pdf [accessed 25th April 2017].

College of Health Care Chaplains (2016) *CHCC Annual Report 2016*. Available from: https://www.healthcarechaplains.org/wp-content/uploads/2016/08/CHCC-Annual-Report-2016.pdf [accessed 19th April 2017].

Dearnley, H. (2016) Prison Chaplaincy. In: Swift, C., Cobb, M., Todd, A. (eds) *A Handbook of Chaplaincy Studies*. Abingdon, Routledge, p.247.

Department of Health (2003) *NHS Chaplaincy: Meeting the Religious and Spiritual Needs of Patients and Staff*. Available from: http://www.merseycare.nhs.uk/media/1855/chaplaincy-guidance.pdf [accessed 18th April 2017].

Durairaj, S. (2015) *NHS England Chaplaincy Guidelines 2015: Promoting Excellence in Pastoral, Spiritual & Religious Care: Equality Analysis*. Leeds, NHS England.

Available from: https://www.england.nhs.uk/wp-content/uploads/2015/03/equality-a nalysis-nhs-chaplaincy-guidelines-2015.pdf [accessed 19th April 2017].

Guest, M., Aune, K., Sharma, S., Warner, R. (2013) *Christianity and the University Experience*. London, Bloomsbury Academic.

Harting-Correa, A.L. (trans.) (1996) *Wahlahfrid Strabo's Libellus de Exordiis et Incrementis Quarundam in Observationibus Ecclesiasticus Rerum: A Translation and Liturgical Commentary*. Leiden: E.J. Brill.

House of Commons Library (2017) *UK Prison Population Statistics*. Available at: http://researchbriefings.parliament.uk/ResearchBriefing/Summary/SN04334 [accessed 29th December 2017].

Howson, P. (2013) The British Churches and the Chaplains: Standing Back to Back and Walking in Opposite Directions. In: Todd, A. (ed.) *Military Chaplaincy in Contention*. Farnham, Ashgate Publishing.

Independent (2013) The Importance of Pastoral Care: A Caring, Sharing Way to Educate. Available from: http://www.independent.co.uk/news/education/schools/ the-importance-of-pastoral-care-a-caring-sharing-way-to-educate-8494596.html [accessed 26th April 2017].

Jones, R. (2010) Characteristics of Chaplaincy: A Methodist Understanding. *Epworth Review* December. Available from: http://www.methodist.org.uk/media/2572/epworth-review-characteristicsofchaplaincy-1210.pdf [accessed 8th April 2017].

Kavanagh, M. (2016) Contextual Issues: Justice and Redemption. In: Swift, C., Cobb, M., Todd, A. (eds) *A Handbook of Chaplaincy Studies*. Abingdon, Routledge, p.256.

King, P. (2013) *Faith in a Foxhole? Researching Combatant Religiosity amongst British Soldiers on Contemporary Operations*. Defence Academy Yearbook 2013. Available from: https://www.da.mod.uk/publications/Defence-Academy-Yearbook-2013 [accessed 12th December 2017].

Markfield Institute (n.d.) MA in Muslim Chaplaincy. Markfield, Markfield Institute of Higher Education. Available from: https://www.mihe.ac.uk/course/ma-muslim-chaplaincy [accessed 7th May 2017].

Ministry of Defence (1996) *The Queen's Regulations for the Army 1975*, Amendment No 26. Available from: https://www.gov.uk/government/uploads/system/uploads/ attachment_data/file/440632/20150529-QR_Army_Amdt_31_Jul_2013.pdf [accessed 20th April 2017].

Ministry of Defence (2017) UK Armed Forces Biannual Diversity Statistics: 2017. Available from: https://www.gov.uk/government/statistics/uk-armed-forces-biannual-diversity-statistics-2017 [accessed 30th December 2017].

National Offender Management Service (2016) Faith and Pastoral Care for Prisoners, PSI 05/2016. Available from: https://www.justice.gov.uk/downloads/offenders/ psipso/psi-2016/psi-05-2016-faith-and-pastoral-care-for-prisoners.doc [accessed 26th November 2017].

National Offender Management Service (n.d.) *A Guide to Religious Practice in Prison*. London, Ministry of Justice, National Offender Management Service, Chaplaincy. Available from: https://static1.squarespace.com/static/58359f279de4bbe7aba10e31/t/ 58456a32197aeafb4a20a4b3/1480944191187/Prison+Faith+Booklet [accessed 10th April 2017].

NHS (2016) *NHS Standard Contract 2016/17 Service Conditions (Full Length)*. Available from: https://www.england.nhs.uk/wp-content/uploads/2016/04/2-nhs-fll-length-1617-scs-apr16.pdf [accessed 10th April 2017].

Noblett, W. (2001) A Multi-Faith Prison Chaplaincy: A Paradigm Shift? *New Life, The Prison Service Chaplaincy Review* 15, 39.

Office for National Statistics (2011) Religion Data from the 2011 Census. Release 16 December 2014.

Olumide, O. (1993) Toward equitable provision of spiritual, religious and cultural care within the NHS. *Journal of Healthcare Chaplaincy* September, 12–16.

Orchard, H. (2000) *Hospital Chaplaincy: Modern, Dependable?*Manchester, Lincoln Theological Institute for the Study of Religion and Society.

Polisano, D. (2015) *ACCE: From 1993 to the Present Day.* Association of Catholic Chaplains in Education. Available from: http://www.acceuk.org.uk/aboutacce.html [accessed 26th April 2017].

Queen's Regulations (1999) *The Queen's Regulations for the Royal Air Force*, Fifth Edition 1999, Amendment List No. 42. Available from: http://www.raf.mod.uk/rafcms/mediafiles/369A5A48_5056_A318_A87DEF0BF23E746C.pdf [accessed 20th April 2017; no longer available online].

Royal Navy (2016) Religion and Belief. In: *BR 3 Vol. 1 – Naval Personnel Management*, version 6. Available from: http://www.royalnavy.mod.uk/-/media/royal-navy-responsive/documents/reference-library/br-3-vol-1/chapter-31.pdf [accessed 20th April 2017].

Scottish Executive (2006) *Transfer of Healthcare Chaplains to NHS Employment.* NHS HDL 67/2006. Available from: http://www.sehd.scot.nhs.uk/mels/HDL2006_67.pdf [accessed 19th April 2017].

Scottish Government (2009) *Spiritual Care and Chaplaincy.* Available from: http://www.gov.scot/Resource/Doc/259076/0076811.pdf [accessed 30th November 2017].

Sedgwick, P. (2013) Terrorism and Interrogation, as an Issue for Chaplains on Operations. In: Todd, A. (ed.) *Military Chaplaincy in Contention.* Farnham, Ashgate Publishing, p.80.

Slater, V. (2015) *Chaplaincy Ministry and the Mission of the Church.* Norwich, SCM Press.

Swift, C. (2015) *NHS Chaplaincy Guidelines 2015: Promoting Excellence in Pastoral, Spiritual & Religious Care.* Version 1. Available from: https://www.england.nhs.uk/wp-content/uploads/2015/03/nhs-chaplaincy-guidelines-2015.pdf [accessed 12th June 2018].

Swift, C., Cobb, M., Todd, A. (eds) (2016) *A Handbook of Chaplaincy Studies: Understanding Spiritual Care in Public Places.* Abingdon: Routledge.

The National Archives (2016) Health and Social Care Information Centre, Provisional Monthly Workforce Statistics. Available from: http://webarchive.nationalarchives.gov.uk/20180328130852tf_/http://content.digital.nhs.uk/media/19320/Number-of-chaplains-employed-by-the-NHS-2010-2015/xls/Chaplains_employed_by_the_NHS_-_2010-2015.xlsx/ [accessed 22nd April 2018].

Todd, A. (ed.) (2013a) *Military Chaplaincy in Contention.* Farnham, Ashgate Publishing.

Todd, A. (2013b) Prison Chaplaincy. In: Becci, I., Bernts, T., Michalowski, I., Rosati, M., Fabbretti, V., Todd, A. (eds) *The Formatting of Religions: Religious Accommodation in Prisons and the Military*, ReligioWest, 11–12 February 2013. European University Institute. p.36. Available from: https://apps.eui.eu/Events/download.jsp?FILE_ID=3941 [accessed 10th April 2017].

Todd, A., Tipton, L. (2011) *The Role and Contribution of a Multi-Faith Prison Chaplaincy to the Contemporary Prison Service.* Final Report. Cardiff, Cardiff Centre for Chaplaincy Studies. Available from: http://orca.cf.ac.uk/29120/1/Chaplaincy%20Report%20Final%20Draft%20%283%29.pdf [accessed 24th November 2017].

Todd, A., Slater, V., Dunlop, S. (2014) *The Church of England's Involvement in Chaplaincy.* Cardiff and Cuddesdon, Cardiff Centre for Chaplaincy Studies andOxford Centre for Ecclesiology & Practical Theology (OxCEPT). Available from: http://www.rcc.ac.uk/downloads/todd-slater—dunlop-2014-report-on-church-of-england-chaplaincy.pdf [accessed 26th April 2017].

UK Government (1952) Prison Act. Available from: http://www.legislation.gov.uk/ukpga/1952/52/pdfs/ukpga_19520052_en.pdf [accessed 9th April 2017].

Chapter 3

Public perceptions of chaplains and non-religious pastoral carers

In 2016, YouGov carried out a major survey for the British Humanist Association (Humanists UK, 2017).[1] Part of the survey, of over 4,000 adults, was concerned with people's perception of chaplains in terms of their religion or belief, the uptake of chaplaincy services, and people's views on the need for non-religious pastoral care. Finally, people were asked how likely or unlikely they thought they would be to access support from a chaplain or a trained non-religious pastoral carer. Respondents were also asked about their religion or belief with the question 'Do you regard yourself as belonging to any particular religion, and if so, to which of these do you belong?' This was followed by 'Yes' with a list of Christian denominations, non-Christian religions, 'Not sure' and 'No, I do not regard myself as belonging to any particular religion'. 44% responded 'No, I do not regard myself as belonging to any particular religion', slightly lower than the British Social Attitudes Survey.

Perceptions of the religious identity of chaplains

The question aimed at understanding people's perceptions of the religious identity of chaplains was as follows:

> For the following question, please imagine someone said to you they were a 'chaplain'.
> Which, if any, of the following types of people would you think this person could be? (Please select all that apply).
> This was followed by a list of religions, 'A person belonging to another religion', 'A non-religious person', 'None of these' and 'Don't know'.

Respondents could tick any number of boxes. For example, if a respondent thought that a chaplain could be a Sikh, they could tick the Sikh box; if they also thought that a chaplain could be a Buddhist, they could tick that box as well. Hence the total exceeds 100%. Figure 3.1 shows that chaplains are overwhelmingly seen as Christian and *only* Christian. As many as 83% of respondents thought a chaplain could be Christian, and only about 5% of

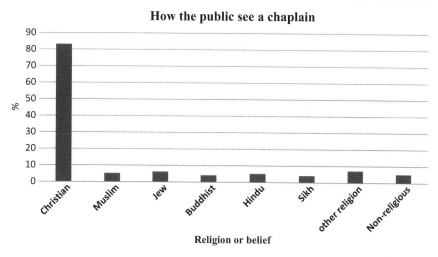

Figure 3.1 How the public see a chaplain
Source: Humanists UK (2017)

respondents thought that a chaplain could be a person of one of the other religious categories or could be a non-religious person.

This finding has significant implications in relation to communications. Clearly, if a person is described as a chaplain, it is likely that most people will consider that person to be a Christian. If a department calls itself a chaplaincy department, or if a leaflet comes from a chaplaincy, then it is likely that most people will consider that these relate to Christians or Christianity. It is quite apparent that, for the vast majority of respondents, the terms chaplain and chaplaincy are not equally inclusive of non-Christian and non-religious people.

Chapter 2 shows that the majority of paid posts in pastoral/spiritual and chaplaincy departments are people with Christian beliefs. In terms of providing care, some have argued that this Christian predominance is not a problem because these Christian providers are there for 'all faiths and none' so all people, irrespective of their religion or belief, get access to the care they need. The next part of the survey examined this argument.

Uptake of chaplaincy services

The survey asked:

> Have you ever personally made use of the support offered by chaplains in a hospital, prison, or university? (If you have never been in, worked in, or visited someone in one of these institutions, please select the 'Not applicable' option.)

Overall, almost one in ten respondents replied 'Yes, I have'. The question was not applicable to about a quarter of respondents. Most of the remainder replied 'No, I haven't'.[2] The percentage making use of chaplains was quite even in all categories of respondent (see Figure 3.2), except for the category of a person's religion or belief.[3]

People describing themselves as belonging to the Christian religion were most likely to have made use of the support offered by chaplains. Those with non-Christian religious beliefs made use of chaplains' support to a lesser extent. But perhaps the most noticeable finding was that very few people who did not regard themselves as belonging to a particular religion had made use of chaplains' support. Those belonging to the Christian religion were more than three times more likely than a non-religious person to have received support from a chaplain.

Such big differences raise very serious questions about current care provision. It might be argued that such differences are to be expected because of our populations' demographics. Older people are more likely to be in hospital, older people are much more likely to be Christian, so it is quite natural that there will be a particularly high proportion of people belonging to the Christian religion receiving support from a chaplain. But the evidence from the survey data does not support this argument.[4] It might be argued that 'chaplains', being predominantly Christian, focus their time and energy on revisiting people belonging to the Christian religion at the expense of people with

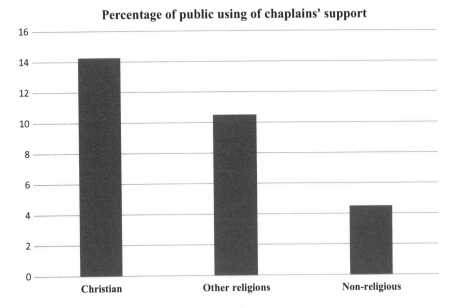

Figure 3.2 Percentage of public using chaplains' support
Source: Humanists UK (2017)

other religions or beliefs, and that this focus helps explain these differences in response. This survey does not explore such arguments and provides no evidence for or against them. However, an audit of 'chaplaincy' visits in one hospital trust found no evidence of such bias (Savage, 2015).[5] 'Chaplains' did revisit Christian patients slightly more often than non-Christian or non-religious patients, but the differences were too small to explain the huge differences found in the YouGov survey. It might be argued that the general public see chaplaincy as Christian, so people belonging to non-Christian religions and non-religious people do not engage to the same extent as people belonging to the Christian religion. Again, the survey does not explore such arguments. However, the response to the previous question does show that chaplain is not a neutral or inclusive term. There may be some validity in this argument.[6]

There have been some attempts to develop a multi-faith 'chaplaincy' service, resulting in some non-Christian 'chaplains' being recruited and their presence as part of the department's team being publicised. Prior to 2016, recruitment to paid posts was almost wholly restricted to religious people. It could be argued that more non-Christian people than non-religious people had received support from a 'chaplain', in part because non-Christian people were employed to provide that support and their availability was publicised. There is some limited evidence to support such arguments. Savage (2015) found that after a trust employed a Muslim 'chaplain' and publicised his availability, the proportion of visits to patients with Muslim beliefs more than trebled.

Recruitment and communication practices may well influence the extent to which non-religious people make use of the support of chaplains. Further research and more targeted surveys of the general public may help improve our understanding. Given the large disparities between Christian, non-Christian, and non-religious access, there is a strong case for such research. The evidence on accessing services does not support the argument that because chaplains and other religious care providers are there for 'all faiths and none', there is no need for non-religious pastoral carers. The responses to the next questions reinforce this view.

Views on the need for non-religious pastoral support providers

The next questions explored people's views about non-religious pastoral support and non-religious pastoral support providers. Before answering the questions, respondents were given an explanation of what was meant by 'pastoral support':

> For the following questions, by 'pastoral support' we mean professional emotional and moral support provided at difficult times. Currently hospitals, prisons, and universities have chaplains working at them to provide pastoral support to patients, prisoners, students, staff, and their families.

These chaplains are all religious and most are Christian. At some of these institutions anyone can access this support, whilst at others support is offered only to people who belong to the same religion as them.

Respondents were then asked:

To what extent do you agree or disagree with the following statement?
'Prisons, hospitals, and universities which have chaplains should also have a dedicated non-religious pastoral support provider as well.'

Overall there was clear-cut agreement, 69% to 12%, in favour of the introduction of dedicated non-religious pastoral support.[7] People belonging to the Christian religion agreed 66% to 16%, as did those belonging to non-Christian religions. Non-religious people agreed 73% to 8%. This solid support for dedicated non-religious pastoral support provision across all groups is most encouraging. There seems to be very little support for the idea that provision should be limited to people belonging to Christian or non-Christian religions. Those institutions that limit pastoral/spiritual care and chaplaincy department recruitment to religious people need to take note of these findings and adapt their policies and practices appropriately.

The final question examined the extent to which people would be likely to use the services of a chaplain or a non-religious pastoral support provider.

As a reminder, some prisons, hospitals, and universities are now introducing trained non-religious pastoral support providers who can give the same help to non-religious people as chaplains give to religious people. Please imagine you were either in, or visiting someone at, a hospital, prison, or university and there was both a chaplaincy service and a non-religious pastoral support service available ...
If you felt unhappy, distressed, or concerned, how likely or unlikely do you think you would be to access support from each of the following? (Please select one option on each row)
- A chaplain
- A non-religious pastoral support provider
For each, people could respond 'Very likely', 'Fairly likely', 'Fairly unlikely', 'Very unlikely', 'Don't know'.

Overall, 39% of respondents said that they were likely to access support from a pastoral support provider or a chaplain, a much higher percentage than those who had actually accessed support. Rather more, 45%, said that they were unlikely to access such care. Interestingly, on balance, there was a slightly greater likelihood of people wanting to access support from a non-religious pastoral support provider than from a chaplain. However, it is important to recognise that the differences are not that substantial (see Figure 3.3).

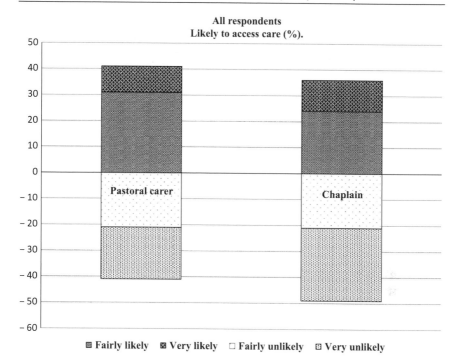

All respondents
Likely to access care (%).

◩ **Fairly likely**   ◪ **Very likely**   ☐ **Fairly unlikely**   ⊟ **Very unlikely**

Figure 3.3 All respondents likely to access care (%)
Source: Humanists UK (2017)

Nearly 40% of religious people said that they were likely to access care from a non-religious pastoral support provider. This suggests that, in general, institutions should find them to be very suitable for providing care to both people with and people without religious beliefs.[8] The responses from people who did not regard themselves as belonging to any particular religion were rather different, as seen in Figure 3.4.

Of non-religious people, 45% were likely to access care from a non-religious pastoral support provider. More significantly, almost three quarters of the non-religious respondents were *unlikely* to want to access support from a chaplain. Indeed, almost half replied that they were *very unlikely* to want to access support from a chaplain.[9] This is an extremely important finding. Many chaplains maintain that they are there for 'all faiths and none' and, quite genuinely, want to provide support to non-religious people. Yet it is quite apparent that many non-religious people are unlikely to want their support. They do want support, probably not from a chaplain.

The implications of this survey are clear. People who do not regard themselves as belonging to any particular religion are not accessing pastoral care to nearly the same extent as those who belong to a religion. There is enormous inequality. In general, chaplains are seen to be Christian, and only

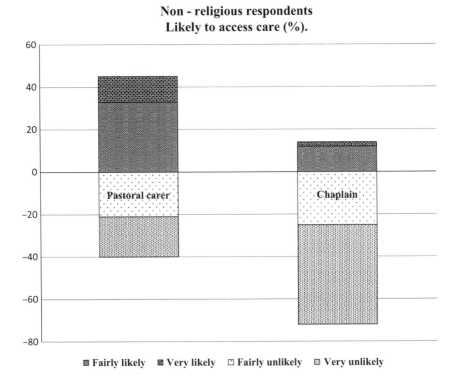

Figure 3.4 Non-religious respondents likely to access care (%)
Source: Humanists UK (2017)

Christian. Chaplains cannot assume that they are meeting the needs of 'all faiths and none'. Merely asserting this does not make it true. Many non-religious people are unlikely to want to receive pastoral support from a chaplain. On the other hand, there is widespread backing, across all groups, that prisons, hospitals, and universities should have a dedicated non-religious pastoral support provider. Both religious and non-religious people are reasonably likely to access such provision. Non-religious pastoral carers can be a real asset to institutions, strengthening their care provision and reducing inequality.

Notes

1 Total sample size was 4,085 adults. Fieldwork was undertaken between 28th - 29th July 2016. The survey was carried out online. The figures have been weighted and are representative of all GB adults (aged 18+).
2 The question was limited to support offered in hospital, prison, or university. The 'Yes, I have' response rate may have been a little higher without these limitations. The percentages were 9% 'Yes, I have', 62% 'No, I haven't', 2% 'Don't know/can't recall', 1% 'Prefer not to say', 26% 'Not applicable'.

3   Other categories included age, gender, social grade, region, marital status, working status.

4   The percentage of respondents replying 'Yes, I have' was similar in all age groups, 9% in the 18–34 and 35–54 age groups and 11% in the 55+ age group.

5   This audit was limited to one hospital trust and the results cannot be extrapolated too far. The number of repeat visits were: Christian, 3.0; Not religious, 2.5; Muslim, 2.3; Hindu, 1.9; Jew, 1.3; Buddhist, 1.3; Other, 2.1; Not specified, 2.7.

6   Such an argument would not fully explain the difference between the percentage of people belonging to non-Christian religions (10%) and non-religious people (4%) who said that they had received support from a chaplain. Both these groups are not Christian, yet far fewer non-religious people had received support from chaplains than people belonging to non-Christian religions.

7   The responses were: 'Strongly agree', 26%; 'Tend to agree', 43%, 'Tend to disagree', 8%; 'Strongly disagree', 4%; 'Don't know', 20%.

8   Of course, it must be fully recognized that non-religious pastoral support providers could not provide sacraments and some other religious functions.

9   The likelihood of non-religious respondents wanting to access a chaplain was: 'Very likely', 2%; 'Fairly likely', 12%; 'Fairly unlikely', 25%; 'Very unlikely', 47%; 'Don't know', 13%.

References

Humanists UK (2017) *Humanists UK Polling on Pastoral Care in the UK*. Available from: https://humanism.org.uk/wp-content/uploads/Humanists-UK-polling-on-pastoral-care-in-the-UK.pdf [accessed 21st January 2018].

Savage, D. (2015) 'All faiths and none'? An Audit of Chaplains' Visits. *Health and Social Care Chaplaincy* 3(1), 63–69.

Chapter 4

Religious and non-religious beliefs in society

On the use of religion or belief surveys

A number of statistics are quoted in this chapter, and throughout the book. They come with a health warning. Statistics and data are essential evidence in support of arguments and explanations, but they do need to be interpreted with some care. The way people are recruited to take part in surveys and how the questions are asked can have a significant impact on the findings.

The Office for National Statistics census question is a good example. The 2011 Census asked the leading question: 'What is your religion?' (ONS, 2012). It presumed that the respondent had a religion. The well respected British Social Attitudes Survey (BSA) asked a similar question, but in a less leading way: 'Do you regard yourself as belonging to any particular religion? IF YES: Which?' (Lee, 2012, p.175). This style of questioning does not presume respondents have a religion.[1] The type of question has a significant effect on the response, as can be seen in Table 4.1.

The difference in response of those ticking the 'no religion' box was particularly marked. In the census question, with its presumption that respondents were religious, only 25% ticked the 'no religion' box. In the BSA question, without this presumption, 50% ticked the 'no religion' box, twice as many. This demonstrates that responses are very sensitive to the details of the question asked. It also shows that departments tasked with providing pastoral, spiritual, and religious care must be extraordinarily cautious in using surveys like the census, which use leading questions. Using census results would

Table 4.1 Responses to questions on religion

Category	Census (%)	BSA (%)
No religion	25	50
Christian	59	35
Non-Christian	9	6
Not stated	7	9

Source: ONS (2012); Lee (2012)

significantly overestimate the potential demand for religious care, and underestimate the potential demand for non-religious care.

The census and the BSA survey differ not only in their phrasing, but also in the nature of the question they ask. The question 'What is your religion' tends to presume that religion is something you *have*. This is reinforced by giving a list of named religions. The BSA question, 'Do you regard yourself as belonging to any particular religion?', presumes that religion is something you *belong to*. But religion as something you have, or something you belong to, are not the only ways in which religion can be perceived. A YouGov survey commissioned by the British Humanist Association (n.d.a) demonstrates this. It compared two questions. The first, 'What is your religion?' was followed by a list of boxes to tick, as in the census. The second, 'Are you religious?', was followed by 'Yes, I am', or 'No, I'm not', or 'Don't know' responses. An important difference is that the first question relates to something you *have*, and the second question relates to something you *are*. A person may *have* a traditional religious affiliation but consider themselves to *be* non-religious. The results of the survey were:

'What is your religion?' Christian, 53%; No religion, 39%
'Are you religious?' 'Yes, I am', 29%; 'No, I'm not', 65%

The percentage answering 'No, I'm not' religious is markedly higher than the percentage answering 'No religion', yet these are the same people, taking part in the same survey.[2]

Similar evidence is found in an insightful 2010–11 survey of over 4,000 undergraduate university students (Guest et al., 2013). In one question, students were asked 'To what religion or spiritual tradition do you currently belong?' from a list of 'None' and six world religions. It found that over half of all respondents said that they *belonged* to the Christian religious or spiritual tradition.[3] The same respondents, in the same survey, were also asked to choose one of the following: 'Religious', 'Not religious but spiritual', 'Not religious or spiritual', 'Not sure'. Only a quarter of the students responded as 'Religious'. Hence over half of the students were Christian, but only a quarter were religious. This apparent contradiction is explained because many respondents ticked the Christian box in terms of *belonging*, but when given the opportunity to say what they considered themselves to *be*, they said they were not religious. Only 34% ticked the 'None' box in response to the first question, but 62% said they were not religious in response to the second question (p.213).[4][5]

All these survey questions provide some useful information. For example, the census information may help an institution check if its recruitment policies and practices are discriminatory, or if there is equality in access to care. The BSA information may give institutions a crude indication of the level of resources that should be allocated to religious and to non-religious care. But it is worth reflecting on what sorts of questions may be most relevant in a pastoral, spiritual, and religious care context. Here, questions that ask people what they consider themselves to *be* may be the most relevant. This relates to how a person sees themselves, to a part of their identity. Issues of identity and sense of self can be very important in good pastoral, spiritual, and religious care. Asking people if they consider themselves to *be* 'non-religious', 'religious', 'spiritual', 'none of these', or 'don't know', and allowing them to tick more than one box, may give a more useful insight into their pastoral, spiritual, and religious care needs.

Belonging, belief, and behaviour

Belief is considered not only in terms of belief in a God, but also in relation to some religious tenets and some current moral issues. The aim here is not to give a comprehensive review, but to emphasise that it is not possible to put people into simple categories.

The BSA has been measuring people's religion in terms of belonging since 1983 (NatCen Social Research, 2016) The changes from 1983 to 2015 are shown in Table 4.2.

It can be seen that there has been a dramatic decline in affiliation to Church of England/Anglican. Roman Catholic and Other Christian affiliation levels have remained more stable. Affiliation to non-Christian religions has grown from 2% to 8%, made up of a number of different religious affiliations. Almost half responded to the question, 'Do you regard yourself as belonging to any particular religion?' by saying no. The 'No religion' category at 48% is larger than the Christian category at 43%. Within the population there are big differences by age (NatCen Social Research, 2016) (see Figure 4.1).

Younger people are more likely than older people to respond by saying that they do not belong to a religion. Longitudinal studies show that, in aggregate, people do not change such affiliation over time (Voas, 2015). Hence it is likely that the proportion of people in the 'No religion' category will grow over

Table 4.2 Responses to the question: 'Do you regard yourself as belonging to any particular religion? IF YES: Which?'

	1983 (%)	2015 (%)
Church of England/ Anglican	40	17
Roman Catholic	10	9
Other Christian	17	17
Non-Christian	2	8
No religion	31	48

Source: NatCen Social Research (2016)

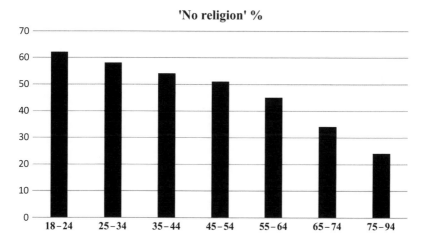

'No religion' %

Figure 4.1 No religion (%)
Source: NatCen Social Research (2016)

time. This means that long-term planning should be developed to properly understand and meet the pastoral and spiritual care needs of these people.

In terms of beliefs, it may be rational to assume that Christians believe in heaven and life after death, and that non-religious people don't believe in God or reincarnation. The reality of life is rather different. Some Christians do believe in heaven and life after death, but some evidence indicates that most don't. That same evidence indicates that whilst most non-religious people do not believe in God[6] or reincarnation, a surprisingly high number do (Theos, 2013). Table 4.3 shows a selection of the data.

Table 4.3 illustrates that an understanding of a person's beliefs cannot be deduced from their ticking a particular box asking about their religious affiliation. There are other surveys that have different absolute numbers, but most draw broadly similar conclusions.[7] It is critically important not to make assumptions about someone's pastoral, spiritual, and religious care needs based on their stated religious affiliation. Just because a person ticks a box

Table 4.3 Some examples of people's beliefs

Beliefs in:	Christian (%)	Non-religious (%)
God	87	21
Life after death	41	16
Heaven	38	5
Reincarnation	17	12
Hell	18	3

Source: Theos (2013)

saying they affiliate to, or belong to, a particular religion or belief, it does not mean that person would want to receive care only from someone of that religion or belief.

Ticking boxes is one thing; behaving according to religious (or non-religious) beliefs and values may be quite another. Measuring behaviour, for example, in terms of church attendance, rather than using tick box results, shows that attendance is very low compared with, say, the census results. Church attendance has declined dramatically from about 12% of the population in 1980 to just 5% in 2015 (Brierley, 2017).[8] For many, one of the purposes of attending a place of worship is to take part in that worship and to receive the sacraments. People in prisons, hospitals, and conflict zones cannot readily attend their local place of worship, so the provision of the sacraments and opportunities to worship can be an important part of religious care in these institutions. In the absence of reliable, independent evidence of the specifically religious care needs of such people, church attendance figures may give a rough-and-ready guide to the proportion of service users who may require this form of religious care.[9]

The Church of England, as the established church, with a parish system covering the whole country, sees itself as there for all members of the community, not just those who attend church. It provides rituals such as baptisms, marriages, and funerals. About 17% of people have their infant or child baptised in the Church of England, 20% have a Church of England wedding, and 30% a Church of England funeral.[10] This suggests that the public use the Church of England for ritual events to a much greater extent than they use it for regular worship. Even so, only a minority of the public use the Church of England for such rituals and, as with church attendance, the numbers are declining. The steepest decline is in the number of funerals, which has fallen by about a quarter between 2006 and 2016. It is not clear how much of this decline is caused by the much greater availability of humanist or other non-religious funerals. Most people in institutions will be able to arrange to have these rites conducted in their own communities, according to their own beliefs and values, but there are emergency situations where this will not be the case. It should not be assumed, as some sort of default case, that the Church of England should conduct those rites. In person-centred care, every effort should be made to make available a rite that meets the needs of the individual and those close to them. This may, for example, be an emergency non-religious baby-naming, or a humanist contract funeral.

Many people prefer a ceremony that is in empathy with their own beliefs and values. The number of people writing to Humanists UK to say how much they appreciated a humanist funeral bears testament to that. This need for empathy with one's own beliefs and values can also be very important when providing people with pastoral care. When people are facing existential issues, this need may be more acute.

Caroline was in a hospital high-dependency unit waiting for an operation the next day. She had a 50:50 chance of surviving the operation. The chances of survival without the operation were even less attractive. Caroline wanted to talk. She was not religious and didn't want to talk to a chaplain. Caroline wasn't in any way anti-religious, but her views about God and life after death were completely at variance to those she thought a chaplain would have. She would have been most uncomfortable talking to a chaplain. Fortunately, there was a non-religious pastoral carer available. This carer listened to Caroline.

There were practical difficulties. Caroline could not speak through her oxygen mask, so she took it off to talk. Her blood oxygen would then fall. At a certain oxygen level conversation would stop, she replaced her mask and waited for the oxygen to return to a good level. All this was monitored by an understanding nurse and one of several machines. Conversation took time, but pastoral carers have time – it is one of their key assets.

Caroline considered what her life's priorities would be if she survived the operation. Having experiences like hers can prompt people to re-evaluate what is important, what really gives their lives meaning and purpose. She also contemplated what may happen the next day. Whilst Caroline was quite sure that death was the end, having the opportunity to reflect on her life, on how aspects of her life would live on in some ways, may have provided some comfort.

This was not a morbid conversation; it was punctuated by a series of Caroline's irreverent religious jokes. Being like-minded, Caroline and the non-religious pastoral carer were able to build a level of empathy and trust that allowed Caroline to explore her thoughts and feelings properly. Perhaps that non-religious pastoral carer was able to help at an important and emotional time.

Caroline was non-religious and wanted to talk to a like-minded non-religious pastoral carer. In the same way, a person with Hindu, Buddhist, Jain, Sikh, Jewish, Muslim, Christian, or other religious beliefs may want to talk to a like-minded pastoral, spiritual, or religious carer. It would obviously be quite wrong to assume that a Hindu 'chaplain' can always meet the pastoral care needs of a Christian patient, or that a Christian chaplain can always meet the pastoral care needs of a non-religious patient.

A person's religion or belief can influence their social attitudes (and vice versa). Some of these social attitudes can be contested within society: assisted dying and same-sex marriage are some current examples. Different individuals make different judgements on such social issues, and these can vary irrespective of their religion or belief. For example, according to 2013 YouGov polls cited by the British Humanist Association (n.d.b), 78% of those who attend a place of worship at least monthly, and 62% of strongly religious people, support assisted dying for the terminally ill. Jayne Ozanne (2016), a leading gay evangelical Anglican and member of the General Synod, commissioned a survey that asked 'Do you think same-sex marriage is right or wrong?'. Most Anglicans who expressed a view said that same-sex marriage was right.[11] Some non-religious people oppose assisted dying and same-sex marriage.

However, the judgements of a religious body such as the Church of England or the Catholic Church, at any point in time, are more unequivocal. On assisted dying, the Church of England (2015) said 'The Church of England cannot support the Assisted Dying Bill' and the Catholic Church in England and Wales (2014) stated 'We remain opposed to any form of assisted suicide'. On same-sex marriage, the Church of England (2012) asserted 'The Church of England cannot support the proposal to enable all couples, regardless of their gender, to have a civil marriage ceremony' and the Catholic Church in England and Wales (2012) stated 'We strongly oppose [the same sex] Bill'. These views are well known by the public. Of course, such church bodies have every right to assert these views, but it is important to recognise the effect such statements can have on pastoral care. Good pastoral care is dependent upon building up empathy and trust, and on being non-judgemental. Many pastoral care providers are chaplains, are ordained clergy, and often wear a clerical collar. They are seen by many as representatives of their church and to represent their church's views on, say, same-sex marriage. For some people wanting to access pastoral care, this can be an insurmountable barrier to receiving non-judgemental care from a chaplain.

George arrived in hospital very seriously ill. The doctors had saved his life and he was going to be discharged in about a week's time. The physiotherapists had been helping with rehabilitation, and he could now get to the ward toilet and back with the help of a Zimmer frame. Before he became ill, George had been passionate about keeping fit. He was a member of a cycle racing club and went on surfing holidays with his friends. All of this was no longer possible. More importantly, being fit and athletic had been a central part of his identity. Now he walked with the help of a Zimmer frame. George wanted to talk, perhaps he needed to talk, to articulate how he felt, to help explore what his identity was now and what it could be. George did not feel comfortable talking to a chaplain. For almost all his adult life he had fought for gay rights, and for almost all his adult life he had felt that the church had condemned and opposed him. He could not see a chaplain as non-judgemental, so building trust and empathy would have been extremely difficult. A non-religious pastoral carer was volunteering at his hospital, and was able to actively listen to George and to be alongside him.

Of course, many chaplains would not have been judgemental about George's homosexuality, indeed some chaplains are homosexual (Hancocks, Sherbourne and Swift, 2008). However, if George and people like him see chaplains as being there to represent their church's social attitudes, then the problem of being seen as judgemental will remain. The churches that chaplains represent have formed judgements on a number of social issues that may be relevant to people who may want to receive pastoral and spiritual care. These include assisted dying, contraception, abortion, and gay marriage. In many of these areas the judgements made by the churches are different from those of most of the public, and from most people who have a religious affiliation (British Humanist Association, n.d.b; Ozanne, 2016). Of course, some people may want to talk to a chaplain, or a member of their own religious community, *because* they see them as representing their own social attitudes.

People's beliefs do not always align neatly with their affiliation as declared in a survey, so careful attention is needed to avoid assumptions. Here, the significant differences between the levels of affiliation and of behaviour need to be carefully considered. Care providers' attitudes to social issues, or perhaps more importantly their perceived social attitudes, may encourage or discourage some service users from accessing pastoral, spiritual, and religious care. Framing a care service that is seen as non-judgemental will require careful thought. With such a multiplicity of beliefs and values, the concept of constructing a pastoral, spiritual, and religious care service only in terms of religion or belief categories needs to be contested. However, it should also be recognised that such categorisation exists, and the reality is that many institutions will view pastoral, spiritual, and religious care provision in these terms. This is one reason for including the following discussion on the 'non-religious' category. Having a better understanding of people who describe themselves as 'non-religious' may help improve their access to appropriate care.

Non-religious people

Many surveys allow respondents to self-identify that they do not belong to or have a cultural affiliation by ticking the 'No religion' or 'None' box. Many reporters interpret 'No religion' only in terms of a lack of identity or lack of affiliation with a religion. Yet for many people ticking the non-religious box can be a positive statement, declaring that being non-religious is a part of their identity.

Some evidence that this identity is important to people comes from surveys that look at how people describe themselves in relation to the strength of their religion or belief. Voas and Ling (2010, p.17) found that 26% of respondents described themselves as very or extremely non-religious compared with only 7% of respondents describing themselves as very or extremely religious (see Table 4.4).

A more recent European Social Survey (2014) asked people in the United Kingdom: 'Regardless of whether you belong to a particular religion, how religious would you say you are?'. People could respond in 11 bands from 'Not at all religious' to 'Very religious', with the centre band being neither

Table 4.4 Respondents' description of themselves (%)

Very or extremely religious	7
Somewhat religious	30
Neither religious nor non-religious	22
Somewhat non-religious	11
Very or extremely non-religious	26

Source: Voas and Ling (2010)

religious nor non-religious. The responses from people who said that they belonged to a religion can be compared with responses from those who did not (see Figure 4.2).[12]

The responses of religious and non-religious people in the European Social Survey (2014) are quite different. Again, a relatively high proportion of non-religious people declared that they are 'Not at all religious'. This suggests that, overall, being non-religious mattered more to people who identified themselves as such than being religious mattered to people who identified themselves as religious. Bullivant (2017)[13] has analysed the 'no religion' population of Britain based on British Social Attitudes Survey and European Social Survey reports. He notes that 'Three-fifths of Nones say that they were brought up with a religious identity' (p.12). This suggests that in moving away from the religious identity they were brought up in, these 'nones' have had to make some decisions to change their beliefs and actions. For example, this

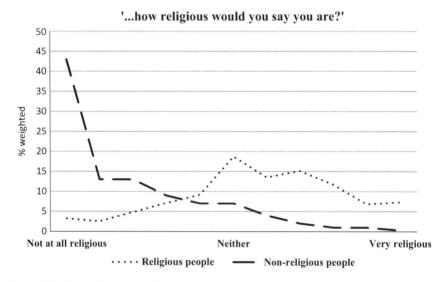

Figure 4.2 How religious would you say you are?
Source: European Social Survey (2014)

may have been a decision to have a civil marriage, or to stop going to church. It may have been to conclude that miracles don't happen, or that there are no gods. This is not merely a lack of affiliation. In a society with an Established Church and a strong Christian legacy, being non-religious is not something that is irrelevant or unsubstantial, but something tangible and consequential.

Some non-religious people may identify themselves as atheists, agnostics, secularists, and humanists. Atheism is about *belief*. Not believing in the existence of gods is sometimes called soft atheism; believing that gods don't exist is sometimes called hard atheism. People who are not sure whether or not they believe in gods are often described as agnostics: they are sitting on the fence. However, this is to misunderstand the nature of agnosticism. Agnosticism is not about belief, it is about *knowledge*. An agnostic is someone who claims that one cannot *know* if gods exist or not. If a person claims that they cannot *know* that gods exist but still *believes* that one or more do, then that person would be an agnostic theist. In the context of this book, the term secularist has nothing to do with belief in or knowledge of gods. A secularist is a person who advocates the separation of the state from religious institutions.[14] Such people could be religious. For example, some people fleeing religious persecution set up a secular state with a constitution that separated the state from religious institutions. This subsequently developed into the United States of America, a secular state where religion has flourished. Humanism is described in chapter 5. Many of these terms are not mutually exclusive. One person may be non-religious, atheist, humanist, and a secularist. Another person may be religious, agnostic, and a secularist. Care is needed in using these definitions.

Great care is also needed in describing people who define themselves as non-religious. A non-religious patient may be recorded as 'NF' meaning 'no faith'; a non-religious prisoner may be categorised as 'nil' religion; a 'chaplaincy' brochure may declare that 'we are here for all faiths and none'. These practices are not uncommon, yet they can be harmful. As Day (2013) says,

> The word 'none' seemed to imply an absence of beliefs, faith or values and undermines the complex identities of people, such as secular humanists, who hold many beliefs and values, albeit not religious ones. (p.107)[15]

Day points out that the word 'none' can imply an absence of belief or values, that it can be seen as an absence of something, a negative. Much more importantly, she highlights the *effect* of using 'none' on people and their sense of identity. Using words like 'none', 'nil, 'no faith', and 'unbeliever' may undermine people's identities. This is particularly important in pastoral, spiritual, and religious care because people seeking such care may well have concerns relating to their identity. To provide good pastoral care it is essential to understand terms like 'non-religious' and its cognates as positive. A non-religious person is not someone *without* religious beliefs, but someone *with* non-religious beliefs and values.

It is important to stress that we are talking about individual people, not Christians, atheists, Buddhists or *the* non-religious, but people. Good pastoral, and spiritual care is person centred. It is not about patients, it is about people with … (illnesses, hopes, anxieties, etc.), it is not about soldiers, it is about people with … (courage, fears, doubts, etc.), it is not about prisoners, it is about people with … (no freedom, regrets, lost relationships, etc.), it is not about Sikhs, Jews or humanists, it is about people with … (Sikh, Jewish or humanist beliefs, and values). Of course, in day-to-day life it is often necessary to think and write of categories of people, but we should remember that these categories are made up of individuals. People may not fit exactly into a category or they may find that categorisation to be irrelevant to their lives. With this health warning, we will look more closely at 'non-religion'.

Lee (2015)[16] considers non-religion in the following sense:

> It is used to indicate not the absence of something (religion) but the presence of something (else), characterized, at least in the first place, by its relation to religion but nevertheless distinct from it. Non-religion is therefore any phenomenon – position, perspective, or practice – that is primarily understood in relation to religion, but which is not itself considered to be religious. (p. 32)

Non-religion is a contradistinction to religion. To help understand this, consider the term 'non-selective school'. We speak of 'non-selective schools' but not 'non-selective shops' or 'non-selective playgrounds'. Shops and playgrounds are not selective, but we do not think of them in this way. We do have selective schools, so a 'non-selective school' can be seen as a contradistinction to a selective school. It is distinctly different from a selective school in that it has an admissions policy that is contrary to that of a selective school. A 'non-selective' school can be seen as a negative in the sense that it has an absence of selection. But it can also be seen as a positive, in the sense that it opposes selection and has values and policies that support equality of access and opportunity. In the same way, the term non-religious can be seen as positive. For example, many non-religious people believe that there are no gods, devils, or djinn; they believe this is the one life we have; that the scientific method is better at explaining the natural world than the revealed truth of ancient sacred texts, and so on. These beliefs are a contradistinction to many beliefs held by some religious people, but many non-religious people see these beliefs as positive and meaningful.

Being non-religious is not just a default or indifferent position, it is a positive aspect of the lives of many non-religious people. Hence the pastoral and spiritual care needs of people with non-religious beliefs and values need to be taken just as seriously as the needs of people with religious beliefs and values.

People with non-religious beliefs and values need to have the same opportunities as religious people to access non-religious pastoral care, and non-religious pastoral carers need to have the same opportunities to provide it.

Notes

1 The BSA survey was conducted in 2010 and the Census in 2011. However, this does not have any material effect on the comments about the difference between the two surveys. The Census had a 'Christian' box to tick, whereas the BSA survey had a list of Christian denominations, Church of England etc. The BSA survey has a list of specific religions and a general category 'no religion'. These differences may have had some effect on the responses.

2 In a similar survey, the Humanist Society of Scotland commissioned a separate poll asking the Scottish census question, 'What religion, religious denomination or body do you belong to?'. In response, 42% of the adult population in Scotland said 'None'. When asked 'Are you religious?' 56% of the same sample said they were not and only 35% said they were (British Humanist Association, n.d.a). The 56% figure falls between the British Humanist Association and BSA survey figures.

3 The percentage of Christians (51.4%) seems to be very high. A 2011 survey of 64,000 adults by YouGov@Cambridge found that only 38% of the 18–34 age group described their religion as Christian (Guest et al., 2013, p.214) In the university survey, randomly selected students were sent an email inviting them to take part in an online survey on student faith. Further emails were sent, with the offer of a prize draw as an incentive to participate. As these careful researchers point out, in a survey on understanding student faith, 'the religiously indifferent may have opted out of the survey so inflating the percentage of students recorded as Christian' (p.215). It seems reasonable to expect that people will respond to take part in a survey on a particular subject if they have an interest in it. But this means that the sample may be biased. This bias was not critical to the analysis these researchers were conducting, and the researchers were fully aware of the issue. However, there is a problem when the figures are quoted out of context, without proper reference to the survey methodology. For example, Davie (2015, p.119) notes that 'a surprisingly high number (just over 50 per cent of undergraduate students) self-identified as Christian, recognizing that the category "Christian" is blurred'. The probability that the survey methodology influenced the number was not mentioned.

4 Only 40% of respondents ticking the Christian box said they were religious.

5 31% said they were 'Not religious but spiritual'. This is an important insight and is considered later.

6 The figures quoted are the total of three descriptions of God: God as a universal life force, God as a personal being, and a higher spiritual being that can be called God.

7 Theos explored 'the faithless' in *Post-religious Britain? The Faith of the Faithless* (Spencer and Weldin, 2012). Woodhead (2013) explored religious identity and belief in *Telling the Truth about Religious Identity in Britain*, which was part of a major study. For more details see www.faithdebates.org.

8 The fall in church attendance at about 58% is greater than the fall in belonging at about 33%, as measured by the BSA survey (NatCen Social Research, 2016). This fall is expected to continue. (Brierley, 2017).

9 Where the age profile is older than that of the average population, the demand may be higher, and vice versa. Hence demand may be higher in hospices than universities, prisons, and the armed forces.

10 These percentages are calculated from Office for National Statistics and Church of England (2017) data.

11 A person's religion was determined in response to the question 'Do you regard yourself as belonging to any particular religion?'; 45% of Anglicans said same-sex marriage was right, 37% wrong, and 19% don't know. Of those who responded 'No, I do not regard myself as belonging to any particular religion', 70% said same-sex marriage was right, 16% wrong, 14% don't know.

12 The 'none' responses are quoted in Bullivant (2017) in his report of the 'no religion' population of Britain. He does not quote these responses for religious people or for Catholics. His report *Contemporary Catholicism in England and Wales: A Statistical Report Based on Recent British Social Attitudes Survey Data* (Bullivant, 2016) refers to England and Wales. The European Social Survey data are for the UK.

13 Bullivant is currently co-Principal Investigator of the three-year Understanding Unbelief project (with colleagues at Kent, Coventry, and Queen's University Belfast), funded by a £2.3 million grant from the John Templeton Foundation.

14 For a fuller discussion, see *The Case for Secularism: A Neutral Sate in an Open Society* (British Humanist Association, 2007).

15 Day successfully campaigned for the census question to be changed from 'none', used in the 2001 Census, to 'no religion' in the 2011 Census.

16 Lee is a founding director of the Nonreligion and Secularity Research Network, https://nsrn.net.

References

Brierley, P. (2017) *UK Church Statistics 2010–2020*. Second edition. Tonbridge, Brierley Consultancy. Information available from: https://faithsurvey.co.uk/uk-christianity.html [accessed 9th May 2017].

British Humanist Association (n.d.a) Loose cultural affiliation: Census data. YouGov Survey Results. London, British Humanist Association. Available from: https://humanism.org.uk/campaigns/religion-and-belief-some-surveys-and-statistics/ [accessed 6th May 2017].

British Humanist Association (n.d.b) On Assisted Dying. London, British Humanist Association. Available from: https://humanism.org.uk/campaigns/religion-and-belief-some-surveys-and-statistics/ [accessed 6th May 2017].

British Humanist Association (2007) *The Case for Secularism: A Neutral Sate in an Open Society*. London, British Humanist Association.

Bullivant, S. (2016) *Contemporary Catholicism in England and Wales: A Statistical Report Based on Recent British Social Attitudes Survey Data*. Catholic Research Forum Reports 1. Twickenham, Benedict XVI Centre for Religion and Society, St Mary's University. Available from: https://www.stmarys.ac.uk/research/centres/benedict-xvi/docs/2018-feb-contemporary-catholicism-report-may16.pdf [accessed 13th June 2018].

Bullivant, S. (2017) *The "No Religion" Population of Britain*. Catholic Research Forum Reports 3. Twickenham, Benedict XVI Centre for Religion and Society, St Mary's University. Available from: https://www.stmarys.ac.uk/research/centres/benedict-xvi/docs/2017-may-no-religion-report.pdf [accessed 18th May 2017].

Catholic Church in England and Wales (2012) Statement on the government response to the same sex marriage consultation. News 11th December. Available from: http://

www.catholic-ew.org.uk/Home/News/2012/Statement-Catholic Church in England and Waleson-Same-Sex-Marriage/ [accessed 11th May 2015].

Catholic Church in England and Wales (2014) Plenary Resolution: Assisted Suicide. News 9th May. Available from: http://www.catholic-ew.org.uk/Home/News/Bishops-Plenary-Meetings/Plenary-May-2014/Assisted-Suicide/ [accessed 11th May 2017].

Church of England (2012) *A Response to the Government Equalities Office Consultation – 'Equal Civil Marriage' – from the Church of England*. Available from: https://www.churchofengland.org/sites/default/files/2017-11/GS%20Misc%201027%20government%20consultation%20on%20same%20sex%20marriage.pdf [accessed 11th May 2017].

Church of England (2015) *Assisted Suicide*. Available from: https://www.churchofengland.org/our-views/medical-ethics-health-social-care-policy/assisted-suicide.aspx [accessed 11th May 2015; no longer available online].

Church of England (2017) *Statistics for Mission 2016*. London, Church of England Research and Statistics. Available from: https://www.churchofengland.org/sites/default/files/2017-10/2016statisticsformission.pdf [accessed 5th January 2018].

Davie, G. (2015) *Religion in Britain, A Persistent Paradox*. Chichester, Wiley Blackwell.

Day, A. (2013) Yes, but Not in the North: Nuances in Religion and Language Cultures. *Studies in Ethnicity and Nationalism* 13(1), 105–108.

European Social Survey (2014) Dataset: ESS7 – 2014 Data Download. Edition 2.1. Available from: http://www.europeansocialsurvey.org/data/download.html?r=7.

Guest, M., Aune, K., Sharma, S., Warner, R. (2013) *Christianity and the University Experience*. London, Bloomsbury Academic.

Hancocks, G., Sherbourne, J., Swift, C. (2008) 'Are They Refugees?' Why Church of England Male Clergy Enter Health Care Chaplaincy. *Practical Theology* 1(2), 163–179.

Lee, L. (2012) Religion: Losing Faith? In: Park, A., Clery, E., Curtice, J., Phillips, M., Utting, D. (eds) *British Social Attitudes 28*. London, Sage. Available from: http://www.bsa.natcen.ac.uk/media/38958/bsa28_12religion.pdf [accessed 5th December 2017].

Lee, L. (2015) *Recognizing the Non-Religious; Reimagining the Secular*. Oxford, Oxford University Press.

NatCen Social Research (2016) *NatCen's British Social Attitudes Survey: Change in Religious Affiliation among Adults in Great Britain*. Available from: http://www.natcen.ac.uk/media/1236081/religious-affiliation-over-time-british-social-attitudes.pdf [accessed 8th May 2017].

Ozanne, J. (2016) YouGov/Jayne Ozanne Survey Results. Available from: https://d25d2506sfb94s.cloudfront.net/cumulus_uploads/document/pwwbcqwbmx/JayneOzanne_Results_SameSexMarriage_160121_GB_Website.pdf [accessed 11th May 2017].

ONS (2012) *Religion in England and Wales 2011*. London, Office for National Statistics. Available from: https://www.ons.gov.uk/peoplepopulationandcommunity/culturalidentity/religion/articles/religioninenglandandwales2011/2012-12-11 [accessed 6th May 2017].

Spencer, W., Weldin, H. (2012) *Post-religious Britain? The Faith of the Faithless*. London, Theos.

Theos (2013) *The Spirit of Things Unseen: Belief in Post-religious Britain*. London, Theos. Available from: https://www.theosthinktank.co.uk/cmsfiles/archive/files/Reports/Spirit%20of%20Things%20-%20Digital%20(update).pdf [accessed 13th June 2018].

Voas, D. (2015) *The Mysteries of Religion and the Lifecourse.* CLS Working Paper 2015/1. London, Centre for Longitudinal Studies, Institute of Education.

Voas, D., Ling, R. (2010) Religion in Britain and the United States. In: Park, A., Curtice, J., Thomson, K., Phillips, M., Clery, E., Butt, S. (eds) *British Social Attitudes: The 26th Report.* London, Sage.

Woodhead, L. (2013) *Telling the Truth about Religious Identity in Britain.* AHRC/ESRC Westminster Faith Debates. Available from: http://static.westminster-abbey.org/assets/pdf_file/0009/69192/Telling-the-Truth-about-Religious-Identity-in-Britain-HANDOUT.pdf [accessed 9th May 2017].

Part II

Non-religious care practice

Chapter 5

Beliefs and values

Some of the underlying principles of non-religious pastoral care outlined in this part of the book are grounded in humanism, and in forms of counselling that have humanist thinking as part of their approach. Of course, it is recognised that pastoral care can also be grounded in religious theologies, in philosophies, and in other life-stances. As will become apparent in the following chapters, good pastoral care providers need not be limited to people with a recognised religion or a recognised belief. However, humanist beliefs and values, humanist counselling, humanist organizations, and people with humanist views have been at the forefront of the development of non-religious pastoral care. Pastoral care is often required in circumstances where people experience loss. This may be a loss of freedom, a loss of identity, a loss of hope, a loss of purpose, to mention just some aspects. Sometimes it is loss of life. We can all be deeply affected by such losses. It is also the case that our responses are affected, in part, by our beliefs and values. Most non-religious people believe this is the one life they have, and this belief inevitably colours their attitudes to death. Chapter 7 reflects on loss and death from a non-religious perspective.

History shows us that rituals have always been important to people irrespective of their religion or belief. Ritual seems to be a part of our common humanity, but the form of ritual may vary depending on our beliefs and values. The provision of non-religious rituals as a part of pastoral care is discussed. Pastoral care provision should meet the highest ethical standards. It is relatively easy to make this statement, but the realities of practice raise a number of challenges. These vary from 'how to say hello', through responding to requests to say prayers, to controversial topics such as assisted dying. These challenges are explored, not to provide answers but to suggest approaches to answering such challenges. Finally, the advocacy role of a non-religious pastoral carer is elucidated.

Humanist values and beliefs found expression over 2,500 years ago, long before the words humanism and humanist came into usage (Copson, 2015). This shows that humanism is different from religions not only in terms of its beliefs and values, but also in terms of its nature. Humanism is a word that captures beliefs, values, and attitudes which already existed. Hence people could be humanists before the word existed. Similarly, today people can be humanists without knowing the word or its meaning, rather like being a member of *Homo sapiens* without necessarily being aware of it.[1] This contrasts with religions and many non-religious philosophies the existence of which can be traced to a particular point in time and which could not have existed before that time, for example Christianity and Marxism. Given the nature of humanism, there is a wide spectrum of humanists, from those who don't know they are humanists to those whose humanism is an important part of their identity and who have a fully developed and explicit humanist worldview. This worldview is a set of values, beliefs, and approaches to life that come together to form a fulfilling, coherent whole. Several writers have described humanism and its worldview, and it is possible to give only a brief summary here (Copson and Grayling, 2015, Law, 2011, Herrick, 2009, Norman, 2012). There are excellent free publications and a free online course, 'Introducing Humanism: Non-religious Approaches to Life'.[2]

The International Humanist and Ethical Union has an agreed definition of humanism:

> Humanism is a democratic and ethical life stance that affirms that human beings have the right and responsibility to give meaning and shape to their own lives. It stands for the building of a more humane society through an ethics based on human and other natural values in a spirit of reason and free inquiry through human capabilities. It is not theistic, and it does not accept supernatural views of reality. (IHEU, 2009)

This definition is in a bylaw of the International Humanist and Ethical Union, not on a tablet of stone.[3] It may be modified and improved over time using the spirit of reason and free enquiry mentioned in the definition.

In essence, humanism can be seen as the combination of three views. The first is a view of the world, and of ourselves within it. The second is how we see the basis of our ethical decisions. The third is about purpose and meaning in life. Humanism sees the world as comprising such things as galaxies, trees, air, quantum particles, and other physical entities still to be discovered through observation and use of the scientific method. It also comprises our sense of awe and wonder as we look into the skies; it includes our love for others; feelings of sorrow, and happiness; our thoughts, fears, and hopes. But the humanist world does not include otherworldly or supernatural places, forces, or beings. This world does not include gods, the 'evil eye', heaven, immortal souls, or life after death. Humanists live their lives without recourse to these beliefs.

Humanists base their ethical decisions on a concern for human beings and other sentient animals. Those decisions are based on reason, compassion, and empathy. Indeed, humanists believe that empathy and compassion can help make the world a better place. There is a sense that we should care for each other because we share a common humanity. Religious ethical beliefs are often based on what philosophers refer to as an appeal to authority. Here, ethical decisions are determined by reference to religious authorities. These may be instructions or guidance in ancient sacred texts, the actions and words of prophets and gurus, or the pronouncements of religious leaders' or gods' views as revealed through prayer.

People in distress or difficult circumstances can often raise questions about meaning and purpose with those providing pastoral, spiritual, and religious care. A religious person may ask the question 'What is the purpose of life?'. The purpose of life is out there, it is something to be searched for and discovered. For some, there is comfort in knowing that God has a purpose for us. Whatever life's difficulties, it is all part of God's plan. In the absence of an afterlife and any discernible purpose to the universe, humanists would tend to ask a different question. Instead of asking 'What is the purpose of life', they would ask 'How can I give my life meaning and purpose?'. Often the answer to this question encompasses the view that meaning and purpose can be achieved by seeking happiness in this life and helping others to do the same.

The relationship between humanism and counselling is considered next. Schuhmann (2015) gives an excellent overview of this subject. The term 'humanist counselling' as used here refers to a range of counselling practices based on, or inspired by, a humanist worldview. They include, but are not limited to, the humanist*ic* psychology of Maslow and Rogers, described below.

In the Netherlands, humanist counsellors have been developing and practising humanist counselling since the end of the Second World War, operating in the armed forces, prisons, and hospitals. Today's non-religious pastoral care can build on the foundations they have established. There are many different approaches to counselling in different settings, for different purposes, and using different methods, but each embodies a way of seeing what it is to be a person (McLeod, 2009). Hence, a counsellor's worldview may influence the approach and methods they use. Two approaches are considered here, the person centred and the existential.[4]

Humanistic counselling

Carl Rogers developed person-centred counselling, the so-called humanistic approach, in the middle of the twentieth century. Initially he joined a theological seminary in 1924 to prepare for religious work, but he lost any religious conviction and decided to work in a field where his freedom of thought would not be curtailed. By steps, he moved to psychology. In his early years, Rogers (2004) would ask questions like 'How can I treat, or cure, or change this person?' (p.32). He was there to fix things for the client, but his experiences taught him 'that it is the *client* who knows what hurts, what directions to go, what problems are crucial, what experiences have been deeply buried' (p.11).

His approach became person centred. The counsellor's role is to facilitate a process of growth or flourishing by the client by creating conditions for this to happen naturally. Those conditions are congruence, unconditional positive regard, and empathy. Rogers describes congruence as follows:

> It has been found that personal change is facilitated when the psychotherapist is what he *is,* when in the relationship with his client is genuine and without 'front' or façade, openly being the feelings and attitudes which at that moment are flowing in him.[5] We have coined the term 'congruence' to try to describe this condition. (p.61)

Often, if someone makes a statement, our first reaction is to make a judgement or some sort of evaluation: 'That's good', 'I'm so pleased', 'That's so upsetting', or 'That's wrong'. It's not easy, and quite rare, to react differently and, instead, try to *understand* the meaning of what that person has said, to be with or alongside that person in the sense of being completely and empathetically in their frame of reference. Rogers found that the more accepting he was of a person, the more he could create a relationship which that person could use. For Rogers, acceptance meant having a warm regard for a person as someone of 'unconditional self-worth' (p.4). This acceptance and unconditional positive regard should be there even when a person has attitudes, beliefs, and values that may be different from, or even contrary to, your own; or that may be quite different from those the person has expressed before. It is by understanding those thoughts and feelings as the person sees and feels them that a person is really free to explore themselves at a conscious and unconscious level.

Empathy is where one senses 'the feelings and personal meanings which the client is experiencing in each moment, when he can perceive these from the "inside", as they seem to the client, and when he can successfully communicate something of that understanding to his client' (p.62).

Creating conditions of congruence, unconditional positive regard, and empathy is not only important in humanistic psychology, it can also be important in pastoral care.

Existential counselling

The aspects of congruence, unconditional positive regard, and empathy are largely common to both humanistic psychology and existential counselling. Existential counselling integrates with other methods and schools of counselling, but with a different way of viewing the world. Existential counselling clearly recognises human limitations and existential constraints. Some aspects of these constraints can be quite apparent in different institutions: constraints on a person's freedom in prisons; limitations on their physical and mental functioning in healthcare; limitations on safety and security in military conflict zones. Common across all of these are existential constraints caused by events such as loss, isolation, death, grief, and anxiety. In the existential approach, people are not defined or determined by these constraints, they have the ability to make sense of their lives by responding actively to them. They do this not by turning to some external, perhaps supernatural, power or to some 'inner natural force', but by exercising their freedom to give meaning to their own situation. Van Deurzen (2012), in her preface to *Existential Counselling & Psychotherapy in Practice*, states that

> the fundamental objective of existential work is to enable people to rediscover their own values, beliefs and their life's purpose ... This means that you come to know yourself in light of human limitations and possibilities and that you engage wholeheartedly with life in the way that is most satisfactory to you. (p.xii)

Behind this is a view that before making sense of problems or of themselves, people need to make sense of life. This often comes to the fore at times of crisis and/or at times when human limitations and existential constraints have changed. These times can appear chaotic and confusing. People may want to turn to someone with an existential approach, to help them understand their life better and to find meaning and purpose.

At this point it should be stressed that non-religious pastoral carers are not employed as counsellors, and in their role of pastoral carers they are not acting as professional counsellors. Of course, some non-religious pastoral carers are also professionally registered counsellors.[67]

The purpose of outlining these humanistic approaches to counselling is to show that non-religious pastoral care has strong foundations in appropriate counselling practices, and to give non-religious pastoral carers some insight into approaches and methods that they may find helpful in their role.

Notes

1 Indeed, a poll for Humanists UK (2017) found that more than one in five people (22%) have humanist beliefs and values. 5% readily identified with the term humanist – meaning there are more people who readily describe themselves as humanists than, for example, Muslims.
2 The free online course is available via https://www.futurelearn.com/courses/intro ducing-humanism. A free Short Course on Humanism eBook is available at https:// humanism.org.uk/humanism-short-course-ebook/
3 The International Humanist and Ethical Union's Amsterdam Declaration (IHEU, 2002) also gives a list of the fundamentals of humanism.
4 A third approach that could be included is the cognitive. The cognitive-behavioural approach was founded by Beck and Ellis. Often using the idea of a Socratic dialogue, Ellis used the term 'rational-emotive therapy' and placed this form of counselling within the humanist tradition (Ellis, 1973).
5 Many writings of this time refer to 'his' or 'he'. It is good to see this changing.

6 Some 'chaplains' are also registered counsellors.
7 As described in chapter 6, those entering postgraduate existential and humanist pastoral care training will explore these areas in much greater depth.

References

Copson, A. (2015) What Is Humanism? In: Copson, A., Grayling, A.C. (eds) *The Wiley Blackwell Handbook of Humanism*. Chichester, John Wiley & Sons, p.1.

Copson, A., Grayling, A.C. (eds) (2015) *The Wiley Blackwell Handbook of Humanism*. Chichester, John Wiley & Sons.

Ellis, A. (1973) *Humanistic Psychotherapy: The Rational-Emotive Approach*. New York, McGraw-Hill.

Herrick, J. (2009) *Humanism: An Introduction*. New York, Prometheus Books.

HumanistsUK (2017) *Humanism*. Available from: https://humanism.org.uk/wp-content/uploads/Results-for-BHA-Humanism-313-18.04.17.xlsx [accessed 6th July 2017].

IHEU (2002) *The Amsterdam Declaration*. London, International Humanist and Ethical Union. Available from: http://iheu.org/humanism/the-amsterdam-declaration/ [accessed 6th July 2017].

IHEU (2009) *International Humanist and Ethical Union, Bylaws*, 1.2. London, International Humanist and Ethical Union. Available from: http://iheu.org/about/organization/bylaws/ [accessed 6th July 2017].

Law, S. (2011) *Humanism: A Very Short Introduction*. Oxford, Oxford University Press.

McLeod, J. (2009) *An Introduction to Counselling*. 4th Edition. Maidenhead, Open University Press.

Norman, R. (2012) *On Humanism (Thinking in Action)*. 2nd Edition. Abingdon, Routledge.

Rogers, C.R. (2004) *On Becoming a Person*. London, Constable & Robinson. First published in 1961.

Schuhmann, C. (2015) Counselling and the Humanist Worldview. In: Copson, A., Grayling, A.C. (eds) *The Wiley Blackwell Handbook of Humanism*. Chichester, John Wiley & Sons, p.173–193.

Van Deurzen, E. (2012) *Existential Counselling & Psychotherapy in Practice*. Third Edition. London, Sage.

Chapter 6

Roles, skills, and competencies

The role of the non-religious pastoral carer

Staying with

Three approaches to expressing compassion are discussed here. These are to *cheer up*, to *sort out*, and to *stay with*. They help to give some insight into what the role of the non-religious pastoral carer is, and just as importantly, what it is not.

At times when people are anxious or distressed, those with compassion – with concern for the sufferings or misfortunes of others – are likely to want to help. Friends or family may, quite naturally, want to cheer up their friend or relative. 'You managed to walk to the hospital shop today', 'at last your PIN is sorted out, there is money on it, so you can ring home', 'only a month to go before you get some R&R', 'you're doing really well'. Finding and emphasising positives and progress might give them something to look forward to and make them feel better. Sometimes it does. To cheer up is a common way in which we try to support those we are close to. Cheering up can help, but if people are upset, worried, and anxious, then just trying to cheer them up may make it more difficult for them to express, reflect on, or share those anxieties and concerns. Instead of being able to talk meaningfully to someone about what is really concerning them, they may have to put on a brave face and be cheerful. This may leave them even more upset.

One way to give support is to help sort out the practical problems someone may have. 'I don't know when I'm going to get my test results', 'My husband phoned to say they're threatening to cut off the electricity', 'I put in an APP asking to be allowed to send a card to Tracy, and I've heard nothing', 'I'm going to have to sell my house and go into a care home'. It may be possible for someone to provide some practical help in all these circumstances. With the person's permission, the non-religious pastoral carer might ask the nurse about the status of the test results; contact the unit welfare officer about the electricity bill, and so on. To sort out these practical problems will be helpful but, with very few exceptions, sorting out such problems will not be the main part of the role of the pastoral carer. One reason is that, in general, the pastoral carer will not have, and will not have access to, the information and expertise needed to help sort out many of these problems. Solving such problems is normally the responsibility of relevant professionals within the institution.

With the person's consent, it may be helpful to bring such practical problems to the attention of the relevant professional or to the head of the department of pastoral, spiritual, and religious care. From the deeper understanding the pastoral carer has of the person requiring support, they may be able to explain the context and emotional impact of that person's practical problems quite well, and act as an effective advocate on their behalf. This is an important role, but it comes from gaining an *understanding* of a person's deeper needs, not from an ability to fix practical problems. Many people coming into non-religious pastoral care come with significant experience in a caring role. They may have worked for a mental health charity, be a trained psychotherapist, or have been a pastoral care tutor to students. They are good, often very good, at listening to people, analysing the problem, and suggesting courses of action to help sort it out. But, in many cases, this is not the essence of the pastoral carer's role.

Table 6.1 Comparing the treatment and pastoral care domains

Treatment domain	Pastoral care domain
Symptoms	Signs
Problems	Dilemmas
Solutions	Choices and meaning
Facts	Beliefs and feelings
Diagnosis	Exploration
Professional distance	Closeness
Explaining causal links	Understanding the meaning of things
Intervention	Presence
Treatment objective	Open process
Focus on recovery	Focus on resilience
Getting better	Being able to stay in control
Treatment restrictions	Life choices
Discontinuation of treatment	Accepting that life is finite
Evidence based	Value based
Patient/client	Person
Doing	Being with

The reasons for this can be illustrated by comparing
domain with the pastoral care domain. This comparison, s
6.1, also helps to highlight key aspects of pastoral care.
the two domains shown here was developed in a medical c
a medical perspective, but the concept can be applied tc
institutions.

The treatment domain has some sort of objective, which could be a
successful treatment, recovery, rehabilitation, reducing reoffending, mini-
mising deterioration, or managing a pain-free end-of-life process. Counsellors, medical practitioners, and other care professionals try to help
meet those objectives. To do this they may collect information, make
analyses or diagnoses, and follow courses of action. Pastoral care works
in a different domain. Non-religious pastoral carers will try to create an
environment where people can feel, articulate, reflect on, and explore
their hopes, fears, dilemmas, and anxieties. Trying to cheer someone up
or trying to help sort out their practical problems will not necessarily
create an environment that allows them to properly engage with
their feelings, anxieties, hopes, and fears. So the pastoral carer has to
develop a relationship with the person. Various terms are used to try to
encapsulate this relationship, such as staying with, walking alongside,
being with, and presence. It is this aspect of staying with, rather than
cheering up or sorting out, which is key to understanding the role (see
Figure 6.1).

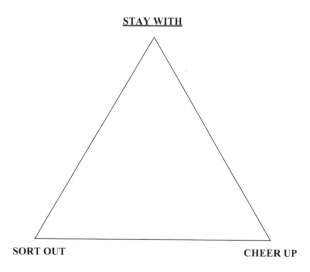

Figure 6.1 Pastoral care relationship

The patient in bed 22 was recovering well following a routine operation. From the perspective of a treatment domain, this statement is probably quite correct. The hospital carried out several operations of this type every week, and staff were very experienced in nursing such patients. This patient was healing well, and was expected to make a full recovery and to be discharged by the weekend.

The patient in bed 22 was a *person*, a middle-aged woman called Mary. It was clear that she wanted to talk to the pastoral carer who was visiting patients on the ward. Mary told her how frightened she had been before the operation, she had never had an operation as big as this before, she had learned that some people [not many] die from the operation. This operation may have been routine for the hospital staff; it was anything but routine for Mary. She said that she felt that the operation had gone well, the nurses were wonderful, and her husband was coming to visit her later that afternoon. Then Mary started to talk about what was on her mind. Mary had had elective surgery. She could have decided not to have the operation or to wait and have it later. It was a big decision for her. Of course, there were medical reasons for the decision, but for Mary they were not the main reasons she had decided to have the operation without delay. Mary had the operation in the hope that it would improve her relationship with someone close to her. For the next 40 minutes, Mary talked of what was going through her mind in making the decision, what had happened to her relationships in her life, and her feelings about them. Then, having had the operation, she talked about her hopes that the relationship would improve, and her fears that it may not. In reality, the conversation did not follow the clear structure of the above sentences; rather, feelings and thoughts came and went throughout the encounter.

Mary wanted, perhaps needed, to talk, to have the opportunity to say out loud some of the things that were important to her, that she felt deeply, that she was concerned about. Through talking to someone else about them, perhaps they became clearer in her own mind, and perhaps by sharing them, some of her anxieties were reduced. Whatever the outcome, Mary thanked the pastoral carer for 'their help'.

But what did the pastoral carer do? During the conversation, some practical problems came up but, whilst acknowledging them, the pastoral carer didn't focus on these. She did not try to sort out those problems. Nor did she try to cheer Mary up. The pastoral carer could have said 'Oh I'm sure you took the right decision, things seem to be working out quite well'. But to do so may have closed off the possibility of Mary sharing and exploring her own thoughts and anxieties about how things were working out. Instead the pastoral carer *stayed with* Mary. The pastoral carer also played another crucial role. That was to behave in a way that created an environment where Mary was able to share and explore her thoughts and feelings. This can be achieved by 'active listening' and is one of the roles at the heart of good pastoral care.

Active listening

The key elements of active listening discussed in this section are: building trust and intimacy; being present; having unconditional positive regard; listening; questioning; and giving feedback. All of these feed into and support each other. The reasons why each element is important are discussed, followed by reflections on how they may be achieved.

Building trust and intimacy

It is essential to help create a safe and supportive environment in which to stay with or walk alongside the person being cared for. Mary did not start to talk about her deeper thoughts and feelings until she felt safe and supported. Building trust and intimacy will help create that environment.

Being friendly is a good beginning: a smile can convey a lot, as can body language. Body language is often a better form of communication than words. Showing genuine concern can start to build a closer relationship. Part of this comes from listening very carefully and responding appropriately. When Mary was asked 'How are you getting on?' she replied 'Oh, sort of OK, thanks', but what does 'sort of' mean? Being concerned means being aware of and wondering about the use of phrases like 'sort of'. Authenticity is important in building trust. Knowing oneself, being oneself, and communicating in a way that is true to oneself will help build intimacy. Sometimes staying with someone can be very emotional. Recognising these emotions is part of being authentic. Clearly, demonstrating integrity, honesty, and sincerity is critical to building trust. Having the highest ethical standards is essential. There is a discussion of ethical issues in chapter 8. Keeping promises is an important part of that integrity. If a promise was made to get some rosary beads for a prisoner, this should be a priority. If there are none available, it is important to get back to the prisoner and explain what has happened. With a busy schedule and the interruptions that often occur, this may not be as easy as it sounds, but keeping promises like these is an important part of building trust.

As trust and intimacy build, information and thoughts of a very personal nature may be shared with the pastoral carer. Maintaining confidentiality is inherent in good pastoral care (some safeguarding and legal exceptions are considered later in this chapter). If it would be helpful to share information, for example with a prison officer, nurse in charge, or managing chaplain, explicit consent should be sought. It is for the person being cared for to decide whether or not this information should be disclosed. They are in control.

Being present

Terms such as 'being present' and 'walking alongside' are much easier to feel or experience than to write about. They are about creating a spontaneous relationship that is open, flexible, and confident. Perhaps it starts with self-understanding and an awareness of one's own resources, such as the ability to give the person being cared for full attention. Non-religious pastoral carers and 'chaplains' are often in the fortunate position of being relatively free of time constraints and rigid work patterns. They can focus on pastoral and spiritual care needs and have the time to give their full attention. That attention includes accessing one's intuition. Words are spoken, some words are left unspoken, particular words are used; body language may be communicating something different; photographs, cards, and books may be expressing something. This is not some rational, analytical encounter. The pastoral carer's feelings and intuition play an important role. In one sense, the pastoral carer is helping to create a space for the person being cared for to explore their issues, thoughts, and feelings. That person may choose to talk about some aspects of their life but not others. The pastoral carer must be comfortable not knowing everything. They may feel curious about other aspects of a person's life, but they are not there to satisfy their own curiosity, they are there to care for the person. It is for the person being cared for to choose what to reveal and what to keep private.

Being present does not necessarily mean being serious, sombre, or earnest. Humour and laughter can play an important part. At first sight, it may seem strange that someone being admitted to prison to serve a ten-year term, or a patient having a life-threatening operation the next day, would want to laugh and tell jokes, but sometimes that is the case. Humour can create a lightness and energy that can be most helpful. Being present means being ready to shift perspectives at any time. The person being cared for may want to explore or reveal different aspects of their life or concerns at any time. Being attentive and fully conscious helps to maintain that spontaneous relationship.

Having unconditional positive regard

It is necessary to introduce a caveat about the term 'unconditional positive regard'. Some people may behave in institutions in ways that cannot and should not be tolerated by those institutions. The pastoral carer simply cannot accept these behaviours or have positive regard for them.

Carl Rogers (2004) talks of having a warm regard for a person as someone of 'unconditional self-worth (p.4)'. Showing someone that they are regarded as a person of unconditional self-worth can help create a sense that they feel respected, giving them a sense of security, which can make them stronger. In turn, this allows the person being cared for to be authentic and to express what they really think and feel. Then, with the pastoral carer being alongside, they can gain a better understanding of who they really are, and explore their thoughts and feelings. Having positive regard means giving support regardless of what the person being cared for does or has done. They may have beliefs, values, and attitudes that are quite different from those of the carer, or with which the carer profoundly disagrees. If the pastoral carer regards that person as someone with unconditional self-worth, then good quality care can be provided.

Clearly, it is important to be non-judgemental. Being non-judgemental means not judging the sex offender as a bad person, or not judging the obese alcoholic with liver problems as irresponsible because she refuses to take her medication. But it is more than that. It is seeing someone not as a 'sex offender' or not as an 'obese alcoholic', but first and foremost as a person, and as a person of self-worth. Judgement is often considered in a negative context: this person is bad, irresponsible, sinful. But judgements can be positive: this person is kind, gener-ous, considerate. In some cases, it is important to be non-judgemental in this positive sense. Take the case of Mary, described above. If, at an early stage, the pastoral carer had expressed the judgement that in electing to have the operation Mary had shown courage and love for those close to her, then Mary may have found it more difficult explore her own thoughts about what she felt when she took the decision, or to explore her true feelings towards those close to her. Care needs to be taken about expressing positive as well as negative judgements.

Showing empathy and understanding is central to demonstrating that a person is valued for who they are. In turn, good listening skills can be used to demonstrate that empathy and understanding. Three aspects of listening skills are discussed below: listening, questioning, and feedback.

Listening

Listening to a person gives them the opportunity to be heard; it also enables them to experience or feel that they are being heard. If listening is done with trust and intimacy and in a non-judgemental way, it can be a rare and pow-erful experience. This type of listening does not occur often in our everyday lives. With this form of active listening, people can feel affirmed and less defensive, sometimes one can sense a sort of internal shift in them. Feeling heard in this way can be an enriching experience and may be very beneficial.

Active listening means focusing on their agenda. It is very person centred. In institutions, those receiving care meet many people who they perceive to come with some sort of agenda. This may be the prison officer who has an agenda to maintain high levels of security, the nurse or doctor with a treatment agenda, or the chaplain with a religious care agenda. Of course, each these people could put aside the agenda of their role and just focus on the individual. However, it may be difficult for someone seeking pastoral care to recognise this change in focus. Often, the prison officer and nurse wear a uniform, the doctor wears a badge and stetho-scope, the chaplain wears a clerical collar. This dress is used to identify a particular role. Inevitably roles have agendas associated with them. In good pastoral care, it is necessary to communicate that the carer is there to focus on the agenda of the person seeking care. Communications are also considered in chapter 11.

As described above, being present is critical to good care, yet the pastoral carer is also absent in the sense that they are *neutral*. Of course, no-one is totally neutral; we all have our opinions, preferences, dislikes, and a range of life experiences. The very fact that we want to provide pastoral care shows something about us. However, a good pastoral carer will try to listen without constantly referring back to their own context, or making comparisons with their own opinions; rather, they will stay neutral by staying within the context of the agenda of the person being cared for.

Active listening means paying very close attention to what is said, but it also means looking behind the words, trying to pick up on feelings and emotions. Sometimes the spoken words will be different from the body language, and the tone of speaking may be different from the tone of the words. It also includes the way the carer responds to what they have heard. Skills such as summarising, paraphrasing, and reiterating are very powerful ways to show someone they have been heard. For people to hear back what they have said helps them to recognise or clarify their thoughts.

Sometimes there will be silences. Although there may be a temptation to fill these silences, it is often best to avoid this temptation. The person being cared for may need time to recognise and reflect on what they have said. They may not be saying anything, but they may be thinking or feeling a lot. Allowing time is essential. There may be occasions when the person being cared for describes a situation similar to one the carer has experienced: they may have gone through a 'similar' divorce or had the 'same' operation. On almost all occasions, it is inadvisable to compare notes on such experiences. Firstly, the 'similar' divorce or the 'same' operation are not similar/the same because the carer's feelings, thoughts, and circumstances cannot have been identical to those of the person receiving care. They are two different people. Secondly, talking about one's own experiences introduces another, different agenda into a conversation. Sometimes mentioning some similarity in one's own life can help build trust and empathy, but this should be done with much care. Avoid pious platitudes such as 'I know how you feel'. It is most unlikely that the pastoral carer will really know how another person feels, and platitudes like this will make it more difficult for the person being cared for to explore or recognise what their real feelings are. Good listening is 'heart work', it takes skill and experience.

Questioning

Asking questions can show that the carer has been listening. They can help the pastoral carer, perhaps to confirm, clarify, or better understand something that has been said. Sometimes questions create a wider perspective, or help link thoughts and situations together; they can help people reflect on the effects of their actions and learn from events and situations.

Broadly there are two types of question: open and closed. Closed questions have definite answers: 'Are you married?', 'How many children do you have?', 'Did Joe visit you yesterday?'. Closed questions can be used to good effect. They can be used to confirm important information and, sometimes, to help move a conversation along. However, it is often unhelpful to ask too many closed questions; the non-religious pastoral carer should not be on a fact-finding exercise or conducting some sort of interview. They are not carrying out some sort of spiritual diagnosis. Closed questions tend to elicit short answers and have a tendency to close down conversations. Open questions can be more encouraging: 'What did that seem like?', 'How did you feel about that?', 'What do you want to happen next?'. Open questions invite a response and encourage expansion. Using questions starting with 'why' may be less encouraging: 'why' questions tend to ask the responder to provide a reason. 'Why did you do that?' may seem to be asking for some justification and may appear judgemental. Of course, tone of voice and body language can help change the nature of a question, and using 'why' questions should not be avoided completely. Open questions are less directional and can allow the person being cared for to explore and reflect. They can be influencing without being controlling. Good questions are simple, inoffensive, and have purpose.

> The ability to ask fabulous questions consistently is uncommon enough to seem like a rare talent … a beautifully timed, perfectly worded question can remove barriers, unlock hidden information and surface potentially life-changing insights. (Starr, 2016)

Giving feedback

Good feedback can work in many ways. The feedback may reflect back what has been said. This shows that the pastoral carer is hearing what has been said and provides an opportunity for the person being cared for to correct any misunderstanding, but it also shows that the pastoral carer has noted a particular part of the discussion. Feedback can help to summarise what has been said, or interpret it. With the right support from the carer, feedback can be challenging, and this can sometimes help the person explore or question their thoughts and feelings. New perspectives may be offered, which can reframe the discussion. Feedback can also be affirming. Often in these types of conversation the person being cared for will, in talking out loud about their thoughts and feelings, find in themselves strengths and values that they had not recognised before. Affirming these can be very helpful. In the discussion with Mary, she came to realise, or at least to consciously confirm to herself, that she was quite a brave person not only in opting for the operation, but in other aspects of her life. In acknowledging and praising this bravery the pastoral carer can help affirm Mary's self-worth. (This is quite different from the carer telling Mary that she was brave.)

A particularly powerful form of feedback is touching. Holding the hand of the person being cared for can express quite deep feelings. This must be done with their permission, and it is imperative that the institutional rules and code of practice are followed; in prisons, for example, such contact will not be allowed. Once trust and presence have been established, touching can give very positive feedback.

Feedback needs to be clear, articulate, and specific, using respectful language appropriate to the person. Often it can be helpful to use metaphor or analogy: 'You seem to be saying that you've been on a scary roller-coaster ride'; 'So it's a bit like being out on a cold, damp day'. The feedback should be based on what the person being cared for has said (in its broadest sense) and on behaviour, rather than on personality. Choosing the time in the conversation to give feedback does require some skill and experience. Whenever and however feedback is given, it should be given with positive intent.

Working in a team

In most cases, non-religious pastoral carers will be working in departments tasked with providing pastoral, spiritual, and religious care. Since the development of specific non-religious pastoral care provision is relatively new, it is likely that almost all the people, volunteers, and paid staff in those departments will be religious. For the non-religious pastoral carer, working in a team comprising mainly religious people may be a new experience. The same could apply to religious members of that team; the concept of a non-religious pastoral carer may seem strange or, at least, unusual. The central point to note at this stage is that the discussion is about a team, one team. One of its common aims should be to provide excellent pastoral, spiritual, and religious care, an aim all members of the team can work together to achieve. In good departments, the head or lead manager will create an opportunity, for example at a team meeting, to introduce the non-religious pastoral carer and express their support for such care provision. For their part, the non-religious pastoral carer needs to play a full and constructive role, including attending team meetings and training events. The existing team members have, collectively, a huge amount of experience and a good knowledge of the institution they belong to. The non-religious pastoral carer needs to recognise this and appreciate the enormous help these team members can provide. There will be times when all members find their role emotionally challenging. Sometimes *they* will need care. Team members, particularly the lead manager, can play a key role in providing that care.

Prisons and large hospitals may have several paid staff as part of a team, but pastoral carers working in the community, care homes, higher education, hospices, and geographically diverse hospital trusts may see colleagues only occasionally. In such circumstances, robust arrangements need to be made with the department to ensure there is support and care for the carers. Members of the Non-Religious Pastoral Support Network can receive emotional and other support from within the network. This may be in the form of monthly supervision and liaison with local members.

Diverse teams have the advantage of bringing together different cultural, religious, and non-religious perspectives. This can be a great opportunity for all members of the team to learn and to understand what others believe and value by letting them express this in their own terms. This is facilitated by avoiding adversarial or confrontational language, by recognising that it is fine to disagree and being honest about differences. This honesty includes expressing feelings and encouraging other members of the team to express theirs, perhaps by actively listening. It is worth remembering that all of us at times fall short of the ideals of our own traditions. Comparing our own ideals with other people's practices can show a lack of empathy and understanding. Avoiding generalisations is helpful. 'I think ...' is better than 'humanists think ...'. These approaches should help build dialogue and trust between team members, whatever their perspective in terms of religion or belief. If properly utilised within a cooperative team, these different perspectives can be used to help build a more informed, inclusive, and stronger care service.

Advocacy and education

The prime role of a non-religious pastoral carer will always be to provide care. Initially this is likely to be achieved through one-to-one care and active listening as described above. Once the non-religious pastoral carer has experience in this role, and is recognised and respected, then aspects of advocacy and education can be developed.

The purpose of advocacy and education is to improve care. The non-religious pastoral carer will have a particular perspective that results from trying to live a life that is consistent with their non-religious beliefs and values. Ensuring that those beliefs and values are properly understood by their team and their institution, for example by giving talks and participating in the education of new trainees or by providing literature for service users, will help to improve understanding and should be encouraged by department managers.

There has been much discussion on improving religious literacy. For example, Professor Hordern (2017) spoke on 'Religious literacy in health and social care' in response to the report of the All Party Parliamentary Group on Religious Education (2016)[1]. The need for improved religious literacy was stressed but the need for improved non-religious literacy was not mentioned. Yet the need for education to improve non-religious literacy is clear. This would include gaining a better understanding of beliefs such as humanism, including humanist ceremonies. The need for better education about the beliefs and values of non-religious people is readily apparent, especially when one sees such people being referred to as of 'no faith', 'nil' or 'none'. Education is vital to explain why such perceptions can be damaging, for example, seeing non-religious people in this negative way is judgemental and lacks positive regard. Education is needed to demonstrate that non-religious people can hold beliefs and values with great sincerity and conviction, and that these beliefs and values have meaning and purpose in their lives. This education is about changing the ways in which some people perceive non-religious people. Changing such perceptions can be more difficult than, say, explaining religious dietary requirements or a funeral ritual. Nevertheless, it is vital. Fortunately, a powerful way of educating people is through our behaviour and actions.

An important part of the advocacy role is likely to be working to ensure people with non-religious belief and values have the same opportunities as religious people to access appropriate pastoral care. Such advocacy can cover many areas. Some of these are considered in greater depth in part III of this book. In one sense, this could be seen as an equality issue and, indeed, being able to challenge inequality is an essential capability.[2] Inequality damages care provision and care outcomes, so advocating a reduction in inequality should primarily be seen as a means of improving care. Whilst it may often be the case that the non-religious pastoral carer may be advocating greater equality for non-religious people, it should be recognised that this is also likely to benefit other groups who are suffering from inequality in care provision or outcomes. Moving from a multi-faith, wholly religious, pastoral, spiritual, and religious care service to a fully inclusive service that embraces non-religious care provision is a very significant change. Making such changes after decades of a different established practice is not without its difficulties. Non-religious pastoral carers need to be cooperative and constructive members of the team, while at the same time challenging some of the attitudes, policies, and practices that may have become established over many years. This make take time, tact, and perseverance, but advocating such change is an essential role.

Roles in institutions

The roles of active listening, working in a team, advocacy, and education are common to all institutions. However, the scope and practice of non-religious pastoral care can vary quite markedly both between institutions and within institutions. Hence it is only possible to give some general guidelines. Non-religious pastoral carers should seek further guidance initially from their department lead, and from the Non-Religious Pastoral Support Network. Large institutions have a range of policies, guidelines, procedures, and practices that apply to all staff and volunteers. Institutions should make pastoral carers aware of these and give appropriate training. All pastoral, spiritual, and religious care departments are likely to have record- and time-keeping systems and other administrative procedures that staff and volunteers should follow. Many procedures and, indeed, the role itself relate to the specific nature of the institution.

Prisons

The title of a non-religious pastoral care volunteer in prisons is 'volunteer chaplain' not 'chaplaincy volunteer'. This distinction is very important. A 'volunteer chaplain' is part of the core 'chaplaincy' team. They must be nominated and endorsed by a 'faith' adviser. A chaplaincy volunteer is part of the extended team, working under a 'chaplain' and helping to carry out many support and administrative roles. Depending on the prison, the non-religious pastoral carer may help with religious registration during the reception visit of new prisoners (Ministry of Justice, 2011, p.5). There are many generic activities where any endorsed member of the team will give pastoral care to any prisoner. Hence a Muslim 'chaplain' may give pastoral care to a non-religious prisoner, or a non-religious pastoral carer will provide care to a Christian prisoner. Often this care will not be centred on matters that relate directly to a person's religion or belief. One example, in the following personal account from a non-religious pastoral carer, is the giving of bad news.

As I arrived in the prison 'chaplaincy' office, the phone rang. A representative from a state agency explained that the previous day she had been scheduled to tell a prisoner about the outcome of a court case regarding the custody of his child. She had missed the meeting because something more important had come up. Would I talk to the prisoner about the results of the case? The court case had not gone in the prisoner's favour, his child had been adopted. Although he could appeal, there was little chance of an appeal succeeding. He would be able to write to his child … but only once a year … and the letter would be vetted before it reached his child. The agency worker had not contacted the prisoner to apologise or to explain why she could not make the meeting. She would send an official letter. Although I had been offering pastoral support in prisons for over three years I was still dismayed at the disregard shown for the feelings of those confined to prison.

I located the prisoner's wing and landing, and introduced myself to the landing officer, a kindly man who had not been impressed by the previous day's fiasco. He needed to know that the prisoner may be more vulnerable after my visit. I was given permission to unlock the prisoner's cell and take him to an office, so I could break the news in as much privacy as the institution afforded. The prisoner was a man called Freddie, he was in his mid-twenties, slight of build, reduced to a dull anonymity in his regulation grey tracksuit bottoms and beige sweatshirt. His gratitude on seeing me was plaintive; I had met a promise that someone from the pastoral care team would return with news. He looked almost devoid of hope. I asked him to sit down and prepare himself for bad news. I broke the news succinctly, adding that an appeal had little chance of success, and that he was allowed one vetted letter to his child each year.

I listened to Freddie as he detailed a litany of being let down. His girlfriend couldn't get straight (she had a heroin addiction), so wasn't able to care for their child. Freddie had tried to provide for his siblings after his dad had left. He was pleased that he had been able to help his sister get through college. He had hoped that she would step up to look after Callum, his three-year-old son … but she hadn't. No-one had been there for him as a child. Now he couldn't be there for his child. There was never going to be another chance.

My job was to sit with Freddie's despair. He cried and talked. I listened. When he talked and cried out, I checked how he thought he would be, alone in his cell later.

'I will be OK miss.' I knew we had to wrap up, we were within the prison schedule. I handed him tissues. Freddie needed to be able to gather himself to leave the room, to allow me to walk with him to his cell, to the banalities of the prison routine. I asked him if he had anything on in the afternoon. 'No.' What would he do to occupy himself. He didn't know. I told him that I would open a precautionary ACCT[3]. He didn't object. I said that I would be in the following week and could look him up, and if he wanted I could ask one of the team to see how he was tomorrow. He'd like that. And despite the news he had to hear me deliver, he thanked me again for coming.

I took Freddie back to his cell and reported his vulnerability to his landing officer. He agreed that I should open an ACCT. It meant that Freddie would be monitored so that he didn't harm himself. I completed the paperwork and delivered it to the landing officer, then wrote up the facts from the telephone call on the computer in the 'chaplaincy' office. I sat back and acknowledged how sad I felt. Later I reflected on it with a colleague from our team. It was good to talk to her.

This account shows that this role can have an emotional impact on those providing pastoral, spiritual, and religious care.[4] These sorts of situation can also be emotionally challenging for staff. The increasing number of deaths in custody can place huge strains on staff. The non-religious pastoral carers' role is not limited to providing care to prisoners. It is just as important that they support staff at difficult times. The effectiveness of the role can be increased by building cooperative links with the prison governor, some relevant management committees, and charities that provide care services to the prison.

The turnover of prisoners is much higher in some prisons than others. This influences the balance of activities; for example, registration can be a significant activity in remand prisons. It may also limit the time available to build trust and confidence with a prisoner.

In all prisons, the 'chaplaincy' department must make daily visits to all prisoners in segregation or receiving healthcare. Non-religious pastoral carers can help with these visits. However, giving one-to-one pastoral care to prisoners in their cells or on their wing may be restricted to providing care to prisoners declaring themselves as 'nil religion'. Good practice should ensure that such prisoners are fully aware of the non-religious pastoral care provision, but this is not always the case. Where requested by the prisoner, the non-religious pastoral carer may act as an advocate for the prisoner in their meetings with prison management. It can be very important to provide support at a time of bereavement. For example, for security reasons some prisoners may be unable to attend the funeral of someone close to them. If that prisoner is not religious, meeting with the chaplain in a chapel at the time of the funeral may be inappropriate: the prisoner could feel quite uncomfortable. The non-religious pastoral carer can offer a more meaningful alternative.

Pamela, a volunteer non-religious pastoral carer, was asked to see John. John had put in a request to visit his grandfather, who was seriously ill in hospital. He had heard nothing and was getting upset. Pamela listened as he told her about not getting a response to his visit request. She explained that she did not have the authority to grant such a request, but if he wanted her to, she would explain the situation to the managing 'chaplain', ask him to follow it up, and check on progress when she was in the prison the following week. John agreed. That was about the extent to which Pamela could help sort out the practical problem.

Pamela asked how he was feeling. John was quite young to be in an adult prison, but he was tough, or at least that's what he wanted to project to the other prisoners and prison officers. John never knew his father; it was his grandparents who loved him and tried their best to bring him up. By being present and giving unconditional positive regard, Pamela gave John the security and confidence to take off his mask of toughness and talk about his real feelings. He so wanted to be able to say sorry to his grandfather for getting into prison. John talked a lot about his life and his hopes. Pamela built up trust and helped create a space for John to think about his strengths as well as his weaknesses, and to explore what he truly wanted from his life.

A couple of weeks later, his grandfather died. John didn't get the chance to visit him. On the day of the funeral, Pamela met John in a small, quiet room, not easy to find in a noisy prison. She brought a portable CD player. They played one or two of grandfather's favourite records, the ones they used to play when John was a child. Pamela read a poem and lit a candle – well, switched on a battery-powered candle – real candles were not allowed. John read a poem. They sat silently for a while. Although John wasn't physically present at the crematorium, he could take part in his grandfather's funeral in a very meaningful way. Afterwards, he could tell his grandmother what he did, and talk about what he felt. Pamela continued to see John.

Prison Service Instructions state that prisoners who register themselves as belonging to a religion should have the opportunity to attend corporate worship, celebrate religious festivals, and take part in religious classes (Ministry of Justice, 2011). Quite rightly, the Ministry of Justice recognises the importance of such activities. Such occasions not only allow prisoners to manifest their religious beliefs, they offer them a chance to leave their cells and meet like-minded prisoners and, in religious classes, to discuss and explore their beliefs and values. Whilst the Prison Service Instructions make no similar provision for people with non-religious beliefs and values, Her Majesty's Prison and Probation Service positively supports similar opportunities for such people. Non-religious pastoral carers can organise discussion groups on ethical issues. For example, one discussion group included speakers from a local council's support group for gay, lesbian, and transgender employees. It is possible to celebrate Darwin Day, World Humanist Day, and Human Rights Day.[5]

A developing area is where non-religious pastoral carers can help facilitate ongoing care and support once a prisoner has been discharged, and for prisoners' families. This can be most helpful, but needs to be done so that trained, reliable support can be maintained whilst ensuring high levels of security and safeguarding.

Healthcare

A popular model of care provision is that of 'generic chaplaincy'. In this model, the care provider covers the needs of all patients, carers, and staff in a particular location, irrespective of their religion or belief. That location may comprise designated wards within a hospital, one of several hospitals in a trust, a hospice, or a geographical community area. The 'chaplain' or non-religious pastoral carer may approach all the patients within their location on a cold-calling basis. Some may decline the approach, some may respond out of politeness and talk briefly, others may be bored and be pleased to have someone to talk to. On some occasions, the conversation will have a deeper significance. Sometimes the nature of the encounter may deepen during the conversation as trust and presence is built up. Clearly, in this model those providing care will talk to people with a range of beliefs and values. One part of this generic role can be to describe the pastoral, spiritual, and religious care available, and if the patient asks, arrange for a 'chaplain' of the appropriate religion and denomination to visit. Sometimes visits will be to patients who want to talk to a non-religious pastoral carer because they are not religious. Of course, 'chaplains' should make arrangements for non-religious pastoral carers to visit such patients on the same basis.[6] However, many pastoral carers' encounters with patients will be generic in the sense that the discussion will be non-specific in terms of a person's religion or beliefs. Aspects of religion, belief, or existential and theological issues may not be part of what they want to talk about. A claimed benefit of this cold-calling generic model is that it informs patients of the care on offer, allowing them to access appropriate care at a time of need.

Part of the role is to provide care to staff, carers, family, and friends. This can be on a one-to-one basis, often via requests made to the department. Memorial and anniversary services play a significant role, bringing together patients, carers, family, and staff. Such services may be for those who have lost babies and young children; to remember those who have died of cancer; for those whose loved ones donated their bodies for medical research; or for many other reasons. Such services need to be fully inclusive, and the non-religious pastoral carer's role can be to advise and help with planning and content, provide suitable poems and readings, and take part in the services. The role includes providing, or helping to arrange the provision of, non-religious rites of passage. The provision of emergency non-religious baby namings is likely to increase; humanist funerals are well established; and there is increasing legal recognition of humanist weddings.[7]

For those with time and interest, becoming a member of one or more of the institution's committees can be an effective way of increasing understanding and helping shape policy. Some institutions have equality and diversity committees, spiritual care groups, patient liaison groups, etc. Non-religious pastoral carers who have the training and expertise could be effective members of ethics committees.

Military

The provision of specific non-religious pastoral care in the military is not well established, so the role has not been developed and defined to the same extent as in prisons and healthcare. Currently there are two broad types of role: the advisory, non-operational role of civilian Buddhists, Hindus, Jews, Muslims, and Sikhs, who are there to ensure their religion is properly considered; and the operational role of commissioned Christian chaplains to provide pastoral, spiritual, and religious care together with the promotion of moral welfare (see chapter 2). It is clear that the Ministry of Defence and the armed forces would benefit from someone having the role of ensuring that the pastoral and spiritual care needs of people with non-religious beliefs and values are properly considered. Such a role would be analogous to a non-religious version of that carried out by the appointed non-Christian civilian staff. However, this role would not actually provide specific non-religious pastoral and spiritual care to people when they need it and where they need it, for example when on operations, overseas, and during military conflicts. This suggests that there is a need for commissioned non-religious pastoral carers in a professional role. As well as providing active listening, advocacy, education, and training, it may be necessary for carers to be trained and authorised to conduct baby namings, marriages, and funerals, especially where they cannot call upon the resources of a local celebrant network. Whilst some aspects may be specifically non-religious, others will be generic, helping to meet the needs of all service personnel and their families. For example, as with chaplains, non-religious pastoral carers would need to be able to help promote moral welfare generally within the armed forces. Of course, there is no reason why people with non-religious beliefs and values cannot help to promote moral welfare, but it is worth giving some thought to what this aspect of the role really means. It will be critical to ensure that this new and developing role is defined and practised in a way that meets pastoral care needs as expressed by service users, rather than being constrained to fit into the form and scope of current chaplaincy roles.

Universities

In universities, non-religious pastoral carers work in a looser structure than some other institutions, so they may have to be more proactive in determining a role that best fits their local circumstances. University or college can be a place where students meet others with different beliefs and values from those of their parents and their upbringing. This may cause some students to reflect and form their own views. For example, many young people with a Christian upbringing described themselves as non-religious by the time they became adults (Lee, 2012, p.176). This can be both empowering and challenging. For some students, changing from the religion or belief of their parents can be particularly stressful, causing them to re-evaluate their own sense of identity. In some relatively closed religious communities, leaving their religion can result in rejection by family and friends. Such students may also have had minimal exposure to a society with a wide range of beliefs, values, and behaviours. Adjusting to this new environment can be confusing and demanding.

Zia was part of a household that practised Islam – her family were raised to be attuned to the cultural, traditional, and religious needs that the religion deems to be significant. Zia was born and raised in the UK and identified as British before identifying as Muslim. During her adolescent years, she began to rebel against the norms of the household, which sometimes caused her father to become angry. On completing her A levels, Zia was accepted at university – a proud, celebratory moment for their household. Her father shared the news with their extended family: it was a momentous occasion.

Before going to university, Zia informed her parents that she did not believe in Islam, or any religion. Her parents immediately ordered her to leave the household. She was informed that could not contact them, but that she would be informed of significant events that occurred, such as the death of a relative. During this time, she remained in a state of low mood, isolated herself from others, and started to steadily increase her alcohol consumption.

During her first week at university, Zia made friends with people who lived on the same floor as her, and they all attended the freshers' fair together. She read somewhere that the debating society was holding its first meet-and-greet at the Student Union bar. She asked her flatmates whether they would go with her, as she was nervous about meeting new people. They went to the Union bar, and saw a group of people – Zia asked whether they were the debating society. To this they replied that they weren't, they were members of Humanist Students, and they were a group supporting non-religious students on campus.

Zia told them that she was non-religious too. The society president, Arjun, spoke to Zia. For the first time she felt that she was able to talk freely about her journey and how she was abandoned for not being religious.

Faith to Faithless (2017) run training courses to help those involved with student welfare to identify and provide assistance to such students. Members of Humanist Students may also want to provide peer-to-peer support. Some universities provide training for students to provide proactive support as student mentors. Wanting to provide care in this way is a part of a humanist approach to life.

Active listening, education, and advocacy will remain essential. Non-religious pastoral carers, working with their religious colleagues, can play a key role in helping to build understanding and tolerance between people of different religions, beliefs, and values. There should be opportunities for discussion groups, debates, and dialogue events. Non-religious pastoral carers will seek to engage with the humanist and atheist communities on campus and cooperate with other chaplaincy members at freshers' week, inter-faith events, etc., and carers may wish to hold celebration events for Darwin Day, World Humanist Day, and Human Rights Day. Close contact should be maintained with the appropriate student welfare department or its equivalent.

Skills and competencies

Skills and competencies include an individual's ability to do something well, their knowledge and experience, ability to communicate and cooperate – and also their attitudes, willingness to learn and reflect, resilience, and tenacity. Many other skills and competencies are necessary or desirable, and it is not the intention to give a comprehensive account here. An assessment can only be made after the role has been carefully defined and articulated. For example, a civilian non-religious pastoral carer in an advisory role in the Ministry of Defence will require different skills and competencies from a non-religious pastoral carer in a commissioned role in the RAF. A role where there is a genuine occupational requirement for an ordained Church of England priest will need different skills and competencies from a role where there is a requirement for a lay person belonging to a church community. More senior roles involving greater management responsibilities will demand different skills and competencies. One organisation that has paid particular attention to roles, capabilities, and competencies is the UK Board of Healthcare Chaplaincy (2009, 2015). The organisation's documents are grounded in experience, carefully considered, and well thought through. They show how capability and competency criteria can change for different job grades. Their scope is limited to healthcare, and they were developed from a religious perspective, but for those with an interest in this area, they are well worth reading.

Many non-religious pastoral carers will have non-professional voluntary roles. As the essence of the role is one of care, previous experience in a caring role, particularly one involving active listening to people, would be advantageous. There are many caring roles. For example, vets can become very good pastoral carers: as well as treating the medical condition of animals, they have a lot of experience dealing with people's anxieties, emotions, and grief. Some occupations, such as counselling, nursing, education, psychotherapy, and social work, are professionally registered, requiring formal qualifications. Formal qualifications of this type are not needed for non-religious pastoral care volunteers but the experience and understanding is invaluable. Many people have relevant experience through their charitable work. A wide range of charities provide care, including Citizens Advice, Cruse Bereavement Care, Marie Curie, Mind, and Samaritans, to mention just a few. Some will have gained experience from their jobs in care and nursing homes, helping with rehabilitation of those with mental health problems or suffering abuse, working with young people's organisations, and many related activities. Some will have gained experience from helping to care for people close to them. Thus experience can be gained at a personal, volunteer, or professional level.

Whilst such experience can be very valuable, certain personal attributes and characteristics are essential. Clearly, a strong commitment to pastoral care as a means of improving the wellbeing of people in institutions and the community is crucial. High-quality active listening demands a capacity to give full attention to the person receiving support, and an ability to see beneath the surface of a situation and engage more deeply with the humanity within. To achieve this, one must be adept at being non-judgemental and empathetic. Having a good awareness of one's own humanity, beliefs, values, and identity is essential to accompany someone exploring their own deep questions of meaning and identity. A willingness to work with and care for a diverse range of people of different cultures, traditions, beliefs, and backgrounds is vital, as is a willingness to accept advice and criticism, to be able to reflect and learn. At times the role can be challenging, so a gentle, unremitting tenacity and robustness in unfamiliar environments are needed.

The non-religious pastoral carer needs to have a general knowledge of the role of pastoral care and of 'chaplaincy' in their institution. Maintaining some knowledge of human responses to loss, bereavement, incarceration, rehabilitation, and illness is most useful, as is some knowledge of human psychology. Having an understanding of the main world religions, in particular their philosophies and practices around birth, loss, dying, and death, can be very helpful, as is a similar understanding of humanist and non-religious philosophies and practices.

As previously mentioned, the ability to work closely and constructively within a team of colleagues holding very different views is essential. It is also essential to be able to work according to the policies and practices of the institution and abide by appropriate codes of practice. Last, but not least, is a willingness to undertake ongoing learning and development.

This should include regular reflective practice. Essentially, reflective practice is thinking about what one does or has done. But it is not just some spur-of-the moment thought. It is a deliberate, conscious effort to reflect on events and gain some insight from them, to work out what to do differently and better next time. Gibbs (1998) describes a six-stage model of reflective practice. For a particular conversation, the first stage is to recognise and describe what happened, noting all the relevant events, the circumstances, the words used, etc. The second stage describes one's feelings both at the time and afterwards. The third stage is to evaluate what went well, what was a cause for concern, what was said that made one think, what was learned. Stage four is analysis. Here one tries to make sense of it all, drawing on one's knowledge of good practice, understanding causes, perhaps seeking the help of peers. Stage five considers what has been learned from the experience, what was noticed, what was missed, and what could be improved next time. This leads to stage six, an action plan to improve future practice: how to respond to a similar situation next time, and what actions to take to consolidate strengths and reduce weaknesses. Learning and development may include seeking opportunities for further training, sharing experiences, reading, and keeping up with new research and understanding.

Training

Volunteers

Most non-religious pastoral carers will be volunteers, and many will have worked in a caring role or profession. However, there is a need for some induction training. One organisation offering such training is Humanists UK. The main purposes of this training are to:

- give people an awareness and understanding of the non-religious pastoral carer's role and why it is necessary
- explain how such care provision is organised and how it operates in different institutions
- deliver training in key skills, to create an opportunity to practise them and experience 'receiving' active listening
- promote safeguarding and explore ethical issues
- assess trainees' capabilities and potential for ongoing learning and improvement
- grant initial accreditation to support applications to institutions
- foster a network of mutually supportive practitioners.

The purpose of the training is not to produce fully equipped non-religious pastoral care volunteers. Institutions need to provide further training, and volunteers' competency will need to be developed and assessed under the supervision of an experienced manager within the institution. Induction training should help trainees decide if they want to commence this role, and give them a basic understanding, some skills, and the confidence to go forward in a supportive environment. It also gives trainers and organisations some evidence on which to base objective accreditation decisions.

Humanists UK's training is open to all those who can articulate a clear non-religious belief system that is consistent with the values of a modern democratic society.[8] This includes humanists. Applicants must show a commitment to the objective of achieving equality of access to like-minded pastoral, spiritual, and religious care. The application process includes writing about the motivations for applying, names of referees, and a telephone interview. If accepted, there will be advance reading and a pre-course webinar followed by two full days of training. One of the roles, active listening, can be explained, but learning is fundamentally experiential. The course includes demonstrations, analysis of videos, and role plays of active listening, allowing participants to develop their understanding and skills. Then, subject to proper safeguarding in a confidential session, participants are invited to talk about themselves and a loss or concern in their lives and to receive active listening pastoral care. This allows them to experience the great value of such care. Most participants have found this part of the training to be enormously worthwhile. Further written reflections and a post-course webinar follow. Those who have demonstrated an ability to learn and to develop the required skills, competencies, and capabilities are given provisional accreditation. This accreditation is subject to participants successfully meeting the requirements of the institution where they want to provide care and agreeing to the organisation's code of conduct.

Procedures differ, and it is for institutions to confirm that people applying to volunteer meet their criteria. Those applying to volunteer in prisons should ask their accrediting organisation (e.g. Humanists UK) to contact the appropriate prison(s) in their area. An interview with the managing 'chaplain' and a visit to the prison will be arranged. For those who have not spent time in prison, it is good practice to spend several hours in the prison and visit different areas of it. The experience of non-religious pastoral carers is that they are welcomed and valued by staff and prisoners. Initially, the prison environment can seem somewhat raw. Spending time in a prison with, say, the managing 'chaplain' can allow potential volunteers to gain a more accurate impression of what it would be like to volunteer on a regular basis. If they are comfortable, the application process can proceed. This includes both Disclosure and Barring Service checks and a Counter Terrorist Check. The Counter Terrorist Check can take weeks or months, so patience is required. It cannot be stressed too strongly that, in prisons, security is paramount. This is reflected in in-house training, which covers a wide range of aspects from how to lock and unlock doors and how to keep oneself safe, to conditioning- and manipulation-prevention awareness training.[9]

The managing 'chaplain' should provide opportunities to shadow experienced members of the team so that pastoral carers can learn from their experience, explain the various activities of the role, ensure access to appropriate parts of the prison and to relevant information about prisoners, and explain the various prison and 'chaplaincy' office procedures. Once established, volunteers should be offered a place on Her Majesty's Prison and Probation Service (HMPPS) 'Starting Out' training course. This two-day course helps to contextualise pastoral carers' existing skills to ensure they are comfortable within the constraints of security and the prison routine. It is a really worthwhile course, in part because it allows people to share experiences, widen their perspectives, and help develop a support network. A four-day 'World Faiths' course covers the basic beliefs of the six major World Faiths.[10] The Managing 'Chaplain' of a particular prison and HMPPS Chaplaincy Department have a responsibility for the ongoing training of volunteers. Non-religious pastoral carers need to be proactive in seeking and seizing these development opportunities.

Those wishing to volunteer their services to hospitals, hospices, and related healthcare institutions should contact the lead 'chaplain' or volunteer department directly, explaining what they want to do and their accreditation, and asking to take part in the next in-house training course. It would be good practice to invite the applicant for an interview or at least a chat. Some will have a more formalised process. All should arrange for Disclosure and Barring Service checks to be completed. Generally, training courses are run a few times a year, so it may be some months before an opportunity becomes available. Most hospices, being smaller than hospitals, may give individual training. The content and duration of in-house training varies considerably from place to place. All training should cover essential and mandatory items such as infection control and hygiene, fire training, health and safety, safeguarding, information governance, and confidentiality. Many will include listening skills, death, bereavement, trauma, and information about religious rites. Some will include role plays or simulation exercises. All should offer the opportunity to shadow and be shadowed by an experienced practitioner.

The Network for Pastoral, Spiritual and Religious Care in Health (2017) also runs training courses to help potential 'chaplains' and non-religious pastoral carers understand the role in a healthcare context. The course comprises teaching days, writing essays, and a placement of between four and 20 hours in a healthcare setting. It is a most useful course. However, most trusts will also require volunteers to complete their own in-house training, and the course is not an alternative to accreditation as a non-religious pastoral carer. The College of Health Care Chaplains (2017) runs courses and holds an annual conference. It also holds regional meetings where practitioners can meet, compare experiences, and hear authoritative speakers. The UK Board of Healthcare Chaplaincy (n.d.) offers an online training course, which is available at the discretion of the Lead 'Chaplain' for a particular trust . Requests to access the course should not be unreasonably withheld. As with prisons, the Lead 'Chaplain' has a responsibility for the development of volunteers within the department and should make available further in-house training opportunities. Non-religious pastoral carers will also benefit from being proactive in seeking such opportunities.

Non-religious pastoral carers wishing to provide care in universities should contact the lead chaplain and the head of the department responsible for 'chaplaincy'.[11] An invitation for discussions should follow. Discussions should help pastoral carers to gain an understanding of the pastoral care needs of university students and staff, how they can help meet those needs, the functioning within the team, and the training offered. In universities, inclusive in-house training has not developed in the same way as for prisons and healthcare. Local discussions about induction and training needs between those responsible for staff training, the lead 'chaplain', and the non-religious pastoral carer could be beneficial. In time, it is expected that improved, inclusive in-house training will be established.

In the armed forces, there are no voluntary roles.

Whatever the form of training and development, pastoral carers are encouraged to keep a log of their continuing professional development activities. The renewal of Humanist UK accreditation is dependent upon being able to evidence continuing professional development.

Paid, substantive posts

Since the end of the Second World War, the Dutch Humanist Association and the University of Humanistic Studies have developed graduate and postgraduate training and professional standards (Bolsenbroek, Mooren and Reinders, 2013). This work, together with the years of experience of Dutch colleagues working in paid, substantive posts in prisons, healthcare, and the military, has formed a sound basis on which to build in the UK.[12]

In contrast to the Netherlands, until recently in the UK, recruitment into paid substantive posts in pastoral, spiritual, and religious care departments has been restricted to religious people. More recently some non-religious people have been recruited into substantive posts. Typically, such people are registered with counselling, psychotherapy, or related professional bodies and are accredited Humanist Ceremonies[TM] celebrants. However, there is a need to provide opportunities for people with non-religious beliefs to undertake relevant postgraduate training and to put the recruitment of such people into substantive posts onto a sustainable basis. To meet these needs, a Master of Arts course in Existential and Humanist Pastoral Care has been developed in close cooperation with Humanists UK. It has drawn on the experience and expertise generously offered by both Dutch colleagues and the UK Board of Healthcare Chaplaincy's academic adviser. The MA, the first of its kind in the UK, is being delivered by the New School of Psychotherapy and Counselling (2017). It has been validated by Middlesex University and the UK Board of Healthcare Chaplaincy. The course is open to people with at least a second-class first degree or equivalent professional qualification, subject to interviews evidencing personal suitability. It is based on a blend of learning styles with online theoretical modules and face-to-face skills-based training. Philosophical worldviews, religions, and belief systems are studied, and the importance of developing a research capability is fully recognised, with students undertaking a supervised piece of research. Significant placements are included across a range of sectors including healthcare, education, prisons, and the armed forces. The MA also affords probationary accreditation as a celebrant for Humanists UK funerals, weddings, and baby namings.[13]

For most non-religious pastoral carers, it is likely the majority of the ceremonies they conduct will be funerals. Just as different religions have distinct funeral rites and rituals, non-religious funeral ceremonies offer a personal and fitting way to say goodbye to those who have lived without religious beliefs. These different funeral rites reflect some of the basic beliefs and existential ideas about life and death.

Notes

1 The All Party Parliamentary Group on Religious Education (2016, p.44) did recommend 'that central and local governments should take steps to encourage public engagement in local and national dialogue and outreach initiatives between different religious and non-religious groups. They should also take steps to encourage the development of new local schemes which can build long-term relationships between people of different religions and beliefs in local communities' (p.44).
2 The UK Board of Healthcare Chaplaincy (2015) identifies challenging inequality as an essential capability.
3 Assessment, Care in Custody & Teamwork.
4 It also shows the value of the pastoral care provided by another member of the team.
5 12th February, 21st June, and 10th December, respectively.
6 Part of the education role is to help ensure that 'chaplains' understand that appropriate referral to non-religious pastoral carers is part of their role.
7 Humanist weddings are legally recognised in Scotland and the Republic of Ireland. In Northern Ireland the first legal humanist marriage took place in June 2017.
8 For a fuller discussion see the section on 'Inclusive recruitment' in chapter 12.
9 This is not intended to be a comprehensive list; for example, there is mandatory training covering areas such as fire safety and health and safety.
10 At the time of writing this HMPPS course was being reviewed.
11 These reporting lines are not always apparent and online searches or enquiries within the university may be necessary. However, it is helpful if the department the 'chaplaincy' reports to is aware of their interest.
12 The Dutch and UK situations are not exactly comparable because of differences in how some state institutions, including universities, are structured.
13 Some pastoral carers may wish to become accredited Humanist Ceremonies celebrants, but not as part of an MA. To do so they can apply directly to Humanists UK (2017) at https://humanism.org.uk/ceremonies/training-to-be-a-humanist-celebrant/

References

All Party Parliamentary Group on Religious Education (2016) *Improving Religious Literacy*. Available from: http://www.reonline.org.uk/wp-content/uploads/2016/07/APPG-on-RE-Improving-Religious-Literacy-full-report.pdf [accessed 28th July 2017].

Bolsenbroek, A., Mooren, J.H., Reinders, W. (2013) *Beroepsstandaard humanistisch geestelijke begeleiding*. Amsterdam, Humanistisch Verbond. Available from: http://www.humanistischverbond.nl/cms/files/beroepsstandaard.pdf [accessed 10th August 2017].

College of Health Care Chaplains (2017) Information about national courses/conferences and application forms. Available from: https://www.healthcarechaplains.org/training/courses/ [accessed 10th August 2017].

Faith to Faithless (2017) How Can We Help? Available from: https://faithtofaithless.com/ [accessed 5th December 2017].

Gibbs, G. (1988) *Learning by Doing: A Guide to Teaching and Learning Methods*. Further Education Unit. Oxford, Oxford Polytechnic.

Hordern, J.H. (2017) Religious Literacy in Health and Social Care. Remarks at a meeting at the House of Commons on January 31st 2017. Oxford, Healthcare Values Partnership, University of Oxford. Available from: http://www.healthcarevalues.ox.ac.uk/religious-literacy [accessed 28th July 2017].

Humanists UK (2017) Become a Humanist Celebrant. Available from: https://humanism.org.uk/ceremonies/training-to-be-a-humanist-celebrant/ [accessed 11th August 2017].

Lee, L. (2012) Religion: Losing Faith? In: Park, A., Clery, E., Curtice, J., Phillips, M., Utting, D. (eds) *British Social Attitudes 28*. London, Sage. Available from: http://www.bsa.natcen.ac.uk/media/38958/bsa28_12religion.pdf [accessed 5th December 2017].

Ministry of Justice (2011) *Faith and Pastoral Care for Prisoners*. Reference 51/2011 (revised).

Network for Pastoral, Spiritual and Religious Care in Health (2017) Starting Out in Healthcare Chaplaincy Course. Available from: http://hcfbg.org.uk/starting-healthcare-chaplaincy-course/ [accessed 10th August 2017].

New School of Psychotherapy and Counselling (2017) MA in Existential and Humanist Pastoral Care. Available from: https://www.nspc.org.uk/course-directory/nspc-courses/ma-in-existential-and-humanist-pastoral-care.html [accessed 10th August 2017].

Rogers, C.R. (2004) *On Becoming a Person*. London, Constable & Robinson. First published in 1961.

Starr, J. (2016) *The Coaching Manual: The Definitive Guide to the Process, Principles and Skills of Personal Coaching*. Fourth Edition. Harlow, Pearson Education.

UK Board of Healthcare Chaplaincy (2009) *Standards for Healthcare Chaplaincy Services*. Cambridge, UK Board of Healthcare Chaplaincy. Available from: http://www.ukbhc.org.uk/sites/default/files/standards_for_healthcare_chaplaincy_services_2009.pdf [accessed 6th August 2017].

UK Board of Healthcare Chaplaincy (2015) *Spiritual and Religious Care Capabilities and Competences for Healthcare Chaplains Bands 5, 6, 7 & 8*. Cambridge, UK Board of Healthcare Chaplaincy. Available from: http://www.ukbhc.org.uk/sites/default/files/ukbhc_spiritual_and_religious_capabilities_and_competences_bands_5_-_8_2015.pdf [accessed 28th July 2017].

UK Board of Healthcare Chaplaincy (n.d.) Healthcare Chaplaincy Training – Online Learning. Available from: http://learn.ukbhc.org.uk [accessed 10th August 2017].

Chapter 7

Death, rituals, and memorials

Death

Some context

It may be helpful to put a discussion about death in some context. An overwhelming majority of people receiving non-religious pastoral care will not be in situations where they see their lives to be in mortal danger, or where they know they are likely to die in the reasonably foreseeable future. For example, although most people die in hospital, the clear majority of people admitted to hospital go on to make some sort of recovery and return to their home/community (Marie Curie, n.d.).[1] Most of the conversations will be about life and living. Of course, there will be circumstances where aspects of death and dying are more prominent. For example, those providing pastoral care in war zones, hospices, and palliative care wards will be supporting people where the risk or expectation of death is much greater.

However, even where aspects of death and dying may seem to be closer, it would be wrong to assume that the main fears and anxieties of people receiving pastoral care will be about death, at least in an existential sense. Jong and Halberstadt (2016), researching death anxiety, found that most people didn't really fear death that much, even when death was close or getting closer. Death anxiety decreased with age, and research with cancer patients showed that their levels of death anxiety were no higher than those of the general population. Research, which included both non-religious and religious people, found that those who were strongly religious and those who were strongly non-religious had lower levels of death anxiety than those who were in the middle of the spectrum (Jong et al., 2017).[2] These findings are averages, and while some individuals may have a high fear of death, for most people it may be the dying process rather than death itself that provokes most anxiety. Concerns about pain, loneliness, and loss of control may result in higher levels of anxiety.

The National Council for Palliative Care commissioned ComRes (2015) to conduct a public opinion poll on death and dying looking at the factors that would help to ensure a good death.[3] Respondents were asked: 'Thinking about death, dying and bereavement, please rank the following factors in order of how important they are to you to ensure a "good death" is possible'. The factors were: being pain-free, being with your family and friends, being cared for and able to die in a place of your choice, retaining your dignity, being involved in decisions about your care ... and having your religious/ spiritual needs met. The ranking was from 1st to 6th.[4] The most important factors, were being pain-free (ranked first) and being with family and friends (second). The least important, ranked sixth, was having your religious/spiritual needs met.[5] A similar poll by the Demos think tank for Sue Ryder, a hospice and neurological care provider, ranked having religious, cultural, or spiritual needs met tenth out of eleven preferences (Wood and Salter, 2013).[6] Again, being pain-free and being surrounded by loved ones were most important. Taken together, Jong's work and these polls suggest that when considering death, it is aspects of living this life that are uppermost in most people's minds. This does not mean that a person's religious/spiritual needs should be disregarded. In the ComRes poll, 5% of respondents ranked having their religious/spiritual needs met as their first priority.[7] Ranking meeting religious/spiritual needs above being pain-free or being with family and friends implies a very strong and meaningful belief in religion.

A humanist perspective on death

A humanist pastoral carer applying to volunteer in a hospice was asked 'How can you talk to someone who is dying if you don't believe in a soul?' and 'How can you give someone hope if you don't believe in Heaven?'[8] These questions were asked from a genuine concern that people who did not believe in a literal life after death could not provide good pastoral care to dying people and, as a result, patients may be harmed. There was also a genuine lack of understanding about how people who did not believe in their own continued existence after death could have hope. These were sincere questions about the care of vulnerable people and, as such, they deserve considered answers. This section addresses the question of lack of understanding.

This is a humanist perspective, not the humanist perspective. However, almost all humanists would agree in the belief that this is the one life we have, that we did not exist before this life, and that we cease to exist in any literal sense after we have died. The philosopher John Stuart Mill (1874) found no evidence for immortality, noting that conscious life is dependent on neural activity and that once brain activity ceases such life ends.[9] Many years later this essentially remains the clinical view of death. Much earlier, the humanistic ancient Greek philosopher Epicurus (341–270 BCE) had formed the view that we ceased to exist when we died, coining the quotation 'When death is there, we are not: when we are there, death is not'. Epicurus didn't want people to fear death. He thought that after death we cease to exist as a soul or in some other disembodied way, we are not resurrected in some other form, and we do not go to heaven, purgatory, hell, or another supernatural place. We 'are not', so there is simply no need to fear death for ourselves.[10] A fear of pain, loss of control, loss of dignity, anxieties about those who may grieve and how others will cope without us, regrets of things unsaid, and plans unfulfilled are a real part of dying. But that is a part of living through this time, this life. An important outcome of this thinking is that others should not be upset *for our sake* by our death. We are not harmed by our death.

From this understanding, it should be apparent that for many humanists and others who do not believe in a life after death, talk of a soul or of heaven would be quite irrelevant. To try to offer such people hope based on these beliefs would be wholly inappropriate, indeed it could be very upsetting. Dying people may be vulnerable, and to challenge their sincerely held beliefs or their identity at such times could be an abuse. However, if the dying person has the opportunity to talk to a like-minded person, someone who also thinks that this is the one life we have, it could be very beneficial. It may be much easier to establish trust and empathy with someone who knows what it is like to live a life based on that belief than with someone who has totally different beliefs on life after death. A key phrase here is 'to know what it is like to live a life based on that belief'. Similarly, and importantly, the converse is true. A dying person who believes in life after death may want to speak to someone with the same beliefs. If the belief in an eternal soul or the prospect of entering heaven is what is sustaining you, giving you hope and strength, then it may be difficult to have a deep and meaningful discussion *about these things* with someone who has quite different beliefs.

At this point it is worth reminding ourselves of the context of the care. Most dying people do not spend most of their time contemplating the nature of heaven, still less the thoughts of Epicurus. Their thoughts are with the here and now. In this context, some humanist pastoral carers have found that their life stance can be helpful to people with religious beliefs as well as to those with non-religious beliefs. If a person is told that they have six weeks, six months, or six years to live, then there can be a clear realisation that this period of time is very finite. Humanists have learned how to live with the clear realisation that their lifetime is finite. They think, find meaning, and decide priorities on that basis. Working out how to spend that finite time well can be immensely valuable. Yalom (2007), Emeritus Professor of Existential Psychiatry and an atheist,[11] worked over many years with patients facing death from cancer. He found that many patients, rather than falling into despair, were positively transformed. They took more control over their remaining lives, prioritising what really mattered to them and stopping trivial activities. They talked in a deeper, more meaningful way to those they loved. He goes on to say:

'One of my patients commented drolly that "cancer cures psycho-neuroses"; another said to me, "What a pity I had to wait till now, till my body was riddled with cancer, to learn how to live!"'

This latter patient died whilst learning how to live. Many of us go through life learning how to live. Perhaps it is a good way to die.

Cicely Saunders said that 'How people die remains in the memory of those who live on' (Dying Matters, n.d.). Most humanists would recognise the salience of this quotation. Whilst they do not belief in a literal concept of life after death or having an eternal soul, the idea of a symbolic immortality may be very real. In some senses people may live on through their children, in the memories of other people, in the fruits of their labours, and through the recycling of their molecules. Our beliefs, values, and behaviour may all have some effect on the living. Many small acts of kindness, consideration, and thoughtfulness conducted through our lives may live on by benefiting people and our environment. Donating to charity, recycling waste, holding the door open for someone, giving a friendly smile may all have had a positive effect that remains. Perhaps, for some, this concept of a symbolic immortality is one motivating factor to live a 'good life'.

Shneidman (2008), an atheist American clinical psychologist, worked for years on suicide prevention. He developed a concept related to symbolic immortality, that of the 'postself'. He writes, 'the postself is who you are after you are dead. It is your post-mortem reputation, how you are remembered, your place in human history' (p.150). In part, the postself is formed by the activities of the deceased, but this identity is also created by those who remain. Throughout society the need to maintain people's post-mortem reputation is reflected in the importance attached to treating the dead with respect: speaking ill of the recently deceased is seen to be wrong, and attempts are made to meet their wishes. Even where the deceased has no known relatives or friends and little if anything is known about them, their funeral is carried out with consideration and reverence. Their reputation as a human being is maintained, their humanity respected.

Rituals

Rituals are examined in 'reverse order', starting with funerals, then marriages, followed by baby-namings. Finally, community ceremonies such as remembrance and memorial services are considered.

Funerals

Wojtkowiak (2012) picks up the concept of postself in *I'm Dead, Therefore I Am.* [12] She notes that 'mourners also create social representations of the deceased after death in order to keep the memory of the loved one alive' (p.14). This is done in many ways: keeping mementos, talking about the deceased, revisiting places holding happy memories, erecting a gravestone, bringing flowers (and, increasingly, other personal objects) to the grave. Rituals can be influential occasions, not only to demonstrate respect but also to celebrate the individual and to express this postself sense of immortality. Such rituals, at best, are dynamic, creative constructs that reflect, communicate, and validate feelings, perceptions, and ways of viewing the world of both the deceased and the mourners.

Humanist Ceremonies[13] offers funerals for people with non-religious beliefs and values. An essential feature of these funerals is that the celebrant visits the bereaved and helps them decide the form and content of the funeral they want. Under the guidance of the celebrant, the bereaved construct the ritual. Often these rituals will include stories about the deceased, some humour, and playing of their favourite music. It may include hymns if these are included in a non-religious context. For example, 'Jerusalem' was played in one humanist funeral because the deceased liked to attend Labour Party Conferences where it was played.[14] Almost all humanist funerals include a time where the mourners will be offered the opportunity to reflect or say a silent prayer in accordance with their own religion or philosophical belief. Of course, this must be in line with the wishes of the bereaved, but it is an important part of the funeral for most celebrants. Being able to pray may bring some solace. Such funerals are highly personalised, and at the same time have an authenticity that is firmly grounded in humanist beliefs and values.[15]

In some cases, hospitals and the armed forces take responsibility for funerals if the next of kin want this. Many hospitals offer baby funerals for late miscarriages (before 24 weeks), stillbirths (after 24 weeks), and where the baby died shortly after birth. Hospital funeral ceremonies for babies are usually conducted by a hospital chaplain (Sands, 2014).[16] These chaplains are likely to be ordained members of a Christian church, yet most mothers will be non-religious.[17] Hospitals should ensure that people with non-religious beliefs are offered a funeral conducted by humanist or non-religious celebrant on the same basis that they offer funerals to people with Christian beliefs conducted by Christian clergy. Funerals conducted by religious hospital chaplains should not be the default position for non-religious baby funerals. Non-religious pastoral carers have an important advocacy role here. A similar situation arises with hospital contract funerals for patients who have no relatives, where there is exceptional financial hardship or an inability to pay. In some cases, the religion or belief of the deceased will be unknown, but where the deceased is known to be non-religious, or relatives want a non-religious funeral, it would be reasonable to expect the hospital or the funeral director to arrange for a humanist or civil celebrant to conduct the funeral. When military personnel die on duty, the Ministry of Defence will arrange a funeral at public expense, or provide funding towards the cost of a private funeral. With a private funeral, the bereaved can arrange a non-religious funeral in the normal way, if they so wish. If the Ministry of Defence arranges a funeral, and the bereaved want a humanist or other non-religious celebrant to conduct the funeral, then their wish should be granted.[18]

Many non-religious pastoral carers will be accredited celebrants. Accreditation is normally given for each type of ceremony. For example, someone may be accredited to conduct funerals but not weddings. It is expected that non-religious pastoral carers working in the military will be accredited to conduct funerals, weddings, and baby-namings. This is also the case with those completing the MA postgraduate course.[19] Where a non-religious pastoral carer is not accredited they can call upon the networks of accredited celebrants.

Marriages

As of 2017, humanist celebrants can conduct legally binding marriage ceremonies in Scotland, and the Republic of Ireland.[20] It is expected that approval will follow for England and Wales. Humanist marriages have proven to be very popular.[21]

Marriages in institutions are subject to strict rules. In prisons they are covered by PSI 14/2016 (NOMS, 2016). On rare occasions where the marriage ceremony is to take place outside the prison, it will be subject to strict security assessments and limited to a register office or place of worship of the appropriate denomination nearest to the prison (9.5). Hence, it would not be possible for a humanist celebrant to conduct the wedding. The Marriage Act 1983 enables prisoners to marry in the place of their detention.[22] There is provision within PSI 14/2016 for non-Christians to marry in prison with a Registrar present (8.5). However, there is no provision for a humanist marriage followed by a civil registration. The Governor may have discretion to allow such marriages, but the regulations do not make this clear. The armed forces make excellent provision for Christian marriages. They have chaplains who are authorised to conduct weddings, and 190 state-funded military chapels in England and Wales.[23] However, there is no similar provision for people with non-Christian or non-religious beliefs.

In hospitals, marriages can take place when the patient who is requesting marriage is seriously ill, not expected to recover, and unable to be moved to a place that is licensed for the conduct of the marriage ceremony. They must be of sound mind and able to properly understand the vows and promises they will make.[24] The marriage must take place at the patient's bedside. In their publicity, many hospitals say that the Registrar is able to conduct a civil ceremony which can be followed by a religious blessing. But they often fail to make clear that it could be followed by a humanist wedding. Again, there is an advocacy role for non-religious pastoral carers to help ensure that the rules, documents, and publicity make quite clear that options for a humanist marriage or wedding are available as appropriate.

Baby-namings

Words cannot begin to describe the utter sense of desolation on the loss of an expected baby. If the baby has died around the time of birth, there may be few memories or mementos. At such times, a baby-naming can play a very important role in giving the baby their own identity – their own name. The ceremony may remain as a precious memory for the parents, and mementos such as a candle and a certificate given in the ceremony may become treasured keepsakes. Sometimes such ceremonies may be conducted at very short notice. Hospitals normally have very good arrangements for emergency baptisms or Christian blessings as appropriate.[25] These baptisms and blessings are often performed by ordained clergy from the hospital's pastoral/spiritual/religious care department. Having clergy who are trained and experienced to conduct such sensitive ceremonies can be of enormous benefit to both parents and the hospital. However, most of these parents will be non-religious. Given the choice, many may prefer a non-religious baby-naming that is in keeping with their own beliefs and values. They may also prefer the ceremony to be conducted by a celebrant or trained non-religious pastoral carer rather than a religious chaplain.[26] Hospitals rarely have very good arrangements in place for offering the choice of a baby-naming conducted by a celebrant or trained non-religious pastoral carer. Non-religious pastoral carers have an important role to work proactively with hospital trusts, children's hospices, ceremonies organisations, and other relevant groups to develop good quality non-religious baby-naming ceremonies, together with the training and arrangements to deliver those ceremonies.[27]

Memorials

The rituals discussed above are mainly for individuals. Commemorations, remembrance and memorial services, and events can play an important role for groups of people and for communities who share common experiences. These may be people whose children have died in hospital, people who have survived cancer, people remembering those who have donated their bodies to science or have died in an armed conflict. The reasons for arranging such events may vary quite markedly but they may have some common characteristics. They offer the opportunity for those with shared experiences or who want to be associated with them to come together, to reflect, to share their feelings, to know that they are not alone, and to remember.

As part of a team, non-religious pastoral carers can play a key role in helping to construct, organise and, where appropriate, take part in such commemoration events. There are many different aspects to consider. These can be illustrated by comparing two commemorative events, in some ways very similar, in others very different.

At 2:20 pm on 29th March 2017, thousands of people, including children, police, members of the public, and faith leaders, walked across a bridge in London (BBC, 2017). They were paying tribute to the victims of the West-minster Bridge attack. There was a period of silence, hundreds of flowers were laid on the bridge, some lit candles. They were remembering those who had died and been injured. But they were also saying things, many things. The most senior person present, an acting commissioner of the Metropolitan Police, talked of remembering the victims. Those unnamed people leading the procession carried a message of love for all and of hatred for none. An imam expressed the view that whatever your religion, colour, or race, London would never be divided.

On the afternoon of 16th June 2017, the bells of Southwark Cathedral rang out as the Dean welcomed an invited congregation, including the Countess of Wessex, the Home Secretary, and the Commissioner of the Metropolitan Police, as well as representatives of religious communities (Giordano, 2017). They were there to remember those caught up in the London Bridge attack. Candles were lit. The Mayor of London, a Muslim, gave a reading. The Archbishop of Canterbury gave a sermon ending with the moving words, 'Hope flowers in the desert of suffering when it is watered by communities of love, for through them Christ comes, light dawns, and lives shattered in grief and pain find astonishingly that they will live again' (Archbishop of Canterbury, 2017).

The causes of these two commemorations were very similar: terrorist attacks on London's bridges. Both events wanted to remember. The West-minster Bridge event was spontaneous, in effect there was an open invitation to all in the community to take part. The Southwark Cathedral event was more official and organised. Some individuals, officials, and representatives of some religious beliefs were formally invited to attend, other representatives were not.[28] In the Westminster Bridge event people were there as of right, being members of our community. In the Southwark Cathedral event people were there only at the invitation of the Church of England. Where memorial and similar events are held in institutions, it would be good practice for the invitations to attend to be seen by all as fully inclusive of their relevant com-munity. Non-religious pastoral carers can help to ensure that such invitations are fully inclusive, and that the language of the invitation properly reflects this. For example, if the invitation says it is a multi-faith service, or it is 'for all faiths and none', this may not be seen as inclusive to some non-religious people. If the invitation is from a 'chaplain' or a 'chaplaincy' department, this may suggest that it will be a religious service. Hence, some non-religious people who may have benefitted from attending may have been, inadvertently, discouraged.

The Westminster event was held in a neutral public space, a bridge. The Southwark event was held in an inequitable space, an Anglican Cathedral, full of Christian symbolism. Non-religious pastoral carers can help the team ensure that wherever possible commemoration services are held in neutral spaces so that those attending do so on an equal basis. The brigade or university may have a historic Christian chapel, but this does not mean it is a good place for inclusive commemoration events. Halls, canteens, and meeting rooms can all be sensitively laid out for such services. Whilst these events are opportunities for people to remember and reflect, the events themselves make statements to the community. What voices are heard, and the context in which they are heard, can make strong statements. In the Westminster Bridge event, the voice was mainly that of many 'ordinary' members of the public. It was a statement of spontaneity, of a massive community response, and of unity in adversity. In the Southwark event, the voice was mainly that of public officials and the Church of England. It was also making a statement about the Church of England's own centrality as the state's organiser of commemorative rituals. Institutions should consider whose voices should be heard, and what the ritual is saying about their institution. If, as in some institutions, only Christian clergy lead or conduct their institution's rituals, what does this say about that institution's attitudes on equality and diversity?

Finally, the content of commemorations needs to be considered. Despite marked differences between the two events described, there were many commonalities in terms of content. Both included the lighting of candles, some silence, and the opportunity to pray. On Westminster Bridge, everyone could express their tribute according to their own religion or belief, but it was personal and, although as part of a large group of people, essentially private. At Southwark Cathedral, despite inviting representatives of certain religions, the content of the commemoration was principally and overtly Christian. Commemorations in an institution should be for all the members of its community. This raises many questions for the non-religious pastoral carer and for the team constructing the commemoration. What do this community's members want from the commemoration? What aspects are most important for them? How can you find out? What does the institution want? Are they the same? How can those attending be given the opportunity to express themselves according to their own religion or belief? What readings, prayers, and blessings should be included? Non-religious pastoral carers can give practical help and advice, for example by suggesting suitable poems or readings.[29]

Prayers can be important to many people attending such events, but not to all people. For some, prayers would not be relevant and they would not want to be prayed for. Prayers need to be introduced in a way that does not presume that non-religious people (and, where pertinent, people with non-Christian religious beliefs) consent to be the objects of those prayers. For example, rather than saying, 'We will now join together to say The Lord's Prayer', it would be better to say, 'For those amongst us who are Christian, we will now join together to say The Lord's Prayer'. As well as reducing the risk of upsetting people, acting in a way that does not presume people have consented to be the object of prayers would be a responsible ethical approach.

Notes

1 54.8% of people die in hospital, 4.5% in a hospice, 17.8% in a care home, and 20.8% at home.
2 Research (such as much US research) that included only religious people found a more linear relationship, showing that people who were more religious were less anxious.
3 ComRes interviewed 2,016 British adults online between 29 and 30 April 2015 (ComRes, 2015: Table 11). Data were weighted to be representative of all adults in Great Britain aged 18+. ComRes is a member of the British Polling Council and abides by its rules.
4 15% did not believe a good death was possible and 5% preferred not to say.
5 The poll found that being closer to death, in the sense of being older, did not have much effect on the priority of having one's religious/spiritual needs met. The figures ranking this by age group are: 18–24: 60%, 25–34: 56%, 35–44: 63%, 45–54: 60%, 56–64: 62%, 65+: 58%. In some ways, this is surprising as older people tend to be more religious.
6 The research was based on 2,038 adult respondents, who were asked to select four priorities from a list of 11 options and then to rank them from first to fourth. One option was 'Having your religious, cultural and spiritual needs met (e.g. having a priest with you)'. This was ranked tenth overall. The option 'Having other people around you going through the same thing, to talk to and provide support' was ranked eleventh.
7 2% ranked this second and 3% third.
8 Swift (2014) makes a similar point, saying 'With the absence of an implicit belief in eternity, it is no wonder that many people struggle to know what to say to those who grieve.' There seems to be a lack of independent compelling evidence to support the assertion that it is a lack of belief in eternity that causes people not to know what to say to people who grieve, or that a belief in eternity will necessarily help people to know what to say. Humanist Funeral Celebrants (https://funeralce lebrants.org.uk/about-celebrants) meet many grieving people, both religious and non-religious, and the feedback from these people is that humanists, who do not believe in eternity, do 'know what to say' (and how to listen). Humanist pastoral carers operating in a generic way in hospices, caring for both religious and non-religious people, are seen as providing effective care to those who grieve. One may also question how having a belief in eternity helps in knowing what to say to a grieving person who does not believe in eternity. Swift may be right in saying that many people struggle to know what to say to those who grieve. Dying Matters (http://www.dyingmatters.org/) makes available very helpful publications on how to talk to dying and grieving people. Perhaps pastoral, spiritual, and religious care departments could promote the provision of such literature.
9 Of course, a lack of evidence is not evidence of absence. It cannot be shown that immortality does not occur but, for humanists and many others, there is no reason to believe it does.
10 'Not being' is totally different from being unconscious or in a coma. The latter are being something that experiences nothing.
11 Interestingly Yalom, despite being an atheist, was awarded the American Psychiatric Association 2000 Oskar Pfister Award for his important contributions to religion and psychiatry. Yalom's (2000) acceptance speech gives some useful insights into care and existential existence.
12 This research work is based on Dutch society, so some aspects cannot be directly related to the UK. For example, the degree of personalisation of funeral ceremonies between Catholics and Protestants seems to be different in the UK and the

Netherlands. However, the findings in relation to a more secularised society seem to relate to both the UK and the Netherlands.

13 See https://humanism.org.uk/ceremonies for further details. Other organisations offer civil and non-religious funerals, for example Institute of Civil Funerals (2015).

14 It was 'Jerusalem' as a reminder of these conferences rather than the reference to 'the holy Lamb of God' that was relevant.

15 There is some evidence that religious funerals are becoming more personalised. Holloway et al. (2013) examine both humanist and religious funerals.

16 Sands (2014), the stillbirth and neonatal death charity, produces an excellent guide, *Deciding about a Funeral for your Baby*.

17 The ONS (2016) gives the average age of mothers as 30.3 years (on average those experiencing miscarriages and baby deaths will be slightly older). The British Social Attitudes survey (NatCen, 2017) shows 61% of people aged 25–34 as non-religious (56% of 34–44-year olds).

18 Cruse Bereavement Care (2017) provides support to military families and has produced a useful guide on military funerals.

19 Humanist celebrants must complete a peer-reviewed probationary period of actual practice before accreditation is confirmed. This will normally occur after the course has been completed.

20 Humanist marriages are also legal in Australia, Canada, Jersey, New Zealand, Norway, and the USA.

21 Humanist marriages were legally recognised in Scotland in 2005, with 82 couples celebrating a humanist wedding. By 2010 they exceeded the number of Catholic weddings, and in 2015 they exceeded those of the Church of Scotland.

22 Civil partnerships and same-sex marriages are also allowed.

23 However, these chapels are dedicated and set aside as places for Christian worship only. They cannot be used as venues for marriages conducted according to the practice of other faiths (Royal Navy, 2017, 61-5, 16).

24 A doctor must sign a letter confirming that these conditions have been met.

25 For religious people, baptism and blessings may include the naming of the baby but they also have profound theological significance beyond the actual naming. Baptism is a Catholic sacrament.

26 No research has been conducted on the attitudes of expectant parents and baby-namings. However, the YouGov survey (Humanists UK, 2017) discussed earlier does show that a significant majority of non-religious people were unlikely to seek the support of a chaplain, preferring support from a non-religious pastoral carer.

27 A wide range of organisations work in this area. Sands (2016) produces an excellent booklet, *Saying Goodbye to your Baby*, which includes information about baby-namings. The Foundation for Infant Loss Training (http://www.foundation forinfantloss.co.uk) provides education in infant loss and bereavement. There is an All-Party Parliamentary Group on Baby Loss (UK Parliament, 2016).

28 At the time of the bombings, the Diocese of Southwark (n.d.) had guidelines for such events. Guideline 36 stated, 'Invitations to attend as guests, or to participate in, civic services in Church of England churches should not be extended to representatives of New Religious Movements, of pagan groups, of the Church of Scientology, or of secularist and humanist organisations. Members of such groups, like people of any religious faith or none, are to be welcomed as individuals at services or events in churches.' Following representations from Humanists UK, the Diocese expressed regret that the Guideline was still available and removed it. The new Church of England (n.d.) national guidance on civic services does not refer to humanist representatives or indicate that they would be welcome at Church of England civic service events.

29 *Seasons of Life* (Collins, Herrick and Pearce, 2000) and *Humanist Anthology* (Knight and Herrick, 2000) have poems, prose, and sayings that may be suitable for such commemorations.

References

Archbishop of Canterbury (2017) Archbishop's Sermon at the Service of Hope at Southwark Cathedral. Available from: https://cathedral.southwark.anglican.org/worship-and-music/worship/sermons-from-special-services/a-service-of-hope-follo wing-the-terror-attack-at-london-bridge/ [accessed 13th September 2017].

BBC (2017) Bridge tribute to Westminster attack victims, 29 March. Available from: http://www.bbc.co.uk/news/uk-39435074 [accessed 12th September 2017].

Church of England (n.d.) *Presence & Engagement Guidelines: Civic Services or Events.* Available from: http://www.presenceandengagement.org.uk/sites/default/files/Civic%20services.pdf [accessed 4th July 2018].

Collins, N., Herrick, J., Pearce, J. (2000) *Seasons of Life: Prose and Poetry for Secular Ceremonies and Private Reflection.* London, Rationalist Press Association.

ComRes (2015) *National Council for Palliative Care – Public Opinion on Death and Dying.* Available from: http://www.dyingmatters.org/sites/default/files/files/National%20Council%20for%20Palliative%20Care_Public%20opinion%20on%20death%20and%20dying_5th%20May.pdf [accessed 16th August 2017].

Cruse Bereavement Care (2017) Military Funerals. Available from: https://www.cruse.org.uk/Military/military-funerals [accessed 7th September 2017].

Diocese of Southwark (n.d.) Guidelines on Civic Services/Events Involving People of Different Faiths. Available from: http://southwark.anglican.org/downloads/what/Civic-services-guidelines.pdf.doc [accessed 13th September 2017; no longer available online].

Dying Matters (n.d.) Famous Quotes about Death. Available from: http://www.dyingmatters.org/page/famous-quotes-about-death-0 [accessed 29th August 2017].

Epicurus (341–270 BCE) Letter to Menoeceus. Available from: http://www.epicurus.net/en/menoeceus.html [accessed 27th August 2017].

Giordano, C. (2017) You are not alone. *Southwark News*, 16 June. Available from: https://www.southwarknews.co.uk/news/not-alone-southwark-cathedral-hosts-service-survivors-victims-london-bridge-attack [accessed 4th July 2018].

Holloway, M., Adamson, S., Argyrou, V., Draper, P., Mariau, D. (2013) "Funerals aren't nice but it couldn't have been nicer." The makings of a good funeral. *Mortality* 18(1), 30–53. Available from: https://hydra.hull.ac.uk/assets/hull:9785/content [accessed 7th September 2017].

Humanists UK (2017) Humanists UK Polling on Pastoral Care in the UK. Available from: https://humanism.org.uk/wp-content/uploads/Humanists-UK-polling-on-pastoral-care-in-the-UK.pdf [accessed 21st January 2018].

Institute of Civil Funerals (2015) Welcome to the Institute of Civil Funerals. Available from: http://www.iocf.org.uk/ [accessed 7th September 2017].

Jong, J., Halberstadt, J. (2016) *Death Anxiety and Religious Belief: An Existential Psychology of Religion.* Oxford, Bloomsbury Academic.

Jong, J., Ross, R., Philip, T., Chang, S., Simons, N., Halberstadt, J. (2017) The Religious Correlates of Death Anxiety: A Systematic Review and Meta-analysis. *Religion, Brain & Behaviour* 8(1), 4–20.

Knight, M., Herrick, J. (eds) (2000) *Humanist Anthology: From Confucius to David Attenborough*. Third edition. London, Rationalist Press Association.

Marie Curie (n.d.) How changing demographics are affecting end of life care in the UK. Available from: https://docplayer.net/22958215-How-changing-demographics-are-affecting-end-of-life-care-in-the-uk-the-number-of-people-dying-is-increasing.html [accessed 16th August 2017].

Mill, J.S. (1874) [2009] Three Essays on Religion. Nature: Utility of Religion: Theism. In *Theism*. Matz, L.J. (ed.). Peterborough, Canada, Broadview Press.

NatCen (2017) Religion in Britain in 2016. Available from: http://natcen.ac.uk/blog/religion-in-britain-in-2016 [accessed 7th September 2017].

NOMS (2016) *Marriage of Prisoners and Civil Partnership Registration*. London, National Offender Management Service. Available from: https://www.justice.gov.uk/downloads/offenders/psipso/psi-2016/psi-14-2016-marriage-of-prisoners-civil-partnership-registration.pdf [accessed 7th September 2017].

ONS (2016) *Births by Parents' Characteristics in England and Wales: 2015*. London, Office for National Statistics. Available from: https://www.ons.gov.uk/peoplepopulationandcommunity/birthsdeathsandmarriages/livebirths/bulletins/birthsbyparentscharacteristicsinenglandandwales/2015 [accessed 7th September 2017].

Royal Navy (2017) Registration of Births, Deaths and Marriages. In: *BRd2 – The Queens Regulations for the Royal Navy*. Available from: http://www.royalnavy.mod.uk/-/media/royal-navy-responsive/documents/reference-library/brd2/ch61.pdf [accessed 7th September 2017].

Sands (2014) *Deciding about a Funeral for your Baby*. London, Sands. Available from: http://www.uk-sands.org/sites/default/files/DECIDING%20ABOUT%20A%20FUNERAL%20SINGLE%20PAGE%20LINKED.pdf [accessed 7th September 2017].

Sands (2016) *Saying Goodbye to your Baby*. London, Sands. Available from: https://www.uk-sands.org/sites/default/files/Saying%20Goodbye%20To%20Your%20Baby%20-%2006.07.16.pdf [accessed 9th September 2017].

Shneidman, E.S. (2008) *A Commonsense Book of Death. Reflections at Ninety of a Lifelong Thanatologist*. Lanham, MD, Rowman & Littlefield.

Swift, C. (2014) *Hospital Chaplaincy in the Twenty-first Century. Explorations in Practical, Pastoral and Empirical Theology*. 2nd Edition. Farnham, Ashgate.

UK Parliament (2016) All-Party Parliamentary Group on Baby Loss. *Register of All-Party Parliamentary Groups*. Available from: https://publications.parliament.uk/pa/cm/cmallparty/160316/baby-loss.htm [accessed 9th September 2017].

Wojtkowiak, J. (2012) *"I'm Dead, Therefore I Am". The Postself and Notions of Immortality in Contemporary Dutch Society*. Nijmegen, Radboud University Press.

Wood, C., Salter, J. (2013) *A Time and a Place. What People Want at the End of Life*. Report by Demos. London, Sue Ryder. Available from: http://www.sueryder.org/~/media/files/about-us/a-time-and-a-place-sue-ryder.pdf [accessed 17th August 2017].

Yalom, I.D. (2000) Religion and Psychiatry. Speech delivered at the American Psychiatric Association annual meeting, May 2000, New Orleans. Available from: http://www.yalom.com/lecpfistercontent.html [accessed 29th August 2017].

Yalom, I.D. (2007) *Staring at the Sun: Overcoming the Terror of Death*. First Edition. San Francisco, CA, Jossey-Bass.

Chapter 8

Ethical behaviour

Some aspects of ethical behaviour should apply to everyone working in institutions where there may be vulnerable people, where sensitive subjects are talked about, emotional issues are faced, and beliefs and values are thought about. These general aspects are considered first. Ethical behaviour that may relate more specifically to non-religious pastoral carers is then discussed.

General considerations

Ethical behaviour should promote and safeguard the interests of the individual. This means acting with integrity, sensitivity, and understanding. It also means avoiding exploitation, manipulation, intimidation, and causing distress, pain, or harm. A person's right to hold values and beliefs should be respected. Humanists UK has always supported the concept of freedom of religion or belief, and respecting a person's right to hold such beliefs follows easily from this. True respect means taking other people's beliefs seriously, recognising that they are sincerely held and that they are meaningful to that person. There is a distinction between respecting the right of someone to hold certain beliefs and respecting those beliefs. A non-religious person may view the theological belief in the concept of original sin as immoral, and not respect that belief. But they should respect a person's right to hold that belief. Similarly, a religious person may view the belief that God does not exist as tantamount to blasphemy, and not respect that belief. But they should respect a person's right to hold that belief. Atheists Aikin and Talisse (2011) make a compelling case for mutual respect in their book *Reasonable Atheism: A Moral Case for Respectful Disbelief*, saying 'We do not "respect" religious beliefs. We do, however, respect religious believers' (p.41). It is also worth remembering that good active listening is non-judgemental.

It would be unethical to proselytise for humanism or to impose one's own non-religious beliefs and values on others. There may be occasions when someone will ask a non-religious pastoral carer about their beliefs. It should be for the service user to raise the question; the non-religious carer should not prompt it. There is a big difference between explaining what those beliefs are and suggesting that they are the right beliefs or that the service user would benefit from adopting them. With humanism, and most non-religious approaches to life, there is no higher authority commanding people to 'spread the word'. The role of the non-religious pastoral carer is one of care, not one of ministry, so conflicts between the ethical approach of the secular institution and that of the non-religious pastoral carer should be minimal.

Respecting the autonomy of the service user is central. It should be for the service user to determine whether or not they want to see a non-religious pastoral carer, and to decide what information to disclose to that carer. Of course, the same ethical principles should apply to 'chaplains'.[1]

It is worth considering how these ethical principles operate in practice. The service user's right to decide to see, or refuse to see, a non-religious pastoral carer is considered first. Would it be ethical for a non-religious pastoral carer to make an uninvited approach to a service user to say who they are and what they do or offer? Is this an unwarranted intrusion on the service user's autonomy, or a reasonable means of informing them of the availability of a care service? Current thinking in some institutions is that an uninvited approach is inappropriate and all contact should be made via a referral. Other institutions consider that an uninvited approach is a reasonable means of informing service users. In the absence of other effective communications about the availability and content of non-religious pastoral care services, this thinking appears to have some merit. However, this is a contested ethical area. Would it be unethical for non-religious pastoral carers (and 'chaplains') to access service users' records, including sensitive information about their religion or belief, without first obtaining their explicit consent? Again, the practical implications of meeting these ethical principles need thinking through. A Muslim prisoner may be very upset to find that a non-religious pastoral carer has read their personal details on the Prison National Offender Management Information System (NOMIS) without first obtaining their explicit consent.[2] Equally a non-religious patient may be very upset to find that a chaplain has read their medical records without their explicit consent. However, restricting such access may raise other ethical issues. If a non-religious pastoral carer in a prison doesn't know which prisoners are non-religious, how can they approach them to offer appropriate pastoral care? If a Rabbi doesn't know which hospital patients are Jewish, how can he offer them appropriate religious care? Maintaining the ethical principle of service user autonomy may prevent some people being offered care they want. In so far as the law reflects the ethical views of society, the current UK law gives individuals autonomy over their personal information, especially sensitive personal information such as a person's religion or belief, except in specific situations. For example, it is both illegal and unethical for a healthcare non-religious pastoral carer or a 'chaplain' to access a patient's record without first obtaining their explicit consent.[3] Part of the problem is that service users with non-Christian religious beliefs or who are non-religious may not be aware of what like-minded care is available, and how to request it. This problem is compounded if the department is called a chaplaincy department. Non-religious pastoral carers have an advocacy role to help improve communications so that there is much greater awareness of this availability (see chapter 11).

The content of any discussions with service users should also remain confidential, but this confidentiality is limited. It may be necessary to disclose the content of a discussion where there is a legal requirement to do so, or for safeguarding reasons, for example if a person has indicated that they will harm themself or another person. An institution should make clear its policy on confidentiality and safeguarding as part of induction training. If this does not happen, it would be sensible to ask for such training.

Preventing discrimination and championing equal treatment for all are essentials of ethical behaviour. This book focuses on non-religious pastoral care, and many non-religious pastoral carers will want to be advocates of greater equality in the care provision for non-religious people. But ethical behaviour goes beyond this. For example, people with some non-Christian religious beliefs have pastoral, spiritual, and religious care provision which is disproportionately low. Championing equality for people with non-Christian religious beliefs and, indeed, for other protected characteristics should be part of the non-religious pastoral carer's behaviour.

In some areas, carers should seek advice from their department manager or lead about appropriate ethical behaviour. One example is the use of touch. Holding someone's hand or touching their shoulder can be very comforting, but great care must be taken in the use of touch. It may be wrong to use touch if the service user has not consented, or if they are in a separate area from other people. In prisons the use of touch is restricted for security reasons. Some 'chaplaincy' bodies have produced very helpful codes of conduct relevant to a particular area of care (UK Board of Healthcare Chaplaincy, 2014). The Non-Religious Pastoral Support Network (2017) has a similar code, which draws on the UK Board's code. This indicates that there are many common ethical standards that underpin the behaviour of all those delivering pastoral, spiritual, and religious care in institutions.

Good ethical behaviour helps to safeguard those receiving care, and to protect the reputation of both the institution where the care is being provided and the institutions that provide accreditation and references for care providers. Consideration should be given to the carer's own safety and the maintenance of a satisfactory work–life balance. The role can be a demanding one, and attention should be paid to times when one's own physical or emotional state may impact on the effectiveness of the care offered. It is important for each individual to work within the boundaries of their capabilities and to distinguish clearly between the pastoral care role and other forms of support such as professional counselling and therapy. Be willing to seek support, for example from the lead manager, members of the team, or the Non-Religious Pastoral Support Network.

Specific ethical issues

It is worth repeating that the role of the non-religious pastoral carer is to provide care to all, irrespective of their religion or belief. Much of that care will not relate to specifically religious care needs, but there will be occasions when a person's religious care needs must be met. Indeed, part of the non-religious pastoral care role is to try to create an environment where a person can identify and articulate their religious care needs. In most cases where a religious care need is identified, the most appropriate action would be for the non-religious pastoral carer to explain that they are non-religious, to offer to refer the care to a 'chaplain' of the most appropriate religion/denomination, and to give details of the religious care available. Sometimes a person's religious care needs may be limited, for example, to bring some rosary beads or give details of services in the chapel. In these circumstances, meeting such needs is relatively straightforward. However, there are occasions when it will not be possible to refer the care to a 'chaplain'. Where referral is not possible, and someone asks a non-religious pastoral carer to pray for them, saying they need the comfort and strength that being prayed for will give them, is it ethically correct to pray for them? Praying for them will give them the religious care they need. Would it be wrong to refuse to pray for them and deny them the care they have asked for? As with many ethical issues, there are often other ethical concerns to be considered. In this case, one of the beliefs of the non-religious pastoral carer is likely to be that God does not exist, so undertaking to pray to a non-existent God would be to act in a way that is contrary to sincerely and deeply help beliefs. To pray may also be seen as dishonest and misleading to the person asking for the prayer. That non-religious pastoral carer would not be acting with integrity. Hence, on ethical grounds they may feel they must refuse to pray for that person. However, there are ways in which they can still provide care. Obviously, it is important for the non-religious pastoral carer to explain in simple and gentle terms why they cannot pray. But they could offer to bring that person some appropriate prayers and to read them out on the service user's behalf, if required.[4]

A similar situation applies to baptism. In principle, the Church allows anyone to baptise a child in emergency circumstances. However, the wording of the baptism raises ethical and integrity issues for non-religious pastoral carers (Church of England, 2017). Non-religious pastoral carers may feel that they must refuse to baptise children. Instead, a non-religious pastoral carer may offer to try to find someone who could baptise the child, or offer a non-religious baby-naming. The essence of these examples is to show that, whilst it would be far better for people to receive religious care from an appropriate religious 'chaplain', a non-religious pastoral carer can still show empathy and provide some care. However, in delivering this care the non-religious pastoral carer must act with their personal integrity in relation to their beliefs. It is also worth recognising that people with religious beliefs face similar ethical issues, some in relation to dealing with people with non-religious beliefs. Gaining a better mutual understanding of such ethical issues would be beneficial.

In the generic model of pastoral, spiritual, and religious care, non-religious pastoral carers will want to introduce themselves to service users to make them aware of the care available. In general, a service user will not know in advance that the person providing care is non-religious. Through active listening, the pastoral carer will want to let the service user talk about what is on their mind. It is for the service user to decide the 'agenda' for the discussion, not the carer. It would be unfortunate if the carer were to suggest or impose an agenda on the service user. If the non-religious pastoral carer were to say, 'Good morning, my name is Sara, I'm a humanist', experience indicates that the conversation is likely to focus on what a humanist is. The conversation would be about the pastoral carer, rather than being centred on the service user and their needs. The service user's agenda is unlikely to relate to humanism. This situation is clearly unsatisfactory and needs to be avoided. If the non-religious pastoral carer were to say, 'Good morning, my name is Sara, I'm from the Pastoral Care Department and I'm just visiting all the people on the ward to …', the discussion is unlikely to focus on the non-religious pastoral carer, and instead the focus would be where it should be, on the service user's needs. However, the service user may make assumptions about the religion or belief of the carer that are inaccurate, and the non-religious pastoral carer may seem to be remiss for not stating their non-religious beliefs up front.[5] Again, this is not a satisfactory situation. One approach that may be a reasonable way forward is to introduce oneself in a neutral way without reference to one's humanist or other non-religious beliefs, but to make these beliefs clear if the discussion begins to relate to religion in any way at all. For example, if the service user says, 'at least there is someone up there looking on me', it would be necessary to tell the service user of one's own non-religious position in order to ensure that there was no misunderstanding. What is important is for non-religious pastoral carers to pay real attention to what would be the best ethical approach in these and similar circumstances. Of course, 'chaplains' need to pay similar attention. For example, if a 'chaplain' were to dress in a clerical collar, carry a Bible, and say, 'Good morning, my name is Luke, I am a chaplain …', it may well be that the service user would conclude the Luke was coming with a religious agenda. This would have the advantage that Luke was making quite clear what his religion was, but it would have disadvantage. Some service users may think that the institution was only offering a religious care service. Hence, some potential service users may be unaware of, or feel unable to access, other aspects of care, including non-religious pastoral care.

A related ethical dilemma results from the requirement of some institutions and lead 'chaplains' that non-religious pastoral carers adopt the religious job title 'chaplain' in order to be able to be part of the team, and to provide non-religious pastoral care. Does the non-religious pastoral carer refuse to accept a religious job title and forgo the opportunity to provide care for people, or accept a misleading job title on the basis that this will allow them to provide needed care? Since non-religious pastoral carers are motivated primarily by their wish to provide care, almost all will accept the second alternative. Of course, the institutions and lead chaplains should not put them in this situation. Indeed, many of these ethical dilemmas are made worse by the unsatisfactory way in which the service provision is described, and by the poor understanding many potential service users may have of the services provided.

Humanists UK campaigns on a number of public ethical issues, and sets out its position on its website (Humanists UK, 2017). One of the most relevant ethical issues in a pastoral care context is that of assisted dying. The essence of the humanist position is that individuals have the right to live their life according to their own personal values, so they should be free to take decisions about their own life, including decisions to end that life. Hence, it is right to legalise assisted dying where an individual has come to a clear decision, which was free from coercion, and where they are physically unable to end their life themselves. Non-religious pastoral carers cannot encourage or assist people to commit suicide. The British Medical Association (2015) has produced some useful guidance about what this means in practice. Although written for doctors, it is also relevant to non-religious pastoral carers. Of course, it would be entirely appropriate to provide pastoral care to people thinking about assisted dying, but it must be given within the guidance set out.

On abortion, Humanists UK recognises that it is best if every child is a wanted child. Improved education on sex and relationships can help to reduce the number of unwanted pregnancies. The humanist position on abortion is 'pro-choice'.[6] On stem cell research, fertility treatment, and related activities, the ethical position is grounded in the view that the primary consideration on such matters should be the benefit to human beings. Hence, properly controlled and regulated actions should be allowed. As previously discussed, the dead are to be respected, but this should not prevent the deceased's organs being used to help others, except when the deceased has expressed a contrary wish. Indeed, organ donation can be a part of a symbolic life after death. To claim that any treatment or procedure is a 'cure' or 'effective' where there is no good evidence to support that claim is unethical. For such reasons, Humanists UK has consistently opposed homeopathy 'treatments', which overwhelming evidence shows are no better than a placebo.

The above is a brief introduction to the ethical position of Humanists UK on some aspects that may be relevant to non-religious pastoral carers. It should be stressed that these are the ethical positions of an organisation. Religious bodies such as the Church of England and the Catholic Church also have ethical positions as organisations. Individuals who identify with those organisations may, or may not, agree with the ethical position of 'their' organisation. Non-religious pastoral care is person centred, so no assumptions should be made about the ethical positions of individuals based on their declared religion or belief.

Some non-religious pastoral carers may wish to become a member of an ethics committee. Such committees must be independent and impartial; amongst other things, this means that members must be free from the pressures of any institutional affiliation. That includes institutions such as Humanists UK, churches, and religious bodies. Given that the beliefs and values held by many non-religious people are founded on a strong ethical base, playing an active role on ethics committees may be very beneficial.

Before leaving this section on ethics, it is worth reflecting that institutions should also behave in an ethical way. This includes behaving ethically towards people with non-religious beliefs. There are many quite diverse ethical issues to consider. How can institutions best meet their ethical standards in preventing discrimination and championing the equal treatment of both people with religious beliefs and those with non-religious beliefs? Is it ethical for institutions to offer only religious ceremonies? Is it ethical for a 'chaplain' to offer to conduct a non-religious ceremony without first making it quite clear that they are religious? Is it ethical for institutions to require non-religious pastoral carers to call themselves 'chaplains' and adopt a misleading religious title? When a chaplain sees themself as having a dual responsibility, both to their institution and to their church or bishop, and the ethical positions of the two are different, what would be the appropriate ethical behaviour? These are just a few of the questions that institutions may have to reflect on when they consider what sort of pastoral, spiritual, and religious care service they want to provide, and how they should manage that service.

Notes

1 Some aspects of these ethical principles of service user autonomy do not apply to prisoners. For example, in the Prison Act (UK Government, 1952) prisoners are required to see a chaplain on reception and in certain other situations. Prisoners cannot decide not to see a chaplain in these circumstances.
2 The National Offender Management Service (2016) instructions state that 'All Chaplains should have the opportunity to access prisoner details on Prison-NOMIS' (p.7). This includes what the Data Protection Act describes as sensitive personal data, such as information on the prisoner's religious beliefs or other beliefs of a similar nature. The instructions do not state that the explicit consent of the prisoner is required in order to access this information. Again, in this respect, prisoners cannot decide what information they want to disclose to the chaplain. The legal basis of this instruction is unclear, it is not a mandatory requirement.
3 Some chaplains and chaplaincy organisations have argued that patients give inferred or implied consent. This is where the circumstances are such that it would be fair and reasonable to believe that explicit consent has been given, even though no evidence of such explicit consent in the form of spoken or written words exists. With healthcare 'chaplains', such consent cannot be inferred because they are not registered and regulated healthcare professionals. It would be difficult to argue that all or most people with non-religious beliefs give inferred consent for religious

'chaplains' to access their records, when survey results show that most non-religious people would be unlikely to seek the support of a chaplain. Hence, it is contrary to law for healthcare 'chaplains' to access patient records without explicit consent. Further information can be obtained from the Information Governance Alliance (NHS Digital, 2018).

4 Most pastoral, spiritual, and religious care departments will have cards or similar materials with a range of prayers for different circumstances. Non-religious pastoral carers should ensure that they know what and where they are.

5 Anecdotal evidence suggests that this occurs very rarely but there is no well validated evidence.

6 Most people, including 61% of Catholics, support abortion (Harding, 2017).

References

Aikin, S.F., Talisse, R.B. (2011) *Reasonable Atheism: A Moral Case for Respectful Disbelief.* New York, Prometheus Books.

British Medical Association (2015) *Responding to Patient Requests Relating to Assisted Suicide: Guidance for Doctors in England, Wales and Northern Ireland.* London, British Medical Association. Available from: https://www.bma.org.uk/advice/emp loyment/ethics/ethics-a-to-z [accessed 19 June 2018].

Church of England (2017) Holy Baptism. Available from: https://www.churchofengla nd.org/prayer-and-worship/worship-texts-and-resources/common-worship/christian-initiation/baptism-and-confirmation [accessed 21st September 2017].

Harding, R. (2017) Personal Freedom: The Continued Rise of Social Liberalism. In: *British Social Attitudes 34.* Available from: http://www.bsa.natcen.ac.uk/latest-report/british-social-attitudes-34/key-findings/personal-freedom-the-continued-rise-of-social-liberalism.aspx [accessed 22nd September 2017].

Humanists UK (2017) Public Ethical Issues. Available from: https://humanism.org.uk/campaigns/public-ethical-issues/ [accessed 21st September 2017].

National Offender Management Service (2016) *Faith and Pastoral Care for Prisoners, PSI 05/2016.* Available from: https://www.justice.gov.uk/downloads/offenders/psip so/psi-2016/psi-05-2016-faith-and-pastoral-care-for-prisoners.doc [accessed 9th April 2017].

NHS Digital (2018) Contact the IGA. Available from: https://digital.nhs.uk/data-and-information/looking-after-information/data-security-and-information-governance/information-governance-alliance-iga/contact-the-iga/contact-the-iga [accessed 9th July 2018].

Non-Religious Pastoral Support Network (2017) Code of Conduct. Available from: http://nrpsn.org.uk/wp-content/uploads/2016/02/CodeofConduct.pdf [accessed 20th September 2017].

UK Board of Healthcare Chaplaincy (2014) *Code of Conduct for Healthcare Chaplains.* Cambridge, UK Board of Healthcare Chaplaincy. Available from: http://www.ukbhc.org.uk/sites/default/files/ukbhc_code_of_conduct_2010_revised_2014_0.pdf [accessed 20th September 2017].

UK Government (1952) Prison Act. Available from: http://www.legislation.gov.uk/ukpga/1952/52/pdfs/ukpga_19520052_en.pdf [accessed 9th April 2017].

Part III

The role of institutions

Chapter 9

A changing care service

Senior management in institutions have a great opportunity to help to build a stronger, better, and more inclusive pastoral, spiritual, and religious care service. This chapter discusses some of the ways this opportunity can be realised. Key aspects include focusing on service users' needs and priorities, communicating in ways that are relevant to and readily understood by service users, and implementing policies that positively encourage both cultural and practical changes.

Pastoral, spiritual, and religious care provision is starting to change in terms of both culture and practice as the care needs of non-religious people are better understood and skilled non-religious pastoral carers play an increasingly significant role in care provision. The responsibility for encouraging this development cannot be delegated to 'chaplains', 'chaplaincy' departments, faith and belief committees, or religious or special interest organisations. It is essential that the senior management in institutions take ownership. There are many reasons for this. One reason is that it is preferable for pastoral, spiritual, and religious care provision to be guided primarily by current and potential service users, rather than just service providers. However, service users' needs can only be properly determined if they can express those needs in a language that they readily understand, and that the managers of the institution also understand. Terms like 'chaplaincy', 'spiritual care', and (to a lesser extent) 'pastoral care' may not be readily understood. The use of these terms and the development of more effective communication are considered in chapter 11. Another reason for institutions' senior management to take ownership is that, as shown in chapter 12, recruitment has sometimes been improperly restricted. Pastoral, spiritual, and religious care departments have failed to reflect their institution's community in terms of their religion or belief demographics. Better approaches to policy and practice development are discussed in chapter 13. But first, to help position subsequent discussion, this chapter offers a brief review of the past few decades in relation to changes in society; changes in pastoral, spiritual, and religious care practice; and current drivers of change.

Chapter 5 discussed how, over the past few decades, there has been substantial growth in the proportion of people describing themselves as non-religious; about half the population now describe themselves in this way (NatCen, 2017). There has been a corresponding fall in the number of people describing themselves as belonging to a religion. Church attendance has been in long-term decline (Brierley, 2017). At the same time, there has been some growth in the number of people with non-Christian religious affiliations. In terms of religion or belief, there is a greater diversity in our society. Even within a religion (or non-religion) an individual may not hold to the formal tenets of their religion or denomination. Some non-religious people believe in God, some religious people do not, many Catholics support assisted dying. Beliefs have become more personalised. These changes are significant, and institutions need to consider their implications carefully in terms of their pastoral, spiritual, and religious care provision.

A few decades ago, institutions used chaplaincy departments and chaplains to deliver Christian religious ministry. Gradually, the concept of multi-faith 'chaplaincy' was accepted, recognising the religious care needs of people with non-Christian beliefs. At the same time, spiritual care was developed further, partly as a response to the move away from organised religion but recognising those who described themselves as spiritual. 'Chaplaincy' became a provider of both spiritual and religious care, sometimes renaming their departments as 'spiritual care departments'. However, on some measures, about half our population describe themselves as neither religious nor spiritual (Westminster Faith Debates, 2013). As shown in chapter 2, 'chaplains' developed and broadened the types of care offered, increasingly describing the core or heart of their role not in terms of religious or spiritual care, but in terms of pastoral care. This pastoral care is often offered to 'all faiths and none'.

In principle, there is no reason why religious 'chaplains' should not offer pastoral care to people with non-religious beliefs. Indeed, there is much anecdotal evidence, and some quantitative evidence, that some non-religious people are pleased to receive pastoral care from 'chaplains'. The YouGov survey reported in chapter 3 showed that 14% of non-religious people would be likely to access pastoral care from a chaplain (Humanists UK, 2017). But the same survey also showed that 72% of non-religious people were unlikely to want to access pastoral care from a chaplain. For an institution wanting to provide appropriate pastoral care to *all* its potential service users, these finding should prompt serious attention. Whilst departments were now offering pastoral, spiritual, and religious care, it was still the case that the institutions' policies and procedures restricted recruitment to religious people. In general, recruitment of Christians predominated so, together with the bar on non-religious recruitment into paid roles, the result was that few pastoral, spiritual, and religious care departments reflected the make-up of the communities they were there to serve in terms of their religion or belief. For the most part, institutions were happy to accept this situation and exerted very little pressure for substantial change. The number of Muslim 'chaplains' did increase significantly, particularly in prisons, but this may have been driven by other Government agendas. In general, the other non-Christian religions continued to be under-represented, and the institutions did relatively little to help build their capability or ensure that their voice was properly heard.

Meanwhile, the National Secular Society maintained a campaign calling for the end of the state funding of chaplains, contending that state institutions should have no religious role (National Secular Society, 2015). For example, its campaigns manager argued that if chaplaincy in the National Health Service was to be limited to religious care, then the NHS shouldn't pay for it. Conversely, if what was being offered was emotional or spiritual support, then recruitment should be open to anyone with the necessary skills to provide that support, whatever their religion or belief. From about 2010 the British Humanist Association, now Humanists UK, started to develop its own approach. Humanist funerals had become very popular, and it was clear that many people wanted a ceremony that was in keeping with their own beliefs and values, conducted by a like-minded celebrant. Humanists UK had built a large, well trained network of celebrants with good quality assurance procedures, well developed continuing professional development programmes, and effective governance.

Following a careful review, Humanists UK decided to build such a network. It strengthened its links with the prison service, where its proposals to develop a non-religious pastoral support network were well received, supported, and encouraged. After some initial difficulties, the healthcare sector chaplaincy bodies and NHS management are recognising the positive and constructive role non-religious pastoral carers can play. Pilot projects have been initiated in some universities. The Defence Humanist Network is focusing on the provision of non-religious pastoral care in the military (Lindsell, 2017).

Humanists UK has developed a well respected training course for non-religious pastoral care volunteers and has trained about 200 volunteers to date. Progressive pastoral, spiritual, and religious care departments have welcomed them. A postgraduate training course for those wishing to enter paid posts has also been established. Although the legacy of unjustified discrimination in recruitment lingers on, the healthcare and prison sectors have already started to employ non-religious pastoral carers into paid substantive roles.[1] These developments mean that more and more skilled and accredited non-religious pastoral carers are becoming available. They will be needed. The general public have shown a high level of backing for non-religious pastoral care provision. The YouGov survey discussed in chapter 3 showed 69% in favour of the introduction of dedicated non-religious pastoral support to 12% against (Humanists UK, 2017).

The above brief review shows that the provision of pastoral, spiritual, and religious care is changing, and this change will have to continue if institutions are to meet the care needs of all their service users. Institutional management cannot stand on the sidelines and watch, they have a very positive and constructive part to play. Part of this change is cultural, and proactive institutional action will be necessary to ensure this cultural change proceeds smoothly. This will include steps to explicitly recognise and welcome the fact that this care service is no longer only a religious care service, only for those who identify themselves as religious. Nor is it only a religious and spiritual care service, merely for those who identify themselves as religious or spiritual. It is a care service for all, including those who do not define themselves as either religious or spiritual. It is also, explicitly, a care service that is there for those who define themselves as non-religious. This has some obvious implications in terms of the recruitment and training of non-religious pastoral carers. However, there are other significant cultural changes that are needed to inform this positive development. One is to place a greater emphasis on understanding the needs, priorities, and preference of existing and potential service users.

Note

1 Monitoring by Humanists UK of some advertised 250 pastoral/spiritual/religious care posts by UK institutions to October 2017 showed that 80% were restricted to religious applicants. However, the fact that 20% were also open to non-religious applicants shows that real progress is being made.

References

Brierley, P. (2017) *UK Church Statistics 2010–2020*. Second edition. Tonbridge, Brierley Consultancy. Information available from: https://faithsurvey.co.uk/uk-christianity.html [accessed 9th May 2017].

Humanists UK (2017) *Humanists UK Polling on Pastoral Care in the UK*. Available from: https://humanism.org.uk/wp-content/uploads/Humanists-UK-polling-on-pastoral-care-in-the-UK.pdf [accessed 16th October 2017].

Lindsell, A. (2017) *Face to Faith*. *RAF News*10th February, 29. Available from: https://issuu.com/rafnews/docs/raf_news_10_feb_2017 [accessed 9th October 2017].

NatCen (2017) British Social Attitudes: Record Number of Brits with no Religion. Available from: http://www.natcen.ac.uk/news-media/press-releases/2017/september/british-social-attitudes-record-number-of-brits-with-no-religion/ [accessed 14th January 2017].

National Secular Society (2015) Religious Chaplaincy Costs NHS £23.5 million a year. News 8th July. Available from: http://www.secularism.org.uk/news/2015/07/religious-chaplaincy-costs-nhs-gbp235-million-a-year [accessed 7th November 2017].

Westminster Faith Debates (2013) *"No Religion" is the New Religion*. Table 2. Available from: http://faithdebates.org.uk/wp-content/uploads/2014/01/WFD-No-Religion.pdf [accessed 30th October 2017].

Chapter 10

Understanding people's needs

In most areas of care, the views of service users are sought to help understand what is important to them in terms of their needs, priorities, and preferences. By gaining a better understanding of their needs, institutions can adjust or modify the care offered and so improve their care service. Non-religious pastoral carers are person centred, so it is natural that they would want the views of service users to play a large role in guiding service provision. One might expect this to be the case with religious and spiritual care. Yet Kevern and McSherry (2016), reviewing the extensive research into 'chaplaincy', note a significant gap, saying:

> Most obvious of these is the relative paucity of material from the perspective of the patient or client: it is paradoxical that a profession that is so explicitly focused on the 'service user' should apparently overlook the possibilities of engaging them in dialogue. (p.57)

With some justification, Kevern and McSherry see this lack of attention towards service users' needs as paradoxical. Yet viewed from a cultural perspective it is, to some extent, understandable. Historically, chaplains were there to provide religious care. That care was biblically grounded, expressed in the sacraments, and part of the mission of the Church. Hence, it was perhaps natural that chaplains would look to the Church, rather than service users, for guidance on service provision. Some of this cultural legacy remains today. Research has been carried out, but a lot has focused on the views of 'chaplains', that is to say service *providers,* rather than service *users* (Beckford and Gilliat, 1998; Orchard, 2000; Todd, 2013). If the research emphasis on service providers rather than service users is culturally based, then it will require a cultural shift to refocus on service users' needs.

Of course, some research and surveys have tried to understand the views of nurses, students, prisoners, etc. (McSherry, 2010; and Tipton, 2011; Guest et al., 2013). However, they have tended to focus on those with an interest in 'chaplaincy' or spirituality. This may be because they have used optional surveys which were specifically about religion, spirituality, spiritual care, or 'chaplaincy'. Hence, these surveys may have self-excluded a disproportionate number of people who did not see themselves as religious or spiritual. Focus group discussions and qualitative interviews have often been used to help understand service users' views. In some cases, recruitment of people to take part in these interviews was via a 'chaplaincy' department, or of people known to the 'chaplaincy' department. This again may have run the risk of excluding potential service users, for example, those who wanted pastoral care but not from a 'chaplain'. In determining people's pastoral, spiritual, and religious care priorities, it is important to be inclusive and representative. If surveys and researchers contact only those who are currently using the service, then gaps in service provision will go unnoticed and opportunities to create a better, more inclusive service may be lost.

If a cigarette company commissioned a tobacco industry research association to evaluate the part tobacco plays in healthcare based on interviews of people recruited from tobacconists' shops, then questions may be raised about impartiality. Similarly, if a chaplaincy body commissions a chaplaincy study centre to evaluate the part 'faith' plays in healthcare based on interviews of people recruited by chaplains, then questions may be raised about impartiality.[1] Of course, such research could be conducted with the highest levels of integrity, but the perception of bias may remain. It would be far better if research could be carried out in a more overtly neutral way.

Gaining a better understanding of people's pastoral, spiritual, and religious needs and priorities is likely to require a cultural shift to place a greater focus on service users. There should be an evaluation of potential service users' priorities, as well as those of existing service users. That understanding should be based on independent and objective research. Fortunately, all major institutions are well versed in conducting or commissioning such research. Surveys have included determining service users' priorities for family welfare services, housing and accommodation, access to professional counselling, sports/gym facilities, improving meals, visiting arrangements, access to mental healthcare, provision of libraries, better telephone access, and many other services. In principle such surveys and research could be extended to ask service users about their preferences and priorities for pastoral, spiritual, and religious care.

Some examples of research are considered next. They are used to illustrate the challenges and benefits of focusing on service users' needs. All are from the healthcare sector, from large public surveys to small, focused studies.

The first examples relate to understanding people's needs. A survey on death and dying commissioned by the National Council for Palliative Care, reported in chapter 7 (ComRes, 2015), aimed to understand people's service need *priorities*. The survey recruited over 2,000 respondents from the general public and asked them to rank the importance of a range of needs, including religious/spiritual needs. Hence, the survey seemed to fulfil many of the requirements for objectivity and neutrality. Recruitment seemed to be representative of the community, both service users and potential service users.[2]

The range of needs considered was quite broad, including being involved in decision making, and retaining one's dignity. One of the benefits of well structured surveys of this type is that institutions can understand better which areas to prioritise to improve their care service. Of course, it does not mean that needs given a lower priority should be ignored. People do use and value services meeting needs that score relatively low in these rankings. Indeed, the 2016 YouGov survey (Humanists UK, 2017) found that almost 1 in 10 of the people surveyed had used 'chaplaincy' services, even though surveys had ranked spiritual/religious needs rather low.[3] Both these surveys were of the general public, and it would be helpful to obtain a better understanding of people's priorities in specific institutions (the armed forces, prisons) and different areas of healthcare (e.g. hospices versus acute care). Similarly, gaining a better appreciation of the relative importance of different aspects of care within the pastoral, spiritual, and religious care context would be most useful. For example, how many people would value having a listening ear, someone empathic, neutral, and confidential to talk to; having someone to pray with or for them; having access to worship with others, etc. This would allow pastoral/spiritual care or 'chaplaincy' departments to develop their care provision based on an understanding of service users' needs.

The previous example looked at service users' priorities in terms of types of need. The following examples look at service users' priorities in terms of the care provider. Slevin et al. (1996) instigated and conducted a survey aiming to evaluate cancer patients' attitudes to different sources of emotional support.[4] Hence it focused on just one care need: emotional support. Compared with the ComRes (2015) survey, the respondents were tightly defined: those receiving a diagnosis of cancer for at least three months. A total of 431 respondents were given a list of 17 individuals who might give emotional support, including healthcare professionals; non-medical people such as friends, family and other patients; and 'peripheral carers' such as a chaplain/priest, complementary therapist, and psychologist. Respondents were asked to rank them.[5] Family and senior registrars came top, with 73% saying they would definitely use them. Chaplain/priest came 13th out of 17 at about 18%, just above the psychologist and just below the complementary therapist. Again, it is worth stressing that for some patients, seeing a chaplain/priest or psychologist may be important. The survey provided valuable information about patients' likelihood that they would use a particular care provider (and use them again). This example shows that a survey can be quite focused in terms of both the service user group and the type of care. Repeating such surveys over time would allow institutions to understand how service users' care preferences are changing and whether or not a particular service provision is improving.

The 2016 YouGov survey (Humanists UK, 2017) also asked people about care providers, but at the level of the general public. It only compared non-religious pastoral carers with chaplains, and the specific care need was less defined. 36% of respondents said they were likely or very likely to access support from a chaplain, twice the number in Slevin et al.'s research. In some ways this is surprising. One may have expected that cancer patients would have been more likely than members of the general public to want to access support from a chaplain. Of course, there were other contextual differences between the two surveys. For example, the Slevin et al. survey may have tended to emphasise a religious role by referring to a chaplain/priest, not just chaplain as in the YouGov survey. This difference in description may (or may not) have been one of the reasons for the different responses. The YouGov survey did show 41% of respondents were likely or very likely to access support from a non-religious pastoral carer, similar to that from a chaplain.

Although quite different, both these surveys show that it is possible to get a better understanding of service users' priorities in terms of the care provider they would want to access. It would be beneficial to have greater clarity on service users' views about the importance of service providers having to have a religious or a non-religious belief, and the importance of them having a particular religious or denominational affiliation. For example, is having good pastoral care skills more or less important than having good theological knowledge? For those with Christian beliefs, is receiving care from a Christian of any denomination acceptable, or should they be of a definite denomination, if so which? The Dutch armed forces were asked these sorts of questions and the findings helped inform service provision (see chapter 12).

The previous examples looked at service users' priorities in terms of a range of needs, and their preferences from a range of service providers. The final examples explore just one aspect of care in more detail: listening. The relative priority for this aspect of care provision could not be determined from studies focusing on just one type of care. These were essentially qualitative rather than quantitative studies, but in some ways they gave a greater insight into service users' views, and raised important issues in relation to the provision of care. The first study examined a Community Chaplaincy Listening service, a new service offered to some patients by GPs.[6] The chaplains listened to patients but were not there to offer religious care such as sacraments or prayer. A total of 250 patients used the service over the period of study (Mowat and Bunniss, 2011, 2012),[7] and the researchers held semi-structured interviews with 18 of those patients. Notwithstanding some limitations in terms of representation, quantification, and perspective, the study was extremely useful. The study found that patients' experience of the listening service was tremendously positive. As with much qualitative research, these findings are evidenced by patient's quotations:

'Being able to open up has given me a more positive outlook and now I can accept the situation I find myself in.'

'I think it helped me to evaluate my own self-worth ... and have a positive structure for the future.' (Mowat and Bunniss, 2011, p. 14)

The reasons patients used the service were mainly bereavement, relationship issues, stress, and depression rather than what they would describe as spiritual or religious issues. Manzano et al. (2015) found comparable results when they considered what they called active listening in a hospital setting.[8] Their report describes active listening in various ways, for example as empathic, sensitive to emotional needs, non-judgemental, and patient driven. Patient responses were like those in the Community Chaplaincy Listening project. One mentioned that by talking to someone else you listen to yourself as well, and the value of knowing that you are being heard. Another said that offloading things and recognising them helped them find answers for themself. Healthcare professionals and patients highlighted the positive benefits of active listening. This research helps confirm the benefits of active listening discussed in chapter 6.

One value of these smaller qualitative studies is that they can reveal issues which may not be apparent in large scale surveys. Both these studies raised important issues on the use of language, particularly the use of the word chaplain. In the community setting of GP surgeries, some chaplains did realise that to be effective they had to speak to patients from a pastoral care perspective rather than from a religious perspective (Mowat and Bunniss, 2011). Their report also noted comments from both patients and doctors that the words 'spiritual' and 'chaplain' could confuse some people and deter them from accessing the care they may need. This was a significant finding. Exploring this further may have helped to develop a language that was more readily understood and less likely to deter access to care. Instead, in the next phase of their work, more emphasis was placed on the spiritual. It set out to 'explore what makes the [Community Chaplaincy Listening] service distinctly *spiritual* listening and therefore the preserve of healthcare chaplains and spiritual care providers?' (Mowat & Bunniss, 2012, p.11).[9] No attempt was made to define the difference between, say, *spiritual* listening and listening that was empathic, non-judgemental, confidential, and provided by people with good listening skills. The latter could be provided by a non-religious pastoral carer. The assumption appears to be that *spiritual* listening provision should be the preserve of, and limited to, chaplains and spiritual care providers. Manzano et al. (2015) also noted that the use of the word chaplain could be a barrier to people accessing active listening. A physician lecturer observed 'how many patients did not want to speak to the chaplain, just because she's the chaplain. So, it's a barrier' (p.210). A patient said how she had 'been on a ward where the chaplaincy comes round, and you can physically see patients going down [on their chairs]' (p.212). The authors quite properly discuss the possible reasons why the term chaplaincy could cause such apprehension in patients. They identified a fundamental lack of understanding of what chaplaincy means today as a barrier to accessing the active listening service. Their research showed that non-religious people valued visits from active listeners, but that it was very important to remove 'potential subconscious barriers' (p.211). Other evidence presented in this book suggests that the barriers are not just potential, and not just subconscious. Nevertheless, these authors did recognise and consider these important issues.

Kevern and McSherry (2016) were right to point out the paucity of robust, independent research into understanding service users' needs. Gaining a better understanding of these needs seems to be essential if institutions are to provide pastoral, spiritual, and religious care services that are fit for purpose and resourced at an appropriate level. Institutional management can play a crucial role in helping to make the cultural shift towards service user-led provision and initiating independent, high-quality studies into understanding service users' needs and priorities.

Notes

1 There is no suggestion that a tobacco company did commission any such research. It is a purely hypothetical scenario. The Healthcare Chaplaincy Faith and Belief Group did commission the Cardiff Centre for Chaplaincy Studies to conduct research into 'faith' and healthcare (unpublished). Those interviewed were recruited via hospital chaplaincy departments.
2 People's responses may change as they near death. The survey would not be able to determine this.
3 This survey also seemed to fulfil many of the requirements for objectivity and neutrality. Recruitment appeared to be representative of the community.
4 The group initiating and conducting the survey were not exactly neutral. Medics initiated the survey, and the survey itself referred to doctors and other medical staff. 75% of patients returned a questionnaire, a very high response rate. Hence it is likely that the respondents were reasonably representative of this cancer patient community.
5 The rankings were: would definitely use, be likely to use, be unlikely to use, definitely not use. The percentages of 'definitely use' were shown in order. Those who had used an individual were also asked if they would use them again. This could be seen as a measure of satisfaction. Of those who had used a chaplain/priest, somewhat under half said that they would use them again. This was the 13th highest response of 17.
6 The service was set up by NHS Scotland. Patients could refer themselves but most commonly referral was by their GP. GPs decided which patients should be offered the service, and patients were free to take up or decline the offer.
7 This study was conducted from a specific perspective. The two researchers are core members of the Centre for Spirituality, Health and Disability, part of the School of Divinity, History and Philosophy at the University of Aberdeen (https://www.abdn.ac.uk/sdhp/personnel-185.php [accessed 9th July 2018].). The authors state that they 'incorporate[d] the reflective theological eye throughout the analysis' (p.13) and in another publication (Bunniss, Mowat and Snowden, 2013) referred to the project as 'practical theology in action'. The patients in the research may not have been representative of all the patients in the GP practices. GPs offered the service to some patients and not others, some patients did not take up the offer, and only 18 patients out of 250 were followed up with interviews. Only service users were considered. No research was carried out into those who had decided not to use the service, for example, to help understand how many had declined the service and why.

8 This was a very thoughtful study, but numbers were limited and only four patients were included. Hence some care is required in using the results. The development of the study was sponsored by a Christian charity, the Acorn Christian Healing Foundation.

9 The patient questionnaire referred to 'listening' not *'spiritual* listening'. The emphasis the researchers placed on *spiritual* listening did not derive from patients' needs; rather, it was the chaplains who wanted to make a distinction between the sort of listening that they were offering and that of other service providers such as psychotherapists. They thought that the use of the term *spiritual* listening would help make this distinction clearer. Manzano et al. (2015) used the term 'active listening'.

References

Beckford, J.A., Gilliat, S. (1998) *Religion in Prison: 'Equal Rites' in a Multi-Faith Society.* Cambridge, Cambridge University Press.

Bunniss, S., Mowat, H., Snowden, A. (2013) Community Chaplaincy Listening: Practical Theology in Action. *Scottish Journal of Healthcare Chaplaincy* 16, 42–51.

ComRes (2015) *National Council for Palliative Care – Public Opinion on Death and Dying.* Available from: http://www.dyingmatters.org/sites/default/files/files/National%20Council%20for%20Palliative%20Care_Public%20opinion%20on%20death%20and%20dying_5th%20May.pdf [accessed 16th August 2017].

Guest, M., Aune, K., Sharma, S., Warner, R. (2013) *Christianity and the University Experience.* London, Bloomsbury Academic.

Humanists UK (2017) *Humanists UK Polling on Pastoral Care in the UK.* Available from: https://humanism.org.uk/wp-content/uploads/Humanists-UK-polling-on-pastoral-care-in-the-UK.pdf [accessed 16th October 2017].

Kevern, P., McSherry, W. (2016) The Study of Chaplaincy: Methods and Materials. In: Swift, C., Cobb, M., Todd, A. (eds) *A Handbook of Chaplaincy Studies: Understanding Spiritual Care in Public Places.* Abingdon, Routledge.

McSherry, W. (2010) *RCN Spirituality Survey 2010.* London, Royal College of Nursing. Available from: https://my.rcn.org.uk/__data/assets/pdf_file/0017/391112/003861.pdf [accessed 17th October 2017].

Manzano, A., Swift, C., Closs, S.J., Briggs, M. (2015) Active Listening by Hospital Chaplaincy Volunteers: Benefits, Challenges and Good Practice. *Health and Social Care Chaplaincy* 3(2), 201–221.

Mowat, H., Bunniss, S. (2011) *Full Report on the National Scottish Action Research Project First Cycle: March 2010–March 2011.* Edinburgh, NHS Education for Scotland. Available from: http://www.nes.scot.nhs.uk/media/511533/ccl_1_final_report.pdf [accessed 20th October 2017].

Mowat, H., Bunniss, S. (2012) *Full Report of the National Scottish Action Research Project Second Cycle: May 2011–September 2012.* Edinburgh, NHS Education for Scotland. Available from: http://www.nes.scot.nhs.uk/media/1920654/ccl2_final_report.pdf [accessed 20th October 2017].

Orchard, H. (2000) *Hospital Chaplaincy: Modern, Dependable?* Manchester, Lincoln Theological Institute for the Study of Religion and Society.

Slevin, M.L., Nichols, S.E., Downer, S.M., Wilson, P., Lister, T.A., Arnott, S., Maher, J., Souhami, R.L., Tobias, J.S., Goldstone, A.H., Cody, M. (1996) Emotional

Support for Cancer Patients: What do Patients Really Want? *British Journal of Cancer* 74, 1275–1279.

Todd, A., Tipton, L. (2011) *The Role and Contribution of a Multi-Faith Prison Chaplaincy to the Contemporary Prison Service.* Cardiff, Cardiff Centre for Chaplaincy Studies. Available from: http://orca.cf.ac.uk/29120/1/Chaplaincy%20Report%20Final%20Draft%20%283%29.pdf [accessed 24th November 2017].

Todd, A. (ed.) (2013) *Military Chaplaincy in Contention.* Farnham, Ashgate Publishing.

Chapter 11

Effective communications

Chapter 10 argues that focusing on service users and gaining an improved understanding of their needs and priorities is essential to building a better care service. Describing that care service in ways that relate to those needs, and in a language that can be readily understood by everyone, will do much to enhance accessibility. Institutions aim to provide care to everyone, religious and non-religious. In many cases communications will need to change significantly in order to demonstrate that what was once a traditionally religious care service has developed and transformed into a care service for everyone. In this chapter we look at how the care service is often described today, and what those descriptions appear to be saying from a non-religious perspective. Descriptions such as 'chaplaincy' and 'spiritual care' are shown to lack clarity, fail to adequately describe how needs are met, and act as a deterrent to some people accessing the care service. These are serious deficiencies and should be a real cause for concern. 'Pastoral care' is offered as a much better choice, but it also has its own limitations and disadvantages. An alternative approach is suggested. This is based on communications that describe care needs in service users' terms, and then explain how the department aims to meet those needs.

Some current communications

Just as the appearance of a sculpture can change when seen from different perspectives, so can the meaning of a communication. Here some communications are considered from a non-religious perspective. A chaplain wearing a clerical collar can appear to be saying that they are Christian, that they want people to see them as Christian, that they are employed as Christian, and that they have a Christian agenda. If the front cover of a leaflet consists of religious symbols and/or the word 'chaplaincy', it can be seen as a leaflet for religious people and only religious people.[1] If a department notice board is full of details of religious services and photographs of people in religious dress or with religious titles, then the notice board can be seen as declaring that the department is for religious people and only religious people. If a spiritual care department's website gives a list of 'chaplains' as: Anglican, Catholic, Buddhist, Hindu, Humanist, Jewish, Methodist, Muslim, Orthodox, and Sikh, it can be seen as saying that the pastoral care needs of non-religious people are not being taken seriously.[2] If leaflets and books for the non-religious pastoral care of students are held on campus in the chaplaincy office, where non-religious students are unlikely to come across them, then the campus is not seriously trying to reach out to its non-religious students. If a university describes a quiet centre as a multi-faith environment primarily for prayer, worship, meditation, and contemplation, then some non-religious students may hear the university saying that they cannot use the centre for their own reflection and contemplation. If a care service says that it is a multi-faith care service, then it can be perceived as saying that non-religious people are excluded. If a formal ministry document on prisoners describes prisoners who have non-religious beliefs and values as 'nil religion', it can communicate that such prisoners are not regarded with the same dignity and respect as prisoners who have religious beliefs and values. If non-religious people are described as 'no faith', this is to misrepresent them. Non-religious people have faith in many things. If a department or care service says that it welcomes 'all faiths and none', it is welcoming with one hand and discouraging with the other. Categorising non-religious people as 'nones' declares that they are seen in negative terms, as people *without* a religious belief rather than people *with* non-religious beliefs and values.

To a greater or lesser extent, all these forms of communication state that the care service is a service provided by religious people for religious people. Insofar as non-religious people are included, they are to be seen in a somewhat negative way, as people lacking faith or religious belief. Sadly, all the above are real examples and some of them are quite common. It will be impossible to build a robust, fully inclusive pastoral, spiritual, and religious care service on the communication foundations described above. However, there are some signs of progress and good practice. Some chaplains remove their clerical collar when operating in a generic role. Some leaflets have an inclusive front cover whilst retaining important details of the religious care available. But progress is slow, and it is not always driven by service users' needs. Another massive impediment to progress is the way that the care service and care departments are described. Departments may be described as chaplaincy departments, spiritual care departments, pastoral and spiritual care departments', or some combination of these.

Chaplains and 'chaplaincy'

Chaplains have played an important role in both the development and provision of pastoral, spiritual, and religious care in institutions. There is no doubt that they will continue to do so. The *Oxford English Dictionary* (1989) defines a chaplain in religious terms, and *only* in religious terms. For example, it refers to clergy who conduct religious services in a prison, regiment, college, or other institution. For some clergy who conduct religious services in institutions, the title of chaplain is wholly appropriate. It describes how they may think of themselves, and it accurately describes their role to potential service users. The word chaplain has been used in this sort of way for hundreds of years, so it is very well established. There is almost no prospect that the meaning of this word will change to any significant extent over the next several decades. Currently, it would be unthinkable for the Queen or the Speaker of the House of Commons to appoint a chaplain who was a declared atheist.[3] Such moves would be strongly resisted by the Established Church. With powerful bodies resisting changes in the usage of the word, its meaning will remain essentially the same.

The YouGov survey discussed in chapter 3 shows that the overwhelming majority of the general public understand 'chaplain' to refer to a religious person, and *only* to a religious person (Humanists UK, 2017).[4] On this basis non-religious pastoral carers cannot be 'chaplains'. Many non-Christian religions do not have an established, historical concept of a 'chaplain' or chaplaincy. For example, it is not really a Muslim concept. When Muslim pioneers were striving to provide Islamic religious care in institutions, Christian chaplains acted as 'gate keepers' who largely determined the terms under which these Muslims could be members of their departments' teams.[5] These terms included adopting the title of 'chaplain'. The use of 'chaplain' as a Muslim title has continued. Gilliat-Ray et al. (2016) in *Understanding Muslim Chaplaincy* note that some Muslim chaplains have changed their identity badge to include the title 'Imam' next to 'Muslim Chaplain' in order to help those Muslims who do not understand the term 'chaplain'. In referring to the work of Muslim prison 'chaplains', they also report that 'male offenders consistently preferred the term imams' (p. 132). In a person-centred approach to care provision, service users would be asked what titles or descriptions would be most helpful and meaningful to them. Conducting some simple research into service users' views would be most useful. A part of good communications is to have job titles and identity badges that properly communicate the role to service users. 'Non-religious pastoral carer', whilst not ideal, is a far better description than 'chaplain', 'non-religious chaplain', or similar. To require non-religious pastoral carers to describe themselves as some form of 'chaplain' is surely inappropriate, unethical, and could be misleading to service users.

'Chaplaincy' is mainly used to describe a department or service. According to Swift (2004) as cited by Bryant (2013), 'The concept of chaplaincy as the "collected activities, knowledge or theory of being a chaplain" rather than chaplains as individual religious functionaries only emerged in the 1960s' (p.2). The 1960s was a time of a quite rapid increase in the number of chaplains employed in institutions, and a time of expansion of their role beyond that of church ministry and purely religious care for religious people. The role was to encompass pastoral and spiritual care for 'all faiths and none'. Hence the care role had changed but the description of that service had not. The result has been a degree of confusion even amongst 'chaplains'. Orchard (2000) quotes a London chaplain in 1968 saying:

> More and more people are now becoming aware of the various professions at work within hospitals, yet it is sad that so few seem to understand fully the function of the chaplain in such a setting. It is doubly sad, of course, if the chaplain himself is uncertain or vague. (p.9)

Orchard (2000, p.9) also quotes another chaplain in 1999, over 30 years later, asking: 'What is chaplaincy? What is its relevance?'. In *A Very Modern Ministry*, Ryan (2015, p.8) is still asking the very same questions, and concedes that 'there is very little consensus on how to define what a chaplain is' (p.10). If, after almost 50 years of reflection, 'chaplains' are still asking the question about what chaplaincy is, there is little prospect that service users will have a satisfactory understanding of what sort of care service 'chaplaincy' provides. The term 'chaplaincy' is not readily understood, lacks clarity, and fails to recognise or reflect the positive developments in service provision over the past 50 years.

Of course, the main argument against communications using the term 'chaplaincy' as the name of a department or as a service description comes from service users and potential service users. Using terms such as 'chaplaincy' can deter some from accessing the care they need. In the YouGov survey discussed in chapter 3 (Humanists UK, 2017), almost three quarters of non-religious respondents said that they were *unlikely* to want to access support from a chaplain. Indeed, almost half replied that they were *very unlikely* to want to access support from a chaplain.[6] Other research has resulted in similar findings (Manzano et al., 2015). If institutions want to ensure that everybody, religious and non-religious, has access to appropriate pastoral, spiritual, and religious care, then inclusive forms of communication are needed. 'Chaplaincy' is no longer an appropriate description of a truly inclusive care service, and its use is a huge barrier to building one.

Spiritual care

An increasing number of institutions recognise the shortcomings of using 'chaplaincy' and have renamed their pastoral, spiritual, and religious care departments as spiritual care departments. This is a forward step. It specifically describes the department as a care department, and this emphasis on care is to be applauded. 'Spiritual' does not have such a specific historical and cultural association with Christianity, so it may be better suited to today's diverse society. Many people consider the spiritual aspects of their lives to be some of the most important to them. For institutions that have a clear purpose, such as security, rehabilitation, medical treatment, or education, the spiritual aspects of people's lives may not always be front of mind. Those tasked with providing pastoral, spiritual, and religious care can help address people's spiritual needs, and help ensure that institutions give proper consideration to meeting those needs. However, the use of the word 'spiritual' as a description of a care service is problematic. It has very close associations with religion, it has no consistently understood meaning, and may discourage some from accessing the care they need.

Davie (2015) states 'At times, however, the term "spirituality" is used as an awkward proxy for "religion", in an attempt to avoid the (supposedly) negative connotations of the latter' (p.166). Ofsted (2018) defines 'spiritual' by referring to pupils' 'ability to be reflective about their own beliefs, religious or otherwise' (p.40). The NHS England Chaplaincy Guidelines (Swift, 2015, pp.5–6) refer to 'spiritual care' as addressing needs that include both religious and non-religious convictions and practices. Her Majesty The Queen (2000), talking about our sense of the spiritual, mentioned those who believed in God and those who did not. Paradoxically, such attempts to make 'spiritual' an inclusive term highlight its strong religious connotations. In order to be properly understood, it often seems necessary to remind people that spiritual may describe those with non-religious beliefs and values. But the expression 'spiritual care department' gives no such reminder, and many may take the expression to be a proxy for a 'religious care department'.

'Spiritual' means many different things to different people. For some people, spirituality is obeying God's will (Heelas and Woodhead, 2005). Theos (2013) explored spirituality in terms of things unseen, such as angels, God, and higher spiritual entities that can't be called God. McSherry (2012) states that spirituality 'is at the core and essence of who we are, that spark which permeates the entire fabric of the person and demands that we are all worthy of dignity and respect' (p.188). Her Majesty The Queen (2000) in a Christmas Broadcast referred to the spiritual in terms of an awareness of profound meaning and purpose in people's lives. What may be seen by one person as spiritual care could be seen by another as something to be avoided. The offer of a prayer is a simple example. Heelas and Woodhead (2005) found that for some people tai chi, yoga, reiki, circle dancing, aromatherapy, and massage were spiritually therapeutic. Are 'chaplains' in spiritual care departments going to start offering circle dancing and tai chi? Probably not. A related problem is the use of 'spiritual' to describe an activity that many would not consider to be spiritual. To give just two examples of many, Mowat and Bunniss (2012) tried to draw a distinction between 'spiritual listening' and 'listening'. The difference was not fully explained or described, other than the fact that if it was 'spiritual listening', the care provider would *be* religious (a chaplain) or spiritual. Here the use of the word 'spiritual', as in 'spiritual listening', seems to refer to the characteristics of the care provider rather than the care provided. McSherry (2010) asked nurses who decided to respond to the Royal College of Nursing spirituality survey to state if they agreed or disagreed with the statement 'I believe nurses can provide spiritual care by having respect for privacy, dignity and the religious and cultural beliefs of a patient' (p.20). In the statement, McSherry describes respecting a person's privacy and dignity as *spiritual* care. But to many people, respecting the privacy and dignity of a patient would be a part of their care. There would be no need for the adjective 'spiritual'. Inserting the word 'spiritual' may be most unhelpful to those who struggle with the meaning of the word. How in this context does 'spiritual care' differ from 'care'? Inserting the word 'spiritual' could be problematic to those who do not see themselves as spiritual; are they unable to provide such care, unable to respect a patient's privacy and dignity? McSherry (2012) may show great insight when he describes the spiritual as 'that spark which permeates the entire fabric of the person' (p.118). Nevertheless, it is almost totally ineffective in describing, in practical terms, what someone may receive from a spiritual care department. In many senses, 'spiritual care' is like 'holistic care'. It is a good thing and institutions may wish to provide it. But to be meaningful, potential service users need a much clearer description of the specific elements of the care being offered. 'Spiritual care' is too vague and too generalised to be an effective description of what care services are being offered.

As noted in chapter 10, Mowat and Bunniss (2011) reported that some patients and doctors found the word 'spiritual' confusing and put people off. This is very strong argument for not using 'spiritual' and for trying to find alternative and more effective forms of communication. 'Spiritual' can be used as a self-designation. Some may describe themselves as a spiritual person, a religious person, not a religious person, not a spiritual person, or some combination. If care is described as spiritual care, some may see this as care for people who describe themselves as spiritual. Conversely, if someone does not describe themselves as a spiritual person, they may well feel that spiritual care is not relevant to them. The same applies to a department described as a spiritual care department. This could be a serious problem because some surveys show that only about a quarter of the general public describe themselves as 'spiritual' or 'religious and spiritual' (Westminster Faith Debates, 2013). Hence, 'spiritual' descriptions could be a real barrier to accessing care for two groups: those who are religious but not spiritual, and the much larger group who are neither spiritual nor religious – over half of the general public.[7] Institutions who want a care service that is understood and available to all people should be very concerned about departments and services that describe themselves as 'spiritual' and only as 'spiritual'.

Pastoral care

It is clear that describing care or care departments as 'chaplaincy' or 'spiritual' can be a barrier to people being able to access appropriate care. This book uses the terms pastoral care and pastoral carer. Whilst not ideal, 'pastoral' has many advantages over 'chaplaincy' and 'spiritual'. Unlike 'spiritual' and 'religious', 'pastoral' is generally not used by people to categorise themselves. Woodhead could organise a survey that asked, 'Are you a spiritual person?', (Westminster Faith Debates, 2013), but asking 'Are you a pastoral person?' would prove more problematic. Personal categories are exclusive and excluding in a way that 'pastoral' is not. The term pastoral is also in common usage within this care area, indeed pastoral care is seen by many 'chaplains' to be at the heart of the care they give. 'Pastoral' does have some strong religious connotations, an advantage from a religious perspective but a disadvantage from a non-religious perspective. Schools use the term pastoral in a quite non-religious way so, over time, pastoral may become a more inclusive term. The established churches are less likely to defend 'pastoral' than 'chaplain' as a purely religious and Christian description. Importantly, including the word pastoral rather than 'chaplaincy' can be a clear signal that institutions recognise the need to make a cultural shift towards a more inclusive care service. However, in describing the care service in a more inclusive way, that inclusivity must not lose sight of the need to communicate the religious care component of the care service. Using the term pastoral on its own may not do this. The term pastoral has many advantages over 'chaplaincy' and 'spiritual', but it has the disadvantage that is common to them all: it fails to fully describe the range of care activities offered in a way that service users can readily understand. Developing a service user-led description of care activities can form the basis of improved and more inclusive communications.

An alternative approach

Improved communications have still to be developed, so there is an inadequate body of proven good practice to draw on. However, it is possible to outline a few general principles to help guide that development. They include (but are not limited to):

- using communications that emphasise the services provided rather than describing those who provide the service
- basing communications on what service users say their needs are, and describing how the department can help meet those needs
- describing the services provided according to the priorities given by service users
- using words and language that service users say they readily understand
- having a range of communication methods that reach out to everyone, and that continue to remind people of the services offered
- announcing the positive cultural shift towards an inclusive care service, providing non-religious care services as well as religious care services, and using changes in language to reinforce that cultural shift

- being explicit that the care service is no longer only a religious care service, that there is a choice of non-religious pastoral care
- avoiding communications that exclude or marginalise people with non-religious beliefs.

The services may fall into three types: individual care services given on a one-to-one basis; care services given to groups of service users in the institution; and services given to the institution at a corporate or management level. For each type, those care services may be of a religious nature, serving a specific religion and/or denomination; they may be of a non-religious nature, serving specifically those with non-religious beliefs; or they may be of a general nature in that they have no specific religious or non-religious focus. The activities and forms of communication will differ for each type. To give an example, a general care activity for individuals is likely to include the provision of trained people who are empathic and non-judgemental, to be there to listen and to be present with people in difficult times, allowing them to explore deeper questions such as meaning, purpose, and identity. This may be communicated through easily understood introductory phrases such as 'It's good to talk, so we're here to listen'. A specifically non-religious or a specifically religious form of this care service should also be offered and publicised. This would be likely to say that service users could request both non-religious carers and religious carers. Communications may also include the availability of other specifically religious and specifically non-religious individual care services. The specifically non-religious may include arranging non-religious baby-namings and humanist or civil funerals, and providing non-religious books of poems and readings.[8] The specifically religious may include how to request the sacraments, the location of prayer rooms, times of religious services, and the availability of sacred texts. Hence, the communications would include the general, the specifically religious, *and* the specifically non-religious.

A specimen front page of a leaflet is shown in Figure 11.1. It aims to be inclusive with the focus on the main activity in this institution, being there to listen. The name of the department is included on the leaflet, but since the name may be confusing or uninformative to many it is only appears in small type. The A4, three-fold leaflet includes details of specifically religious and non-religious care services, and a tear-off slip to request a non-religious pastoral carer or a 'chaplain' of a particular religion/denomination. It is a simple, straightforward illustration of what can be achieved.

Using inclusive symbols of this kind on leaflets, noticeboards, and websites, rather than religious images, shows a more welcoming attitude towards non-religious people. Rather than saying 'We are here for all faiths and none', it would be more respectful to say 'We are here for everyone, non-religious and religious'. It is important to include 'non-religious and religious' for two reasons. The first is to really flag up that non-religious people are included. The second reason is that if departments are described only as spiritual care

Institution name and logo

We are here to listen, support,
encourage and walk alongside you.

Issued by the Pastoral & Spiritual Care Department

Figure 11.1 A sample leaflet

departments, the religious care element may be rather diluted, so the religious reference is also needed. Similarly, if religious care is being provided, using the word religion rather than faith makes this clear. It also avoids the implication that non-religious people do not have faith. Clearly, using the terms 'no faith', 'none', and 'nil' for those with non-religious beliefs has no place in good pastoral, spiritual, and religious care practice. As a person-centred care service, talking about *people* seems most appropriate. Where possible, talk of people with Buddhist beliefs; people with Christian beliefs; people with non-religious beliefs. If lack of space prevents this, using 'NRB' for non-religious beliefs is preferable to 'Nil', 'None', or 'NF' (no faith). Such a change may

Name......................................

Unit/wing/ward.........................

I would like a visit   Yes/No·

If you have a preference, please circle below

as appropriate:

Non-religious:

       Humanist, Other..................

Religious:

       Anglican, Catholic, Other Christian

       Please specify.....................

       Muslim, Hindu, Sikh, Jewish, Other

       Please specify......................

I would like to hear prayers/receive Holy
Communion/attend worship/get help to get to
worship.*

I would like my own community religion or
belief leader to be informed (Give details)

....

....

* Delete as appropriate

Figure 11.2 A sample tear-off request slip

seem trivial, but it is not. The change signals a recognition that non-religious people are afforded the same dignity and respect as religious people. Similarly, simply removing the word 'multi-faith' as a description of a team, place, or service signals that membership of that team, access to that place, and the service provision are not restricted to religious people. Renaming a 'multi-faith room' as a 'breathing space' or a 'room for reflection' would be more inclusive.

Careful consideration should be given to the wearing of religious dress. Where the care being given is specifically religious, then wearing the appropriate dress can help by indicating the religion of the care provider, showing authenticity, and giving reassurance. However, where the care being offered is general or generic, wearing religious dress may be inappropriate because it may indicate that a specifically religious care service is being provided. In the same way, some thought should be given about using photographs of service providers on noticeboards and in other visual forms of communication. It is a common practice for noticeboards to show photographs of the paid 'chaplains' in religious dress. These are overwhelmingly Christian, so it is perhaps inevitable that the care service may be seen by many as a service provided for Christians. Showing photographs of service users rather than service providers would be an important step in the cultural move from a focus on service providers towards a focus on service users. Listing the services offered would help people gain a better understanding of the types of care available. By mentioning non-religious care as well as religious care services, people with non-religious beliefs may recognise that they are being given proper consideration. Just making a list of religions and beliefs as described above is most unhelpful. Many non-religious people will not read down a list of religions in the vague hope that a non-religious belief is included. The description should first make clear that both non-religious and religious care are available, and then give further details within each of these categories. An example of a tear-off request slip, designed on this basis, is shown in Figure 11.2. This makes clear that service users have a choice of both non-religious and religious care providers. Note also the inclusion of several religious care request options.[9]

Offering the choice of non-religious care on a form is one thing; delivering the resources to make that choice a reality is quite another. Recruitment practices should ensure that appropriate religious and non-religious resources are available.

Notes

1 Some 'chaplaincy' departments and organisations include a humanist symbol amongst the many religious symbols on their leaflets and websites in order to be able to say that they are inclusive. This is tokenism. If anything, it demonstrates a lack of serious intent to communicate with non-religious people.

2 Many non-religious and non-spiritual people would ignore the website. Humanism is listed as though it were a religion when it is not. Non-religious pastoral carers are not included.
3 The Speaker's Chaplain role has been filled by an Anglican cleric since the office was created in 1660. Legal reform would be necessary to allow others to read the daily prayers. In 2010 *The Telegraph* reported that the Speaker backed the creation of a multi-faith chaplaincy team, including representatives of the Hindu, Buddhist, and Jainist religions (Wynne-Jones, 2010). It has not happened. In 2017, the Speaker's Office reported that the current arrangements were working and that they were not aware of any parliamentary appetite for change (Kate Winterflood, Secretary to the Speaker's Secretary, personal communication, 27th October 2017). The Speaker's Chaplain will continue to be an Anglican.
4 Total sample size was 4,085 adults. Fieldwork was undertaken between 28th and 29th July 2016. The survey was carried out online. The figures have been weighted and are representative of all GB adults (aged 18+).
5 To give a more recent example, when the British Humanist Association (BHA; now Humanists UK) started to develop its non-religious pastoral care provision from 2012, it wanted to do so in constructive cooperation with the Multi-Faith Group for Healthcare Chaplaincy. The BHA's request that the group adopt a more inclusive name so that it could become a member was refused, and in 2015 the group offered to grant BHA some funding to help it develop its network of pastoral carers on condition that it would accept the 'chaplaincy' title. This illustrates the pressure early pioneers of a more inclusive care service have come under to adopt Christian descriptions. This offer was declined. In 2016 the group adopted a more inclusive name without the term chaplaincy. The Non-Religious Pastoral Support Network then joined as full members.
6 The likelihood of non-religious respondents wanting to access a chaplain were: very likely 2%, fairly likely 12%, fairly unlikely 25%, very unlikely 47%, don' know 13%.
7 13% were none of these, 6% 'don't knows'.
8 Suitable books include *Humanist Anthology: From Confucius to David Attenborough* (Knight and Herrick, 2001) and *Seasons of Life: Prose and Poetry for Secular Ceremonies and Private Reflection* (Collins et al., 2000).
9 This form is for illustration purposes. The details will vary depending on the service user group and the institution.

References

Bryant, J.R. (2013) Assertion and Assumption: A Single Site Study of Acute Healthcare Chaplaincy. M.Res. thesis, Department of Theology and Religion, University of Birmingham. Available from: http://etheses.bham.ac.uk/4973/1/Bryant14MRes.pdf [accessed 22nd October 2017].

Collins, N., Herrick, J., Pearce, J. (eds) (2000) *Seasons of Life: Prose and Poetry for Secular Ceremonies and Private Reflection*. Third revised edition. London, Rationalist Press Association Ltd.

Davie, G. (2015) *Religion in Britain, A Persistent Paradox*. Chichester, Wiley Blackwell.

Gilliat-Ray, S., Ali, M.M., Pattison, S. (2016) *Understanding Muslim Chaplaincy*. Abingdon, Routledge. First published in 2013 by Ashgate Publishing.

Heelas, P., Woodhead, L. (2005) *The Spiritual Revolution: Why Religion is Giving Way to Spirituality*. Oxford, Blackwell Publishing.

Her Majesty The Queen (2000) Christmas Broadcast. Available from: https://www.royal.uk/christmas-broadcast-2000 [accessed 25th October 2017].

Humanists UK (2017) *Humanists UK Polling on Pastoral Care in the UK*. Available from: https://humanism.org.uk/wp-content/uploads/Humanists-UK-polling-on-pastoral-care-in-the-UK.pdf [accessed 16th October 2017].

Knight, M., Herrick, J. (eds) (2001) *Humanist Anthology: From Confucius to David Attenborough*. Third revised edition. London, Rationalist Press Association Ltd.

Manzano, A., Swift, C., Closs, S.J., Briggs, M. (2015) Active Listening by Hospital Chaplaincy Volunteers: Benefits, Challenges and Good Practice. *Health and Social Care Chaplaincy* 3(2), 201–221.

McSherry, W. (2010) *RCN Spirituality Survey 2010*. London, Royal College of Nursing. Available from: https://my.rcn.org.uk/__data/assets/pdf_file/0017/391112/003861.pdf [accessed 17th October 2017].

McSherry, W., Smith, J. (2012) Spiritual Care. In: McSherry, W., McSherry, R., Watson, R. (eds) *Care in Nursing Principles Values and Skills*. Oxford, Oxford University Press, p. 118.

Mowat, H., Bunniss, S. (2011) *Full Report on the National Scottish Action Research Project First Cycle: March 2010–March 2011*. Edinburgh, NHS Education for Scotland. Available from: http://www.nes.scot.nhs.uk/media/511533/ccl_1_final_report.pdf [accessed 20th October 2017].

Mowat, H., Bunniss, S. (2012) *Full Report of the National Scottish Action Research Project. Second Cycle: May 2011–September 2012*. Edinburgh, NHS Education for Scotland. Available from: http://www.nes.scot.nhs.uk/media/1920654/ccl2_final_report.pdf [accessed 20th October 2017].

Ofsted (2018) *School Inspection Handbook*. Manchester, Office for Standards in Education, Children's Services and Skills. Available from: https://assets.publishing.service.gov.uk/government/uploads/system/uploads/attachment_data/file/699810/School_inspection_handbook_section_5.pdf [accessed 4th July 2018].

Orchard, H. (2000) *Hospital Chaplaincy: Modern, Dependable?* Manchester, Lincoln Theological Institute for the Study of Religion and Society.

Oxford English Dictionary (1989) Second edition. Oxford, Oxford University Press.

Ryan, B. (2015) *A Very Modern Ministry: Chaplaincy in the UK*. London, Theos.

Swift, C. (2015) *NHS Chaplaincy Guidelines 2015: Promoting Excellence in Pastoral, Spiritual & Religious Care*. Version 1. Available from: https://www.england.nhs.uk/wp-content/uploads/2015/03/nhs-chaplaincy-guidelines-2015.pdf [accessed 12th June 2018].

Theos (2013) *The Spirit of Things Unseen: Belief in Post-Religious Britain*. London, Theos.

Westminster Faith Debates (2013) *"No Religion" is the New Religion*. Table 2. Available from: http://faithdebates.org.uk/wp-content/uploads/2014/01/WFD-No-Religion.pdf [accessed 30th October 2017].

Wynne-Jones, J (2010) *Multi-faith chaplains to make House of Commons more inclusive*. The Telegraph. Available from: https://www.telegraph.co.uk/news/religion/8224923/Multi-faith-chaplains-to-make-House-of-Commons-more-inclusive.html [accessed 4th July 2018]

Chapter 12

Better recruitment

Reducing inequality and building opportunity

The YouGov survey discussed in chapter 3 shows strong backing for the provision of trained non-religious pastoral carers in institutions (Humanists UK, 2017). The survey also shows that non-Christian, and particularly non-religious, people have accessed this sort of care much less than Christians. One of the probable reasons for this inequality has been unfair or unsatisfactory recruitment policies and practices. Recruitment requirements have often specified that posts are open only to religious people where there is no justification for such a restriction. Hence, capable non-religious people have been prevented from applying. Before discussing the development and adoption of better recruitment practices, it is worth considering why this inequality in recruitment has persisted.

Historically, institutions recruited chaplains to perform Christian church ministry. Restricting recruitment to Christians would have been consistent with that. Later, institutions included provision of specifically non-Christian religious care. So, they started to recruit individuals of other religions, albeit on a quite limited scale. Since these people were only to provide specifically religious care, restricting recruitment was justified. For example, if the role was to say Muslim prayers every Friday, recruitment would be restricted to an imam. However, from about 50 years ago, care provision expanded, the number of 'chaplains' increased, and pastoral and spiritual care activities were included. Institutions declared that service provision was 'for all faiths and none'. Although the nature and scope of the roles had changed, recruitment policies and practices had not. Unjustified recruitment restrictions remained. One can only speculate as to why often inappropriate recruitment restrictions have remained for so long, and why institutions' senior management and human resources departments have not been proactive in addressing the obvious inequalities. Some possible answers are suggested below.

- Some institutional management may have understood 'chaplaincy' to be a religious care service, provided by religious people, for religious people.

Of course, this view was contrary to their policy statements about equality and inclusivity. The way many pastoral, spiritual, and religious care departments were communicating may have reinforced this flawed perception. This flawed perception may have led institutions' senior management and human resources departments to accept inappropriately restrictive recruitment requirements.

- Perhaps non-religious people were seen in a negative way, just as people without religious beliefs. Therefore, recruiting non-religious pastoral carers would have been irrelevant. Seeing non-religious people as people with non-religious beliefs and values changes this completely.
- Many institutional managers, especially if they were not particularly religious themselves, may not have felt experienced or qualified enough to determine the recruitment policies and practices for religious people. Their thinking may have been that religion is a sensitive area and religious recruitment is best delegated to the experts: lead 'chaplains', 'chaplaincy' committees, or 'chaplaincy' bodies set up for the purpose. Whilst the wish to delegate in this way is understandable, it has proven to be most unsatisfactory. With some notable progressive exceptions, many of these leaders and experts have presided over a recruitment system that has resulted in an employment profile where, in relation to their community, people with Christian beliefs are over-represented, people with non-Christian beliefs are under-represented, and people with non-religious beliefs are almost absent.
- It is quite possible that institutional management were not aware that there was an equality or a recruitment issue. Until recently, there is very little evidence that 'chaplaincy' departments were raising issues about the recruitment of non-religious people with their own management. Equality analyses carried out by 'chaplains' may have failed to even mention inequality in recruitment, let alone bring it to the attention of their management.[1] Some chaplains may have thought that there was simply no need for non-religious carers, that chaplains could provide satisfactory non-religious care.
- There was little or no external pressure to address these recruitment issues.[2]
- Most importantly, there were few non-religious people seeking paid or volunteer roles. This situation has changed. The Non-Religious Pastoral Support Network is now training and accrediting people to take up mainly voluntary roles. Postgraduate training in non-religious pastoral care is in place for people seeking mainly paid posts. If trained and competent non-religious pastoral carers find unjustified recruitment restrictions, they are likely to seek to change the recruitment policies and practices that resulted in those restrictions.

The Non-Religious Pastoral Support Network and Humanists UK are trying to ensure that equality analyses are of high quality. Both try to engage and cooperate with institutions and 'chaplaincy' bodies to promote better understanding and to ensure good recruitment practices. Where engagement and cooperation are not possible, Humanists UK are prepared to challenge unjustified recruitment restrictions, using legal means if necessary.[3] Fortunately, there are growing signs that institutions are beginning to recognise the need to improve recruitment practices and to address inequalities. NHS England has organised workshops on recruitment. 'Chaplains' are increasingly recognising the value of, and positively seeking to recruit, non-religious pastoral carers.

The legal situation

The following section is not an authoritative legal account. It gives an outline of legislation in relation to 'religion or belief' and recruitment.[4] Important pieces of legislation are the Equality Act of 2010 and, within that Act, the public sector Equality Duty.[5] The term 'religion or belief' has a precise meaning within the Act. The term covers religious beliefs and recognised philosophical beliefs such as humanism, but it also includes non-belief or a lack of religion or belief. The term 'faith and belief' is not the same as 'religion or belief'. In common usage 'faith and belief' is often taken to *include* religious beliefs and recognised philosophical beliefs but *exclude* non-belief or a lack of religion or belief. For example, 'faith and belief' may include a humanist but exclude a non-religious person who was not a humanist, whereas 'religion or belief' would cover both.

'Religion or belief' is a protected characteristic. The Equality Duty requires public bodies to have *due regard* to the need to advance equality of opportunity between people who share a protected characteristic and people who do not share it. This includes advancing equality of opportunity between religious people and non-religious people. Having due regard does not mean that public bodies are required to eliminate inequality, but it does mean that consideration of equality issues must influence the decisions they reach. For example, public bodies would need to be able to demonstrate how their consideration of the need to advance equality of opportunity had affected their recruitment policies and practices. They would also need to consider how to remove or minimise disadvantages suffered by people due to their protected characteristics. If, for example, non-religious people wanted pastoral care as much as religious people, but were disadvantaged in receiving that care because they were non-religious, the public body would need to consider how it could eliminate or minimise that disadvantage.

Public bodies must consider encouraging people with protected characteristics to participate in public life or in other activities where their participation is low. An area of activity where participation of non-religious people is disproportionately low is in the provision of pastoral and spiritual care in public institutions. Hence, institutions should be considering how they can encourage greater participation by non-religious people. Some chaplains have argued that they are there to provide care to 'all faiths and none', so the needs of non-religious people are already being met by chaplains and there is no need for non-religious pastoral carers. Leaving aside the doubtful validity of that assertion, their argument cannot be legally justified. Non-religious people should have the same opportunities to provide pastoral and spiritual care as religious people. If recruitment policies and practices have denied them those opportunities, resulting in disproportionately low participation, 'chaplains' and their institutions should be considering how to encourage greater participation.

In limited circumstances employers can legally require a job applicant to be of a particular 'religion or belief'. One such circumstance is where a public body is acting to encourage people with a 'religion or belief' that is under-represented or disadvantaged in a role or activity. Another, called an occu-pational requirement, is where belonging to a particular 'religion or belief' is essential for the job. Where it is considered that a post has an occupational requirement, this needs to be made clear in the advertisement. The applica-tion pack should give the reasoning for the requirement. Requirements must be critical to the role, not just one of several requirements, and they must be proportionate. If there are any other reasonable, less discriminatory ways or arrangements of achieving meeting service users' needs, the occupational requirement cannot be justified. If a post previously had an occupational requirement, it cannot be assumed that the requirement is justified when that post becomes vacant. For example, if a Christian chaplain leaves, auto-matically seeking to recruit another Christian chaplain would be invalid. A reassessment is needed because circumstances may have changed.

There seems little doubt that the Equalities Act 2010 and the Equality Duty will continue to have an important influence on the development of recruitment policies and practices of pastoral, spiritual, and religious carers. This can be seen in a negative sense of having to take care to avoid possible legal action. Far better to see this legislation from a positive perspective. The words of the Government Equalities Office (2011) emphasise this positive perspective:

> The new Equality Duty supports good decision making – it encourages public bodies to understand how different people will be affected by their activities so that policies and services are appropriate and accessible to all and meet different people's needs. By understanding the effect of their activities on different people, and how inclusive public services can sup-port and open up people's opportunities, public bodies are better placed to deliver policies and services that are efficient and effective. (p.3)

Very careful thought needs to be given to the requirements of a role when a vacancy occurs.[6] Have service users' needs and priorities been properly evaluated? Has an assessment been made of the extent to which those needs have been met? If some of the activities of the pastoral, spiritual, and religious care department are specifically religious or specifically non-religious, are the remaining resources sufficient to reasonably and proportionately carry out those activities? Could those activities be carried out in ways which would allow recruitment that would eliminate or minimise disadvantage and create opportunities? Has a record been kept of how these decisions have been made?

Even where the headline job description makes it clear that the role is open to any competent person, irrespective of their religion or belief, the details may unwittingly tell a different story. If the documents say that the applicant should have a theology degree, have received ordination training or equivalent, or be authorised by a 'faith and belief' group, then these requirements may constitute indirect discrimination. Indirect discrimination occurs when a public body works in a way that puts certain people at a disadvantage because of their 'religion or belief'. Having to have a theology degree disadvantages a non-religious person. There is no obvious non-religious equivalent to ordination. Those people who do not belong to a 'faith and belief' group are disadvantaged.[7] If these requirements cannot be objectively justified or are not proportionate, or if satisfactory alternatives are available then including such requirements would risk legal action. More importantly, removing unnecessary requirements would encourage a wider range of competent people to apply, would help reduce inequalities, and would increase the opportunities to build a better more inclusive care service.

Inclusive recruitment

Good recruitment practices should be based on a well grounded understanding of service users' needs, ensuring that those needs are reflected in a range of different job roles and descriptions, job specifications, and person specifications. Applicants for these roles would be responsible for providing evidence that they meet the requirements of a particular role or activity. That evidence may come from various sources, such as personal interviews or statements from third parties. The evidence needed will, of course, depend on the specific role and activities.

Some activities may relate to an identifiable religion/denomination or belief. For example, performing the sacrament of anointing the sick, leading Friday prayers, or conducting a humanist ceremony. In these cases, the institution would need to say what evidence it needs to satisfy itself that an applicant was competent to carry out that activity. Clearly, in these circumstances the institution would need to consult the relevant religion or belief organisation to get a proper understanding of what that evidence should be, and the applicant would need to provide it. This evidence may well be in the form of some authorisation, accreditation, or reference from the religion or belief body.

Some activities, whilst important, may take up a relatively small proportion of the total hours 'chaplains' are employed. In general, using these activities as a basis of a genuine occupational requirement would be inappropriate. These activities may include emergency call outs, conducting weddings and funerals, formal religious services, etc. Various ways of meeting these needs should be considered. These include setting up service-level agreements with local religious bodies and clergy to respond to emergencies, using funeral directors to arrange for 'chaplains' or humanist/non-religious celebrants to conduct funerals, and part-time employment. Some of these options will give the institution more scope to open opportunities to those who are under-represented. Some roles may not require an applicant to perform the sort of activities described above, but may need an applicant to have a certain religion or belief perspective and lived experience. For example, some service users may want religious care only from people with an Anglican Christian perspective and lived experience. As above, the institution would need to consult with the Anglican Church to get an understanding of the evidence that an applicant fulfils these requirements. That evidence may well be in the form of some authorisation, accreditation, or reference. Some service users may want spiritual care from a spiritual carer. It is not entirely clear what evidence an institution would need to satisfy itself that an applicant has a satisfactory spiritual perspective and lived experience.

If a role required someone with a non-religious perspective and lived experience, what evidence would the institution need? Many non-religious pastoral carers are humanists, so the institution could consult with Humanists UK in these cases. Whilst humanists are non-religious, not all non-religious people are humanists. With few exceptions, it is likely that restricting recruitment of non-religious people to humanists would be unjustified and discriminatory. How should the institutions proceed? First it is worth noting that some people who would tick a 'non-religious' box in a survey may also believe in God, attend church regularly, and believe Christian doctrine; but they may dislike a 'religious' designation. They may not want to be associated with some forms of organised religion.[8] They are not considered as non-religious within the context of this recruitment discussion. A workable definition of a non-religious person for recruitment purposes could be 'someone who sustains and upholds a naturalistic view of the world without reference to otherworldly or supernatural places, forces, or beings and who lives their life without recourse to, or the need for, supernatural assumptions and beliefs'. An institution seeking evidence regarding a person applying for a non-religious pastoral care role may want the applicant to convincingly articulate and demonstrate that they genuinely hold the beliefs and values described above. The institution may also require an applicant to provide evidence that their beliefs and values are worthy of respect in a democratic society, compatible with human dignity, and not in conflict with the fundamental rights of others.[9] Such evidence could be supplemented by receiving appropriate references, as is common practice in many areas of recruitment. It would be good practice to ensure that non-religious, as well as religious, people evaluate that evidence.

Many roles and activities are not related to religion or belief, but to other general capabilities, such as having good listening skills or an ability to follow the administrative arrangements of the institution. The institution can seek evidence of these capabilities in accord with its normal recruitment practices. The endorsement or accreditation of an applicant by a religion or belief body may or may not relate to such general capabilities. Where job specifications ask for approval or endorsement by a religion or belief body, the specification should say why the endorsement is required. For example, is it to show the applicant has a certain religion or belief perspective and lived experience, or is it to confirm competence in some general capabilities or some combination of these? It would be good practice for an endorsing body to state the nature and scope of its endorsement or accreditation. Accreditation by the Non-Religious Pastoral Support Network confirms that those accredited have good basic pastoral care skills and competencies, as well as a non-religious perspective and lived experience. They are not necessarily accredited to perform humanist ceremonies. Likewise, those accredited to perform humanist ceremonies are not necessarily accredited as non-religious pastoral carers. However, many accredited non-religious pastoral carers are also accredited as humanist celebrants.[10]

Inclusive recruitment not only provides opportunities for people to provide non-religious pastoral care, it also helps institutions by enabling them to recruit from a large proportion of the population who are non-religious. There is a substantial pool of people with talents, capabilities, and experience to provide first class non-religious and generic pastoral care. Some have been motivated to provide care from their personal experiences, for example from caring for loved ones. Some have been motivated by being unable to access appropriate non-religious pastoral care when they needed it. They include people with professional care experience such as social workers, teachers, and lecturers with pastoral care responsibilities; retired doctors and nurses; vets; people who have worked in care and nursing homes; and people trained in psychotherapy and related disciplines. Many have worked in the charitable sector with organisations such as Citizens Advice Bureau, Clinks, Cruse, Marie Curie, Mind, Samaritans, Sands, or other care and support charities. These charities have welcomed and encouraged suitable non-religious people to provide care. Recruiting from this pool of very able people gives institutions the opportunity to widen the range of experiences and perspectives in their department. This must result in better, stronger, and more inclusive care provision.

To achieve these significant benefits, institutions' recruitment practices need to reach out to everyone, not just religious people. Using existing 'chaplains' and their links with their local religious communities as the main source of recruitment will maintain the existing inequalities. Similarly, institutions need to reach out beyond humanist groups and organisations in their recruitment of non-religious pastoral carers. Recruitment leaflets and websites using inclusive job titles that talk of pastoral as well as spiritual and religious care are likely to reach a more inclusive audience. Explicitly recognising the value and relevance of previous care experience would also help encourage a wider range of applicants, including those who are non-religious. For institutions using volunteers, it may be worth working with Volunteering Matters[11] and similar organisations to ensure they understand the opportunities in pastoral, spiritual, and religious care and to develop suitable recruitment material.

If institutions want to seriously address the massive inequalities in recruitment and provision, then their management will need to proactively help their pastoral, spiritual, and religious care departments to develop and implement improved recruitment policies and practices. Attracting a wider range of motivated, competent people will help build a stronger, more inclusive care service.

Notes

1 Astonishingly, the equality analysis carried out as part of the latest review of the NHS England Chaplaincy Guidelines failed to even mention, let alone address, the massive inequalities in staffing and recruitment in terms of religion or belief (Durairaj, 2015).

2 The National Secular Society was exerting pressure but this was mainly to highlight the costs of 'chaplaincy' and to persuade the NHS to stop funding it, rather than to focus on recruitment practices.

3 In 2015, the British Humanist Association (BHA; now Humanists UK) challenged several NHS Trusts where recruitment was restricted to Christians. Following attempts to promote better understanding and to ensure good recruitment practices that met with little or no positive response, the BHA reluctantly wrote to some Trusts asking them to withdraw the relevant recruitment advertisements or the restrictions, saying that otherwise they would take legal action. All the Trusts decided to accede to the BHA's request, and issues of recruitment and equality in terms of religion or belief are now being taken much more seriously by NHS England and by Trusts. NHS England has been positive and proactive in taking responsibility and in addressing these equality issues.

4 Helpful guidance and advice is available from Acas (2014) and from the Equality and Human Rights Commission (2017).

5 This legislation covers England, Scotland, and Wales.

6 There is no legal requirement to carry out an Equality Impact Assessment (Government Equalities Office, 2011, p.8). However, public bodies do need to show that they have given proper consideration to the effects on different people. The situation is slightly different in Wales. This document usefully lists a number of misconceptions about the Equality Duty.

7 Examples include people who would describe themselves as religious but would not want to define themselves as a member of any particular religion or denomination, nor as a member of a group. Similarly, someone who described themselves as spiritual but not religious may not be a member of a faith and belief group, yet they may be competent to provide pastoral and spiritual care. People with non-religious beliefs but who would not describe themselves as humanists may not be a

member of any faith and belief group, but may be competent to provide non-religious pastoral care.

8   Some people fitting this description have applied for roles as non-religious pastoral carers.

9   Applicants for induction/training with the Non-Religious Pastoral Support Network need to demonstrate that they meet these requirements in order to be accredited. There could be a strong case that, irrespective of religion or belief, all applicants to pastoral, spiritual, and religious care roles should confirm that their beliefs and values are worthy of respect in a democratic society, compatible with human dignity, and not in conflict with the fundamental rights of others.

10   Humanist celebrant accreditation is for a particular ceremony: namings, weddings, funerals. A list of accredited celebrants is available from the Humanists UK website: https://humanism.org.uk/ceremonies/find-a-celebrant/

11   See https://volunteeringmatters.org.uk/

References

Acas (2014) *Religion or Belief and the Workplace.* London, Acas. Available from: http://www.acas.org.uk/media/pdf/d/n/Religion-or-Belief-and-the_workplace-guide.pdf [accessed 9th November 2017].

Durairaj, S. (2015) *NHS England Chaplaincy Guidelines 2015: Promoting Excellence in Pastoral, Spiritual & Religious Care: Equality Analysis.* Leeds, NHS England. Available from: https://www.england.nhs.uk/wp-content/uploads/2015/03/equality-analysis-nhs-chaplaincy-guidelines-2015.pdf [accessed 19th April 2017].

Equality and Human Rights Commission (2017) Religion or Belief Discrimination. Available from: https://www.equalityhumanrights.com/en/advice-and-guidance/religion-or-belief-discrimination [accessed 9th November 2017].

Government Equalities Office (2011) *Equality Act 2010: Public Sector Equality Duty – What Do I Need to Know? A Quick Start Guide for Public Sector Organisations.* Available from: https://www.gov.uk/government/uploads/system/uploads/attachment_data/file/85041/equality-duty.pdf [accessed 10th November 2017].

Humanists UK (2017) *Humanists UK Polling on Pastoral Care in the UK.* Available from: https://humanism.org.uk/wp-content/uploads/Humanists-UK-polling-on-pastoral-care-in-the-UK.pdf [accessed 16th October 2017].

Chapter 13

Policy and practice development

General approaches

Chapters 10 to 12 have outlined some of the problems and opportunities in developing stronger, more inclusive pastoral, spiritual, and religious care services. It should be apparent that the senior management in institutions have an essential and proactive role to play in encouraging this positive change. Some of the change relates to culture, attitudes, and behaviour. In addition, developing and implementing better policies and practices can also play an important part. The review in chapter 2 of the development of pastoral, spiritual, and religious care practice strongly suggests that in some (not all) cases, policy development has been carried out largely by 'chaplains' talking to other 'chaplains' and religious bodies. This is plainly unsatisfactory. Good policy development would benefit from fully involving people with different perspectives and experiences. The contribution of skilled and experienced pastoral, spiritual, and religious care practitioners will be vital. Given that the overwhelming majority of practitioners are Christian, they can also bring this perspective. Non-Christian and non-religious perspectives also need to be included. It is clear from what has been said earlier that the voices of service users and potential service users offer crucial inputs. Possible approaches to obtaining a better understanding of people's pastoral, spiritual, and religious care needs are explored in the sections on different institutions below.

Based on publicly available documents, it is often difficult to see if, or how many, institutions could effectively demonstrate that they have properly considered the need to advance equality of opportunity in pastoral, spiritual, and religious care provision. Policy reviews can be used by institutions to demonstrate that they have shown due regard in considering equality issues. More importantly, they can help bring about changes that will benefit both the institution and service users. The following sections look at the state of policy development in prisons, healthcare, defence, and universities. They offer some opening suggestions as to how improved policies could be developed. They should be regarded as initial thoughts that institutions' senior management can develop in conjunction with service users, potential service users, existing practitioners, and those with different religion or belief perspectives. Humanists UK and the Non-Religious Pastoral Support Network are available to help provide guidance and assistance to institutions in policy and practice development.

Prisons

Published literature gives very limited insight into the pastoral, spiritual, and religious needs of prisoners and prison staff. Todd and Tipton (2011) interviewed 15 prisoners and 16 staff, but their research suffered from some of the problems outlined in chapter 10: numbers were small, interview recruitment was facilitated by chaplains, the voices of those with non-Christian religious beliefs were barely heard, and the research was carried out by a chaplaincy organisation from a multi-faith rather than a fully inclusive perspective (p.13). Whilst the researchers were very conscious of the need to avoid bias, some bias was inevitable. Nevertheless, the researchers concluded that the main role of 'chaplains' was the provision of pastoral care, particularly providing non-judgemental one-to-one support to all prisoners, irrespective of their religion or belief (p.4). Fortunately, our prison services do conduct regular, good quality surveys of prisoners. Commenting on its own survey, the Scottish Prison Service (Carnie and Broderick, 2015) stated:

> The Survey is … directed at improving the quality of service delivery … This approach is predicated on the well-established belief that for change to be effective it is imperative that the views of prisoners are factored into the planning equation. (p.5)

This wide-ranging survey covering living conditions, healthcare, and relationships invited high levels of participation by all prisoners. It covered questions about their religion/belief being respected and questions about wellbeing. Responses include comments such as 'I've been able to make up my mind about things' (p.2). In England and Wales, HM Chief Inspector of Prisons (2016) carried out a similar survey of over 6,000 prisoners, which asked if prisoners had access to a chaplain or religious leader (p.111). Reports of this nature indicate that the Department of Justice could, in principle, gain a better understanding of their service users' pastoral, spiritual, and religious needs and priorities. It may be possible for the Chief Inspector's survey to ask prisoners if they have access to a non-religious pastoral carer, or ask questions of the type used in the 2016 YouGov survey (Humanists UK, 2017), for example: To what extent do you agree or disagree with the following statement? 'Prisons that have chaplains should also have a dedicated non-religious pastoral support provider.' Responses could provide very useful information to help guide policy development.

Prisoners' voices can make an essential contribution to the development of pastoral, spiritual, and religious care policy. Surveys are just one means of providing a voice. If there were some sort of development committee or policy review group, it may be possible to have prisoners' voices represented by a charity working in prisoners' interests. It would be good practice for such a working group/committee to have members bringing in the perspectives of staff, of people with different religion or belief (including non-religious) perspectives, and of those with expertise in the area. Conducting a review of the Prison Service Instructions (National Offender Management Service, 2016) in this way would be an excellent way forward. Apart from a minor update, these instructions date from 2011, and a review is due. In 2011 Todd and Tipton (p.17) were questioning the use of term 'nil', yet the term is still in the instructions and is still being used. The Instructions are largely written from a 'faith and belief' rather than a fully inclusive perspective. For example, they contain appendices about various 'Faiths and beliefs', including humanism, but no appendix about people with non-religious beliefs and values. An outline of what such an appendix may look like is given at the end of this chapter. The Ministry of Justice (2011) has a good approach to ensuring equality. For example, its PSI 32/2011 states:

> Disproportionality occurs when protected groups are under or over represented in a particular function or area; for example, if the data shows that the local IEP [incentives and earned privileges] scheme consistently denies certain privileges to particular protected groups. This does not establish that unfairness is occurring – it is possible that disproportionality represents fair outcomes: for example, there may be differences in the level of need between different groups – but it is a prompt for further investigation. (p.15)

The data presented in chapter 2 clearly show a high level of disproportionality in terms of pastoral, spiritual, and religious care provision, particularly of non-religious pastoral carers. In accordance with its own instructions, the Ministry of Justice should prompt a further investigation, which would look into the causes of the limited provision and consider how provision by non-religious pastoral carers should be encouraged.[1]

Over many years, Her Majesty's Prison and Probation Service (HMPPS) has been supportive of developing more inclusive care provision, at least compared with many other institutions. Conducting a review as described above would be a chance to ensure a common understanding of the nature of this care amongst a range of stakeholders. This common understanding could be publicised, using inclusive language, through revised instructions, for example, an updated *Faith and Pastoral Care for Prisoners* PSI.

Another way in which HMPPS could communicate that it was developing a care service that was in keeping with current society would be to publicly declare its wish to amend the Prison Act (UK Government, 1952). This declaration would send a powerful, positive message to prisoners, prison staff, religion or belief groups, and the wider community that HMPPS seeks to respect the humanity of everyone, equally, irrespective of their religion or belief.[2] It would be a wonderful opportunity for HMPPS to reiterate its wish that *all* prisoners and staff have access to good quality pastoral, spiritual, and religious care. It would also ensure that care provision is based on solid legal and policy foundations.

Healthcare

In healthcare, pastoral, spiritual, and religious care policies are determined at a local level, that of the NHS Trust, the hospice or group of hospices, the Clinical Commissioning Group, etc. However, guidelines have been developed that can help inform policy development. Since most publicly funded healthcare has been devolved, different guidelines have been drawn up in each devolved area. The following discussion on policy development refers mainly to two sets of guidelines, those of NHS Scotland (Scottish Government, 2009) and NHS England (Swift, 2015).

Both sets of guidelines make little or no reference to good quality surveys or research into patients' and staff priorities and preferences in relation to those aspects of pastoral, spiritual, and religious care they most value.[3] Such information is indispensable to good policy development. Our healthcare organisations have a great deal of experience in surveying patients and staff to help understand their needs and experiences. The Picker Institute, Care Quality Commission, Ipsos Mori, and several health-related non-governmental organisations have commissioned or carried out surveys. In principle it should be possible for respected, independent research organisations to include the sort of questions outlined above as a part of one or more of their surveys. In addition, Trusts often invite service users and patient representatives to make an input to service design and development. There seems to be every reason to include both patients and staff in committees or groups drawing up pastoral, spiritual, and religious care guidelines and policies.

NHS Scotland management took ownership of drawing up its guidelines, making it clear that 'Responsibility for a spiritual care service now lies within the NHS' (Scottish Government, 2009, Annex A, p.4). It formed a working group with a range of stakeholders including NHS staff, and religion and belief organisations including the Humanist Society of Scotland. NHS England took a different approach by asking a leading and respected chaplain to undertake the review of its guidelines. Beyond this, NHS England took relatively little ownership when compared with NHS Scotland. A working group of different types of stakeholder was not set up; instead, greater reliance was placed on discussions with existing healthcare 'chaplaincy' bodies. Hence most of the consultation was between 'chaplains'. The British Humanist

Association considered the process for drawing up the guidelines adopted by NHS England to be flawed. Fortunately, since the publication of the guidelines, NHS England has taken greater direct responsibility for the development of pastoral, spiritual, and religious care. With this has come an increased awareness of equality issues. Guidelines should be subject to regular review to reflect the better understanding of service users' needs, changes in society and the development of non-religious pastoral care provision.[4] Carrying out guideline reviews based on service users' needs, and with a working group consisting of a range of stakeholders, would seem to be an effective way forward.

Whilst such guidelines can be influential, they are guidelines. Further action is necessary to ensure that appropriate policies are developed and implemented. Each healthcare body or legal entity should have a pastoral, spiritual, and religious care policy that gives due consideration to the guidelines, to its Equality Duties, and to local circumstances. Local circumstances can best be understood by consulting a range of local stakeholders. In some cases it may be appropriate to have a pastoral, spiritual, and religious care committee, again with a range of stakeholders. The Scottish Government (2009) recommends this sort of approach (Annex B, p.10).[5]

It is clear that, in many cases, NHS senior management need to take greater ownership of their pastoral, spiritual, and religious care policies. This is important in order to expedite the development from a religious to a fully inclusive care provision and to facilitate the cultural change to a care service that is mainly directed by the wishes of service users. One benefit of this would be that hospital and hospice management obtain a much better insight into the value of their pastoral, spiritual and religious care services. Basing policy on service users' needs would be consistent with their ethos to 'put patients first' (but not forgetting staff and carers). Encouraging a range of stakeholders to be directly involved should result in policies and practices that will lead to a stronger, fairer, more inclusive care service.

Universities and colleges[6]

Based on age demographics, most students will be non-religious. Multi-faith 'chaplaincy' departments can provide support to help students explore their religious and non-religious beliefs. But only when such departments are described in an inclusive way, and have adequate non-religious pastoral care provision, will those students who want to explore their non-religious beliefs have the same sort of like-minded support. Identifying student needs is an essential part of building good pastoral, spiritual, and religious care provision. It would be helpful to conduct some independent research to gain a better understanding of the relative importance of pastoral, spiritual, and religious care needs within the various student services offered.

Universities and colleges have a great deal of autonomy in this area. There are no inclusive national representative groups responsible for pastoral, spiritual, and religious care, and no inclusive national guidelines. The Learning and Skills Council (2005) has produced an extensive handbook on 'chaplaincy', partly in response to the growing number of 'chaplains' in the further education sector and partly to reflect the need to move from Christian to multi-faith provision. However, this is largely out of date, and it did not consider the need for, or development of, non-religious pastoral care. Whilst some form of national guidance, developed with a range of stakeholders, would be of value, it is likely that policy development will need to take place at local level. Such development may be encouraged by non-religious pastoral carers, for example by their involvement in equality and diversity committees.

Considering pastoral, spiritual, and religious care provision within the wider equality and diversity agenda may be advantageous. This was the case with the Morgan report for the University of Westminster (2015). [7] As part of its work, an impressive independent panel looked at the role of faith advisers, noting that faith advisers should see their role mainly as supporting students rather than promoting religious opinions. The panel also said that they had heard little of the voice of 'non-believers', surprising given that most students were probably non-religious. Their thoughts about secular advisers resulted in appointment of an in-house Secular Adviser, the first in a UK institution of this type. As well as providing non-religious pastoral care, the role brings an explicitly non-religious viewpoint to the cultural, ethical, and political matters of the university. In terms of policy and practice, this development from a Christian to a multi-faith and then on to a more inclusive provision as at the University of Westminster is a model that other universities and further education colleges are increasingly embracing. It is a very welcome advance.

Whereas the prison service has a central 'chaplaincy' committee bringing together 'chaplains' of different religions, and in healthcare the Network for Pastoral, Spiritual and Religious Care in Health brings together organisations of different religions and beliefs, there seems to be no equivalent body with the same standing in the university/further education sector. It would be very helpful if an inclusive body of this type could be formed for this sector. [8]

Military

In common with prisons, hospitals, and universities, the armed forces talk of meeting the pastoral and spiritual needs of all personnel, irrespective of their religion or belief (Ministry of Defence, 2011, p.11). Like other 'chaplains', military chaplains have a long history of working conscientiously to serve everyone in their military community. But when it comes to recruitment policies and practices, the military finds itself in a different situation from hospitals, prisons, and universities. In terms of pastoral, spiritual, and religious care, recruitment into commissioned posts is restricted to personnel from the main Christian denominations. No other major public institution adopts this approach. The Ministry of Defence (2017) notes that the majority of service personnel are from the main Christian denominations. Indeed, nearly three-quarters do declare themselves to be Christian, but almost a quarter declare themselves to be of no religion.[9] The idea that since *most* personnel are Christian then *all* recruitment into the above roles should be Christian would not withstand scrutiny. If the role of chaplains was limited to activities that could only be carried out by authorised Christians of certain denominations, then there may be some legal justification for these recruitment restrictions, but the Ministry of Defence (2011, p.11) makes it clear that this is not the case. At the height of its activities Camp Bastion, the British army's base in Afghanistan, had over a dozen chaplains, so more proportionate representation in terms of religion or belief should be possible in such circumstances (Coulter and Legood, 2016, p.211). Commenting on the Equality Act 2010, the Ministry of Defence (2011, p.8) states that most of its policies and procedures will require little or no change to comply with the Act. Most – but not all. Its pastoral, spiritual, and religious care policies, including its recruitment policies, may well benefit from a review given the current legal framework.

Whilst reviewing policies and practices for legal reasons may be prudent, it may be more meaningful if they are reviewed with the intent to provide a stronger, more inclusive care service. This is recognised by some military chaplains. Coulter and Legood (2016) note that 'Questions about humanism ... will prevail and need to be addressed' (p.212). Here the need for some sort of review seems to be acknowledged and understood. Of course, the questions should not be restricted to humanism and humanists, nor indeed to those with non-religious beliefs. The views and needs of all service personnel should be considered. A survey of the type discussed in chapter 2 may be very valuable to help determine the probable level of support for non-religious pastoral care provision, and to get an idea of the extent to which the current care provision is being used by different people. A more detailed survey that analyses current activities, time spent, and the main contacts of the Commissioned Chaplains, Officiating Chaplains to the Military, and Civilian Chaplains to the Military may prove useful.[10] However, a survey of this nature is unlikely to identify unmet or potential demand.

The Ministry of Defence could learn a lot from humanist pastoral carers in the Dutch military, both about their role and practices, and about the needs of service personnel. In the Netherlands, 'commissioned humanist pastoral carers' have provided pastoral and spiritual care to the armed forces for about 50 years, including providing support on the front line in conflict areas.[11] In the Dutch military it is more likely that the need for non-religious pastoral care is being met. A survey for the Dutch Ministry of Defence examined many of the areas mentioned above (Bernts et al., 2014). For example, military personnel were asked if they had a preference for 'spiritual support' from a particular religion or ideology; 52% said they had no preference, 16% preferred a Protestant, 15% a Catholic, 13% a humanist, and the remainder non-

Christian or other (p. 35).[12] Its survey of 'spiritual support workers' showed that most of their time was spent on pastoral and spiritual care, and less than 10% on religious ceremonies, celebrations, and rituals (p.11). Whilst the circumstances in the UK are different from the Netherlands, these surveys do show that it is possible to obtain a reasonable understanding of service users' needs. This understanding can help inform policy development, including recruitment and the allocation of resources.

A review could also help explore some of the dilemmas felt by chaplains and probably also by some non-religious personnel. King (2013) found that 87% of agnostics and 79% of atheists valued remembrance services. Most of these services include Christian prayers. Ball (2013) thoughtfully asks if it is right for a military chaplain to assume that all those present (including non-religious people) have consented to be the objects of those prayers. In many memorial and thanksgiving services in civilian institutions, it is good practice to make them inclusive, not specifically and wholly religious or Christian. Chaplains could preface Christian prayers with words to non-Christians that make it clear that their consent is not presumed. Phrases such as 'We will now say the Lord's Prayer' presume consent; saying 'For those who are Christian, we will now say the Lord's Prayer' does not. By developing a constructive dialogue between Christian, non-Christian, and non-religious personnel it should be possible to create forms and words for ceremonies that better meet the needs, beliefs, and values of all those who want to attend. The same sort of dialogue may be useful in managing the moral dilemmas faced by chaplains. When documents say that chaplains are the guardians of the armed forces' moral compass, what does this really mean? Are chaplains there to guard Christian moral values within the armed forces, or to guard the corporate moral values of the Ministry of Defence and the armed forces? Could a guardian role be to encourage all armed forces personnel to think about what their personal moral values should be? Bringing a range of different perspectives to discussions of such questions can be challenging but enormously worthwhile. Civilian Chaplains to the Military and non-religious pastoral carers face the same sort of moral dilemmas. The fact that military chaplains are raising these issues is most heartening and suggests that good progress should be possible.

Reviews into pastoral, spiritual, and religious care policy and practices could be carried out by a particular service (Air Force, Army, Navy) or on a joint forces basis. Whatever the basis, having an independent chair and a committee or working group bringing in a range of perspectives would be advantageous to the review. Such a review could consider the roles of commissioned non-religious pastoral carers, typical job descriptions, and personal specifications. From these considerations it would be possible to determine what training would be required in order to meet these specifications. The armed forces could consider how they might encourage greater participation by non-religious people in these roles. Within prisons, healthcare, and higher education there are established multi-faith structures, with people of different religions working in essentially similar roles. It is relatively easy for these to develop naturally into fully inclusive teams that embrace non-religious pastoral carers. Unfortunately, such multi-faith structures are not developed in the same way in the armed forces, so methods of implementation and deployment will require some thought. Whilst single-service 'cloth-on-cloth' provision (army people providing care for army people, navy people for navy people, etc.) has the benefit that those providing care understand the environment of those they are caring for, if few non-religious pastoral carers are initially available there may be significant advantages in more joint forces cooperation in facilitating non-religious pastoral care provision.

Whatever the way forward, it is important to take the first steps. This is a great opportunity for the armed forces to demonstrate that they recognise the changing demographics of service personnel, that they are committed to meeting their pastoral, spiritual, and religious needs with like-minded provision, and that they will translate that commitment into positive action.

Non-religious pastoral carers and policy development

The heart of the non-religious pastoral carer's role is to care. That care will often be provided in a one-to-one relationship based on empathy and trust. Developing policies and guidance documents is, in many ways, a different type of activity. Some non-religious pastoral carers may feel that becoming involved in such activities is not for them. This is quite understandable. However, developing appropriate policies and practices is often essential to ensure that all service users have access to appropriate like-minded pastoral, spiritual, and religious care. Some non-religious pastoral carers may want to help their institution in such developments. They can try to play a constructive and active part with their team when reviewing policies, guidelines, the wording of leaflets and websites, the content of memorial services, etc. At times it may be necessary to approach their more senior management to make them aware of the need for like-minded non-religious pastoral care and to encourage them to initiate a review or similar activity.

Many pastoral/spiritual care or 'chaplaincy' departments produce guides on faiths and beliefs. These are very valuable in informing staff about dietary requirements, holy days, actions in relation to death and burial, organ donation, and many other items. Some departments and institutions now include information on humanism as a recognised belief. Again, this is helpful, but most people with non-religious beliefs and values do not recognise themselves as humanists. These guides rarely have a section specifically about non-religious people. Perhaps this is partly because those writing the guides see non-religious people as people without religious beliefs. It is difficult to write about non-religious people from this perspective. In conclusion, as detailed in the preceding chapters of this book, the following suggestions may assist non-religious pastoral carers, and others, to help write such guides, and to guide policy and practice development.

- Perceive non-religious people as people *with* non-religious beliefs and values. Recognise that these beliefs and values may be strongly and sincerely held and very meaningful in their lives.
- Treat non-religious people with dignity. In a pastoral, spiritual, and religious care context talk of 'people with non-religious beliefs and values'. Avoid using descriptions like 'no faith', 'none', 'nil', 'unbeliever'. Rather than using the term 'all faiths and none' it is better to refer to 'people with religious and non-religious beliefs and values'.
- When describing care services, use language and descriptions that non-religious people would clearly recognise as inclusive. 'We are here to care for everyone' is better than 'We care for all faiths and beliefs'. Descriptions such as 'multi-faith' and 'chaplaincy' are seen by most people as wholly religious terms and not inclusive.
- Take a person-centred approach, avoiding assumptions. Don't assume that all non-religious people must be atheist or agnostic. Some non-religious people may believe in a God (just as some religious people may not believe in a God). For some non-religious people, both religion and a lack of religion may be of little importance in their lives (as is the case with some religious people).
- Note that non-religious people hold a range of beliefs and values. Where appropriate, ask what beliefs and values are important to them. In terms of diet, some non-religious people may be vegan or vegetarian, some may not eat pork. These dietary choices may be based on preventing harm to sentient animals, rather than for religious reasons.
- When delivering pastoral, spiritual, and religious care, be sensitive to the beliefs of non-religious people. Before offering to pray with or for someone, clearly establish whether they would be comfortable with receiving such an offer. Respect the right of service users not to disclose information about their religion or belief unless required to do so for regulatory or legal reasons. People who see themselves as non-religious or not spiritual may find the use of spiritual assessment tools to be quite inappropriate.[13]
- Treat non-religious people with respect. Don't presume that they are religious. When enquiring about a person's religion or belief, ask a more open question such as 'Do you consider yourself to be a religious, non-religious, or a spiritual person?' rather than 'What is your religion?'.
- Where relevant, ensure both staff and service users receive details of non-religious baby-namings, weddings, and funerals, together with information about how to contact accredited celebrants. Where there are inclusive memorial, remembrance, thanksgiving, and related services, ensure that the invitations to attend are not from (or just from) religious bodies, that

the content is not only or overwhelmingly religious or Christian, and that the introduction to prayers does not presume that non-religious people (and, where pertinent, non-Christian people) consent to be the objects of those prayers.

- Ensure non-religious people have the same opportunities as religious people to access pastoral and spiritual care. Encourage the recruitment and training of non-religious pastoral carers. Make it very clear that care is available to 'people with non-religious beliefs and values'. Put in place effective referral systems for non-religious service users and monitor their effectiveness.
- Foster positive and constructive relationships between institutions and those organisations that help support people with non-religious beliefs and values.

Notes

1 It would be beneficial for the review to consider the recommendations of the Catholic Bishops' Conference of England and Wales, Church of England, and Free Churches Group (2016).

2 Some Churches and the British Humanist Association (now Humanists UK) submitted evidence to the Joint Select Committee of Prison Reform in relation to the 1952 Act. The essence of the British Humanist Association's (2017) submission was 'that pastoral, spiritual and religious care should be available to all prisoners irrespective of their religion or belief and that this should be reflected in legislation. Therefore, we believe that the Prisons and Courts Bill 2016–2017 should amend the Prison Act 1952 to remove references to the Church of England and so put those of all religions and beliefs on an equal footing when it comes to the recruitment of chaplains or pastoral carers in prisons' (p.2). In a joint submission, the Catholic Bishops' Conference of England and Wales, Church of England, and Free Churches Group (2016) made reference to the Act, saying 'The Prison Act 1952 enshrines the presence of chaplaincy in prisons, giving chaplains legal status and statutory responsibilities.' Their submission did not call for the Act to be modified. Neither did their submission address the issues of equality and human rights. However, both submissions stressed the importance of pastoral care. A general election prevented proposed legislative reforms being progressed. HMPPS could declare its own wish to amend this Act at any time; it does not need a formal proposal for a legislative change to do so.

3 The NHS England Guidelines (Swift, 2015) did refer to one aspect of patient experience: 'However, independently gathered information shows that a significant minority of patients who have a particular religion or belief wish to practice it during their episode of care (and are often unable to do so)' (p.14). The Picker data to which the report refers show that in response to the question 'Were you able to practise your religion in the way in which you want to?' 2.3 to 3.4% said 'no' (Clayton, 2010). Some may regard this as a relatively low figure.

4 As the NHS Scotland guidelines were written in 2008, before the Equalities Act came into force, a review would be most helpful. A review of the NHS England guidelines was due in February 2017.

5 The NHS England Guidelines state 'The chaplaincy [should have] a written policy or guidance document describing the service and what care those using the service can

expect to receive' (Swift, 2015, p.12). Whilst a policy should describe the care service and what service users should expect, a good policy would be more extensive than this. For example, it could include reference to service users' needs, recruitment, equality issues, and the processes for reviewing the policy. More importantly, it should be a policy for which the healthcare body feels ownership and responsibility.

6   Policy development in relation to schools is not considered here.

7   A former student was Mohammed Emwazi, known in the media as 'Jihadi John'. Hence, aspects of the Government's Prevent Strategy were a large part of their report. Nevertheless, the panel carefully considered the role of faith advisers. Interestingly, the report did not refer to chaplains or chaplaincy.

8   The Churches Higher Education Liaison Group is an effective body for developing best practice. It is a Christian organisation. Establishing an inclusive body would require the cooperation of the Church of England and other religion or belief organisations.

9   The percentage of personnel declaring themselves to be of no religion is increasing. In the Regular UK forces it has increased from 15.5% in 2012 to 25.5% in 2017.

10 There are three types of military chaplain. Commissioned Armed Forces Chaplains are currently drawn from the main Christian denominations. They are military personnel and work at home, abroad and in conflict zones. Officiating Chaplains to the Military are civilians, normally part-time, and provide local support. Civilian Chaplains to the Military are full-time civilians, one from each of the following religions: Buddhist, Hindu, Jewish, Muslim, and Sikh. They provide support to people of their own religion and give advice to the Ministry of Defence..

11 The phrase 'commissioned humanist pastoral carers' is used here because the providers are members of the armed forces, not civilians, they are humanists, and they provide pastoral support. Their equivalent Dutch title may be closer to 'spiritual support worker'.

12 The survey was administered by the armed forces personnel department, not by 'chaplains'. There were 1,416 responses.

13 For a brief discussion of spiritual assessment see Fitchett (2014). Many spiritual assessment tools ask a series of prescribed questions, often focused on 'faith and belief'. This approach does not fit well with the non-religious pastoral care approach described in chapter 6. McSherry (2010) found very little support for the use of spiritual assessment tools amongst nurses.

References

Ball, J. (2013) 'O Hear Us When We Cry to Thee': Liturgy in the Current Operational Context. In Todd, A. (ed.) *Military Chaplaincy in Contention*. Farnham, Ashgate Publishing.

Bernts, T., Ganzevoort, R., Leget, C., Wojtkowiak, J. (2014) *Omvang en verdeling van de geestelijke verzorging in de krijgsmacht vanaf 2016*. Radboud University Nijmegen. Available from: http://www.ruardganzevoort.nl/pdf/2015_GV_Defensie.pdf [accessed 12th December 2017].

British Humanist Association (2017) Written Evidence Submitted by the British Humanist Association (BHA) (PCB 22). Available from: https://publications.parliament.uk/pa/cm201617/cmpublic/PrisonsCourts/memo/PCB22.pdf [accessed 29th November 2017].

Carnie, J., Broderick, R. (2016) *Prisoner Survey 2015*, 15th Series. Edinburgh, Scottish Prison Service. Available from: http://www.sps.gov.uk/Corporate/Publications/Publication-4565.aspx [accessed 25th November 2017].

Catholic Bishops' Conference of England and Wales, Church of England, and Free Churches Group (2016) Written Evidence from the Catholic Bishops' Conference of England and Wales, Church of England, and Free Churches Group. Available from: http://data.parliament.uk/WrittenEvidence/CommitteeEvidence.svc/EvidenceDocum ent/Justice/Prison%20reform/written/44933.html [accessed 29th November 2017].

Clayton, A. (2010) Religious Need in the NHS in England. The Contribution of Picker Inpatient Surveys. Unpublished report commissioned by the Diocese of Ripon and Leeds. Available from: https://www.researchgate.net/publication/ 260025691_Religious_need_in_the_NHS_in_England_The_contribution_of_Picker_ Inpatient_Surveys [accessed 3rd December 2017].

Coulter, D., Legood, G. (2016) Military Chaplaincy. In: Swift, C., Cobb, M., Todd, A. (eds) *A Handbook of Chaplaincy Studies: Understanding Spiritual Care in Public Places*. Abingdon, Routledge.

Fitchett, G. (2014) Assessing Spiritual Needs in a Clinical Setting. Powerpoint presentation. Chicago, Rush University Medical Center. Available from: http://www. ecrsh.eu/mm/Fitchett_-_Keynote_ECRSH14.pdf [accessed 16th December 2017].

HM Chief Inspector of Prisons for England and Wales (2016) *Annual Report 2015–16.* Available from: https://www.justiceinspectorates.gov.uk/hmiprisons/wp-content/up loads/sites/4/2016/07/HMIP-AR_2015-16_web.pdf [accessed 26th November 2017].

Humanists UK (2017) *Humanists UK Polling on Pastoral Care in the UK.* Available from: https://humanism.org.uk/wp-content/uploads/Humanists-UK-polling-on-pastoral-care-in-the-UK.pdf [accessed 21st January 2018].

King, P. (2013) *Faith in a Foxhole? Researching Combatant Religiosity amongst British Soldiers on Contemporary Operations*. Defence Academy Yearbook 2013. Available from: https://www.da.mod.uk/publications/Defence-Academy-Yearbook-2013 [accessed 12th December 2017].

Learning and Skills Council (2005) *Faiths and Further Education: A Handbook Towards a Whole-college Approach to Chaplaincy for a Pluralist Society.* Coventry, Learning and Skills Council with National Ecumenical Agency in Further Education. Available from: http://fect.org/wp-content/uploads/faiths-and-fe-handbook.pdf [accessed 5th December 2017].

McSherry, W. (2010) *RCN Spirituality Survey 2010*. London, Royal College of Nursing. Available from: https://my.rcn.org.uk/__data/assets/pdf_file/0017/391112/003861. pdf [accessed 17th October 2017].

Ministry of Defence (2011) *Guide on Religion and Belief in the Armed Forces.* London, Ministry of Defence. Available from: https://www.gov.uk/government/uploads/ system/uploads/attachment_data/file/28127/guide_religion_belief.pdf [accessed 6th December 2017].

Ministry of Defence (2017) *UK Armed Forces Biannual Diversity Statistics.* London, Ministry of Defence. Available from: https://www.gov.uk/government/statistics/uk-armed-forces-biannual-diversity-statistics-2017 [accessed 6th December 2017].

Ministry of Justice (2011) *Ensuring Equality*. PSI 32/2011. London, Ministry of Justice. Available from: https://www.justice.gov.uk/downloads/offenders/psipso/psi-2011/psi_ 2011_32_ensuring_equality.doc [accessed 29th November 2017].

National Offender Management Service (2016) *Faith and Pastoral Care for Prisoners,* PSI 05/2016.London, National Offender Management Service. Available from: https:// www.justice.gov.uk/downloads/offenders/psipso/psi-2016/psi-05-2016-faith-and-pastoral-care-for-prisoners.doc [accessed 26th November 2017].

Scottish Government (2009) *Spiritual Care & Chaplaincy.* Edinburgh, Scottish Government. Available from: http://www.gov.scot/Resource/Doc/259076/0076811.pdf [accessed 30th November 2017].

Swift, C. (2015) *NHS Chaplaincy Guidelines 2015: Promoting Excellence in Pastoral, Spiritual & Religious Care.* Leeds, NHS England. Available from: https://www.england.nhs.uk/wp-content/uploads/2015/03/nhs-chaplaincy-guidelines-2015.pdf [accessed 2nd December 2017].

Todd, A., Tipton, L. (2011) *The Role and Contribution of a Multi-Faith Prison Chaplaincy to the Contemporary Prison Service.* Cardiff, Cardiff Centre for Chaplaincy Studies. Available from: http://orca.cf.ac.uk/29120/1/Chaplaincy%20Report%20Final%20Draft%20%283%29.pdf [accessed 24th November 2017].

UK Government (1952) Prison Act. Available from: http://www.legislation.gov.uk/ukpga/1952/52/pdfs/ukpga_19520052_en.pdf [accessed 9th April 2017].

University of Westminster (2015) *The University of Westminster: Diversity and Divergence. A Report by the Independent Panel.* London, University of Westminster. Available from: https://www.westminster.ac.uk/file/15946/download [accessed 5th December 2017].

Index